P9-EDY-495

Praise for *Fun with the Family™ in Northern California*
(first published as *Family Adventure Guide: Northern California*)

"Enables parents to turn family travel into an exploration."
—Alexandra Kennedy, Editor, *Family Fun*

"Bound to lead you and your kids to fun-filled days,
those times that help compose the memories of childhood."
—Dorothy Jordon, Publisher, *Family Travel Times*

Help Us Keep This Guide Up to Date

Every effort has been made by the author and editors to make this guide as accurate and useful as possible. However, many changes can occur after a guide is published—establishments close, phone numbers change, hiking trails are rerouted, facilities come under new management, etc.

We would love to hear from you concerning your experiences with this guide and how you feel it could be improved and kept up to date. While we may not be able to respond to all comments and suggestions, we'll take them to heart and we'll make certain to share them with the author. Please send your comments and suggestions to the following address:

The Globe Pequot Press
Reader Response/Editorial Department
P.O. Box 480
Guilford, CT 06437

Or you may e-mail us at: editorial@globe-pequot.com

Thanks for your input, and happy travels!

FUN WITH THE FAMILY™

in NORTHERN CALIFORNIA

HUNDREDS OF IDEAS
FOR DAY TRIPS WITH THE KIDS
THIRD EDITION

By KAREN MISURACA

The Globe Pequot Press

Guilford, Connecticut

The prices and rates listed in this guidebook were confirmed at press time. We recommend, however, that you call establishments to obtain current information before traveling.

Fun with the Family is a trademark of The Globe Pequot Press.
Cover and text design by Nancy Freeborn
Cover photograph by Julie Bidwell
Maps by M.A. Dubé

Library of Congress Cataloging-in-Publication Data
Misuraca, Karen.
    Fun with the family in Northern California : hundreds of ideas for day trips with the kids / by Karen Misuraca. — 3rd ed.
      p. cm. — (Fun with the family series)
    Includes indexes.
    ISBN 0-7627-0813-1
    1. California, Northern—Guidebooks. 2. Family recreation—California, Northern—Guidebooks. I. Title. II. Series
F867.5.M57   2000   00-056184
917.9404'54—dc21   CIP

Manufactured in the United States of America
Third Edition/First Printing

Thanks to Michael and my girls
for riding along with me in the adventure of family life.

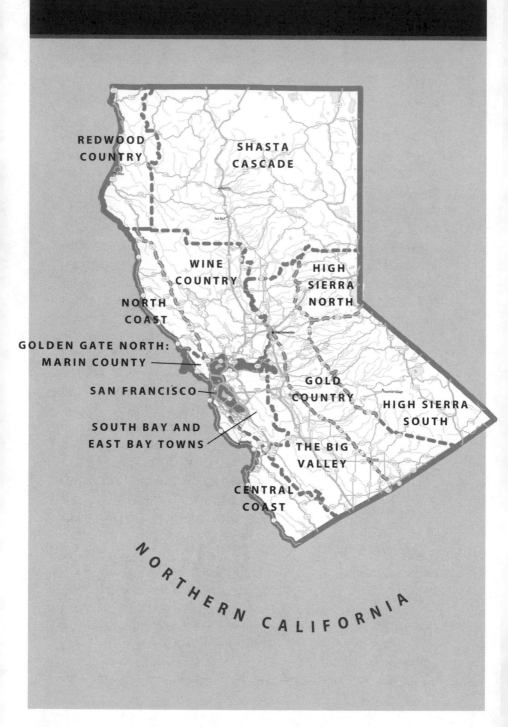

REDWOOD
COUNTRY

SHASTA
CASCADE

WINE
COUNTRY

HIGH
SIERRA
NORTH

NORTH
COAST

GOLDEN GATE NORTH:
MARIN COUNTY

SAN FRANCISCO

GOLD
COUNTRY

HIGH SIERRA
SOUTH

SOUTH BAY AND
EAST BAY TOWNS

THE BIG
VALLEY

CENTRAL
COAST

NORTHERN CALIFORNIA

Contents

Introduction

Think of Northern California as a giant theme park, packed with everything that kids and parents like to do together on vacation. From ocean beaches to ski resorts, from cable cars to canoes, for outdoor fun and living history, it's hard to beat the top half of this state.

The problem is, how can a family decide where and how to spend precious vacation time together? *Fun with the Family in Northern California* will help you choose destinations that are perfectly suited to the ages of your children and the activities your family enjoys.

This book is divided into twelve geographic regions. The major towns in each region are featured, together with information on nearby attractions, family-friendly restaurants, and places to stay that welcome and provide for children.

Does your family like water sports and camping? Consider spending a few days in California's Central Valley, at one of its many lakes and reservoirs, or on the inland Delta waterways, a paradise for families who love to fish, water-ski, houseboat, and camp out.

In the mountains of the Sierra Nevada, pitch a tent in a pine forest or settle into a rustic lakeside resort. Head for Redwood Country and park your RV beneath the tallest trees in the world, or hit the beach with your boogie boards in Santa Cruz.

Near the waterfront in San Francisco, your young scientists will enjoy one of the world's largest hands-on science museums. In the shadow of the Golden Gate Bridge, visit America's newest national park. Shake hands with a robot at the Tech Museum of Innovation in San Jose, the birthplace of the personal computer.

Fancy accommodations can be hard on the family budget, so you'll find suggestions for comfortable, reasonably priced motels, inns, campgrounds, and hostels with amenities such as coin laundries, sofa beds, swimming pools, playgrounds, and games rooms; some offer supervised "kids' camps."

You'll find a strong focus on recreation, nature, and the environment. Many state parks and nature preserves are recommended as places to get close to wildlife and to see a tremendous variety of native flora and dramatic landscapes—images that stay with children for the rest of their lives. In the northernmost reaches of California, in the Shasta Cascade region and around Lassen Volcanic National Park, the trails and roads are lightly used, a key advantage if one of your vacation goals is to spend quiet time together in the wilderness.

Learning about the history of California is something that just happens in many of the towns and villages you will visit. In the perfectly preserved Gold Rush settlement of Columbia, shopkeepers and blacksmiths dress and work just as their forebears did a century ago, and you can still get a sarsaparilla and have your tintype taken. On the plaza in the Spanish mission town of San Juan Bautista, step into the stables to have a look at horse-drawn carriages and wagons from the 1860s, when a dozen coaches a day arrived with travelers from the East, bound for the boomtown of San Francisco.

Amusement parks, playgrounds, rest stops, and easy hiking trails are described in every region. On a driving trip with my children and their children, I like to have a few spots in mind where we can take a fresh-air break and the kids can let off steam.

Have you ever involved your kids in pretrip planning? You'll be surprised how doing so will maximize everyone's good time. The older the children, the more rewarding this undertaking will be. Send away for brochures and maps in advance for everyone to peruse, put the kids in charge of browsing the Internet for ideas, and give them this guidebook for bedtime reading. Once in the car or on the plane, designate the children as navigators and tour guides. While on the trip, have them collect postcards, take photos, and keep a journal; then put it all together in an album when you get home. Seeing through your children's eyes can make your Northern California vacations unforgettable.

"The real voyage of discovery," wrote Marcel Proust, "consists not in seeking new landscape but in having new eyes."

LODGING AND RESTAURANT RATES

In the "Where to Eat" and "Where to Stay" sections, dollar signs indicate general price ranges. For meals, the prices are for individual dinner entrees. For lodgings, the rates are for a double room, with no meals, unless otherwise indicated; rates for lodgings may be higher during peak vacation seasons and holidays. Always inquire about family and group rates and package deals that may include amusement park tickets, ski area tickets, and tickets for concerts and other performing arts events. Visitors bureaus can steer you to lodgings that offer family packages.

Rates for Lodgings

$	up to $79
$$	$80 to $110
$$$	$111 to $170
$$$$	$171 and up

Rates for Restaurants

$	entrees up to $10
$$	entrees $11 to $15
$$$	entrees $16 to $20
$$$$	entrees over $20

Attractions Key

The following is a key to the icons found throughout the text.

 Swimming

 Boating / Boat Tour

 Historic Site

 Hiking / Walking

 Fishing

 Biking

 Amusement Park

 Horseback Riding

 Skiing/Winter Sports

 Park

 Animal Viewing

 Food

 Lodging

 Camping

 Museums

 Performing Arts

 Sports/Athletic

 Picnic

 Playground

 Shopping

Central Coast

Tracing the coastline south from San Francisco to Big Sur, Highway 1 is one of the most spectacular and diverse scenic highways in the world. Sandy beaches, rocky promontories, coves and harbors, dramatic mountain ranges, and farmlands create a rich geography. Along the way are a scattering of fishermen's villages and historic mission-era towns, the honky-tonk of a vintage seaside amusement boardwalk, the sophistication of European-style cafes, and state-of-the-art museums. Take time to stop frequently and make discoveries. Stroll on the beach; peer into tidepools; load up on veggies and fruit at a produce stand.

Whale watching and beachcombing attract weekenders to Half Moon Bay, the Pumpkin Capital of the World. South along the coast from here to Santa Cruz are a chain of redwood parks, dozens of tidepooly beaches, and tiny seacoast hamlets. At Ano Nuevo State Reserve, thousands of elephant seals pose an unforgettable sight.

Fringed with 20 miles of wide sandy beaches, the classic beach towns of Santa Cruz and neighboring Capitola Village offer surfing, boating, seafood restaurants, and a boardwalk extravaganza of rides and games. Just inland from Highway 1, the Santa Cruz Mountains are crisscrossed by country roads meandering through ancient redwood groves and along the banks of the San Lorenzo River. Kids like the campgrounds and Roaring Camp, an 1880s logging settlement with a steam train.

Farther south the rich heritage of Spain is alive in the thick-walled adobes and Colonial haciendas of Monterey. Museums and restored buildings from the days of the conquistadors are found on the "Path of History." The largest in the world, the Monterey Bay Aquarium is the most popular destination on the Central Coast.

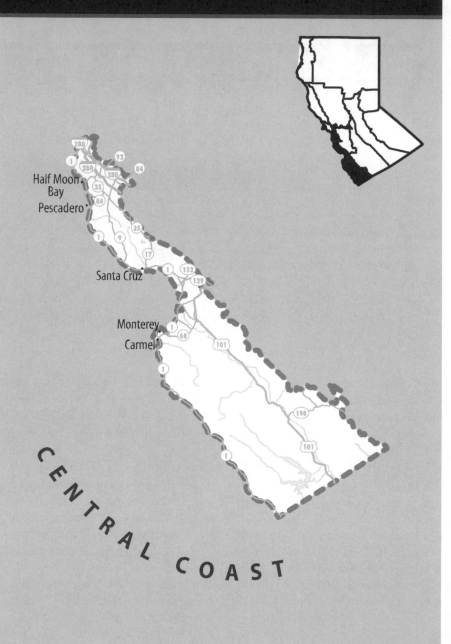

CENTRAL COAST

The fairy-tale village of Carmel-by-the-Sea is chockablock with hundreds of shops. The glorious Carmel Mission and a jewel of a town beach are not to be missed. Carmel Valley is a good choice for a family vacation headquarters in the area, due to dependably warm, dry weather and less expensive lodgings.

Running 90 miles south from Carmel, Highway 1 threads along the Big Sur coast between high cliffs and river valleys above a coastline legendary for its wild beauty. A national forest and four state parks and rocky beaches are worth exploring here.

Half Moon Bay

Good weather, sea air, and lots of outdoor fun near the harbor town of Half Moon Bay lure weekenders from the Bay Area in great numbers. It's worth the drive for a day on a sandy beach or a walk in a silent redwood forest.

Besides commercial ocean fishing and tourism, the main activities in the area are flower and vegetable growing. Within huge greenhouses and in the fields around them, flowers such as carnations, roses, tulips, and iris are grown for shipment all over the world. You can buy plants and produce—and Christmas trees—at several places along the highway. Colorful flower markets take place on third Saturdays, May through September outside on Kelley Avenue, and November through April, inside at La Piazza, downtown.

A stroll through this small Victorian town turns up Western saloons, country stores, and hundred-year-old hotels and homes, many on the National Register of Historic Places. Trendy galleries and shops abound.

In October families come for pumpkin carving, pie eating, a haunted house, an exhibition of a 1,000-pound-plus winner of the Great Pumpkin Weigh-Off, and entertainment galore. You can meet locals at the pancake breakfast and the Halloween costume competition.

HALF MOON BAY NURSERY (all ages)

11691 San Mateo Road, 3 miles east of Half Moon Bay off Highway 92, Half Moon Bay 94019; (650) 726–5392.

Keep a sharp eye out for the turn into the nursery. This is a rambling, gorgeous kingdom of blooming garden and house plants, from orchids and ferns to thousands of geraniums, herbs, azaleas, camellias, climbing vines, hanging baskets, and seasonal bulbs—a veritable flower show. Wintertime, it's cozy in the main greenhouse by the wood stove.

Across the highway, Lemos Pumpkin Patch is popular with little kids, offering weekend pony rides and a play area.

CUNHA'S

448 Main Street, Half Moon Bay 94019; (650) 726–4071.

A country store straight out of the Old West, with wooden floors, cowboy boots, hardware, and hardtack. They also have a scrumptious array of gourmet picnic foods. Look for the nice picnic-table area on the corner across from the store.

PILLAR POINT HARBOR (all ages)

At Princeton, five minutes north of Half Moon Bay on Highway 1; (650) 726–4382.

Watch a fleet of more than 200 fishing boats and yachts go in and out of the marina, fish from the wharf, go shelling on the little beach west of the jetty, and hike or bike for miles. Tiny cafes, bars, and fish markets at the harbor are frequented by the locals. Whale-watching tours depart from the wharf. From December through April you are almost guaranteed to see California gray whales on their 4,000-mile migration from the Arctic to Baja. Surfers from around the world come to Maverick's off Pillar Point, where 30-foot waves breaking over a rocky reef up the ante; some say these are the biggest waves in the world. Boat launch ramps, public restrooms, RV parking.

PILLAR POINT MARSH AND SHORELINE (all ages)

On Capistrano Road at Princeton (pass the Pillar Point Harbor, going left on Prospect Way; turn right onto Broadway, left onto Harvard to the end; go right on West Point, then 0.5 mile to the parking lot); (650) 728–3582.

A 0.5-mile easy walk, perfect for toddlers, where you will see great blue herons, snowy egrets, and red-winged blackbirds, as well as a variety of other sea- and shorebirds. Follow the trail to the breakwater and tidepools on the far side, and watch for sea lions on the offshore rocks. Restrooms, wheelchair access.

HALF MOON BAY STATE BEACH (all ages)

Just south of Half Moon Bay, west on Kelly Avenue; (650) 726–8820.

Buy a kite at Lunar Wind Inventions in town, and head for these 3 miles of adjacent sandy beaches. At Francis Beach, the most popular, are developed RV and tent campsites, cold showers, BBQs, picnic sites, and the ranger station. If the campground is full, try the nice Pelican Point RV Park on Miramontes Point Road (650-726-9100). Notice the skateboard park on the highway at Kelly Avenue.

Water temperature is chilly, even in summer, and the surf can be treacherous, so plan to dip your toes and play on the sand.

COASTSIDE TRAIL (all ages)

From the coastal/west end of Poplar Avenue, 4.2 miles south of Pillar Point; (650) 726–8297.

A flat, easy, paved biking and walking trail along the coastline—beautiful! There is a parking lot here, a picnic area, and a bridge to the southern coastal trail.

HARBOR SEAL COMPANY (all ages)

406 Main Street, Half Moon Bay 94019; (650) 726–7418.

A marine and wildlife shop with unusual sea and birdlife toys, puzzles, soft animals, educational toys, books, and games.

FITZGERALD MARINE RESERVE (all ages)

California Avenue off Highway 1, about ten minutes north of Half Moon Bay, in Moss Beach; (650) 728–3584.

A 0.5-mile easy trail loops through the tangled garden of an old estate, a spooky forest of Monterey cypress, and along a bluff above some of the richest tidepools on the Pacific Coast. At low tide a kaleidoscope of sponges, sea anemones, starfish, crabs, mollusks, and fish emerge. A California sea lion may be watching you, and you can see gray whales offshore December through April.

With a special fishing license, try your hand at rock fishing. For the best tidepooling call ahead to find out when the low tides are expected. Docent tours are available. Restrooms, picnic tables, interpretive center.

Where to Eat

Main Street Grill. *435 Main at Kelly, Half Moon Bay; (650) 726–5300.* Cajun sausage, homemade waffles and muffins, grilled sandwiches, thick shakes, microbrewed beer, and a jukebox. Breakfast and lunch. $

Ketch Joanne. *Pillar Point Harbor, Princeton; (650) 728–3747.* Big breakfasts, clam chowder, and fresh seafood in a booth by the potbelly stove. It's like a ship inside, with hatch covers, old photos, and paintings of sea creatures—and real seamen at the bar.

Breakfast, lunch, and dinner. $–$$

Barbara's Fish Trap. *281 Capistrano Road at Pillar Point Harbor; (650) 728–7049.* A fun, noisy, casual place full of families, overlooking the harbor. Oilcloth-covered tables and a covered patio with outdoor heaters. Try the daily fresh fish specials. $–$$

Miramar Beach Restaurant. *131 Mirada Road, Half Moon Bay; (650) 726–9053.* Formerly a circa-1918 Prohibition roadhouse, this joint jumps on the weekends with live music. Kids like watching the surfers off Miramar Beach. Fresh seafood and steaks, and a kid's menu. Lunch, dinner, and weekend brunch. $$

Half Moon Bay Coffee Company. *20A Stone Pine Road at the north end of*

Main Street; (650) 726–3664. A casual place busy with locals and tourists digging into homemade pies and pastries, pancakes, burgers, sandwiches, and simple, hearty entrees. Breakfast, lunch, dinner. $

Where to Stay

Harbor View Inn. *51 Avenue Alhambra, El Granada 94018; (650) 726–2329.* A Cape Cod–style motel near Pillar Point Harbor; large rooms with two queen beds, bay windows; cribs available. Walking distance to beaches, harbor, restaurants, walking trails. $$

Half Moon Bay Lodge. *2400 South Cabrillo Highway (Highway 1), south end of Half Moon Bay 94109; (650) 726–9000 or (800) 368–2468; www.woodsidehotels.*

com. Eighty spacious rooms with small patios or balconies overlooking gardens; some fireplaces. Large swimming pool, enclosed oversized spa in a glass house, fitness center, sauna. Continental breakfast, and many extras, such as borrowable books, refrigerators, down pillows and comforters, beach blankets, cribs, and extra beds. Less than five minutes from here starts a coastal walking trail. $$$

For More Information

Half Moon Bay Coastside Chamber of Commerce. *520 Kelly Avenue, Half Moon Bay 94019; (650) 726–5202;*

www.halfmoonbaychamber.org; e-mail: info@halfmoonbaychamber.org.

Pescadero

South of Half Moon Bay along Highway 1 are a string of beautiful beaches, several wildlife preserves, and two tiny historic towns. The town of Pescadero is a block or so of clapboard buildings and steepled churches, circa 1850. Peek into a few antiques boutiques and stop at Norm's Market, where the irresistible aroma of warm artichoke and garlic-cheese bread wafts out the door; some of the twenty-four kinds of bread are "half-baked," to take home, stow in the freezer, and bake later.

Just south of here near Ano Nuevo State Reserve, the circa-1870, ten-stories-tall Pigeon Point Lighthouse is open for tours on weekends (650–879– 2120). The Pigeon Point Hostel has inexpensive private and shared rooms, and marvelous views (www.norcalhostels.org).

PESCADERO STATE BEACH (all ages)

Fifteen miles south of Half Moon Bay, on Highway 1; (650) 879–0227.

Two miles of sheltered beach, with tidepools, huge dunes, and trails. The sea lions and the seagulls like it here, as do the fishermen who catch steelhead and salmon at spawning time in Pescadero Creek. Kids love investigating the big tidepools and sliding down the dunes. Restrooms, picnic tables, barbecues.

Just across the highway, Pescadero Marsh is 600 acres of uplands and wetlands, an important stop on the Pacific Flyway and a must for avid birders, or for anyone who likes to walk on nature trails. Fall and spring are the best times to see thousands of birds nesting and feeding. An underpass provides safe access to and from the beach; no pets.

 DUARTE'S TAVERN

202 Stage Road, Pescadero 94060; (650) 879–0464.

Crowded on sunny weekends but worth the wait, Duarte's has for more than fifty years been a family restaurant serving cioppino, seafood specialties with a Portuguese accent, artichoke soup, deep-fried cala-mari, and olallieberry pie. Local ranchers belly up to the Old West–style bar. Daily breakfast, lunch, and dinner. $$

 PHIPPS RANCH (all ages)

1 mile east of Pescadero, 2700 Pescadero Creek Road, Pescadero 94060; (650) 879–0787. Open daily from 10:00 A.M. to 6:00 P.M.

A combination produce market, farm, plant nursery, and menagerie of exotic birds and farm animals, just made for kids. Among the cacophony of sounds are parrots' squawks, green and orange canaries' songs, and peacocks' trumpetings. There are fancy chickens, big fat pigs, a variety of bunnies, and antique farm equipment. You can pick your own strawberries, raspberries and olallieberries, and eat them at a picnic table in the middle of a flower-filled greenhouse. Restrooms.

 ANO NUEVO STATE RESERVE (all ages)

Highway 1 at New Year's Creek Road, Pescadero 94060; (650) 879–0227 or (800) 444–4445; www.anonuevo.org. Admission $4.00 per car, parking $5.00. No pets.

On 1,200 acres of dunes and beaches, the largest groups of elephant seals in the world come to breed from December through April. A moderately strenuous, 3-mile walk through grassy dunes brings you to an unforgettable sight: dozens of two-ton animals lounging, arguing, maybe mating, cavorting in the sea, and wiggling around on the beach. As many as 2,500 seals spend their honeymoons here, and there's lots of other wildlife to see too. During the mating season it is necessary to reserve spaces in guided interpretive tours (800–444–7275). At other times you can wander around on your own. The boardwalk enables wheelchair access.

 ## PURISMA CREEK REDWOODS OPEN SPACE PRESERVE (all ages)

Off Highway 1, 4.5 miles south of Half Moon Bay, west on Higgins-Purisma Road.
   A beautiful path winds up Whittemore Gulch through redwoods along lovely fern grottos for a mile, then climbs out of the canyon into open foothills; take a short ramble or hike the whole way, 2.2 miles to Skyline Boulevard on the ridge.

Santa Cruz

The summer resort town of Santa Cruz is known for a 20-mile string of wide, sandy, warm-water beaches and an old-fashioned waterfront boardwalk with rides and concessions. Here at the top end of Monterey Bay, the climate is mild, and surf's up every month of the year.

The town is composed of hundreds of fanciful Victorian homes. The main street, Pacific Avenue—called the **Pacific Garden Mall**—is a pleasantly tree-shaded boulevard with outdoor cafes and dozens of shops. Musical performances and festivals take place on Pacific all summer long. In this artists' town, notice the many sidewalk sculptures, and watch for building-size murals on side streets.

From the Santa Cruz waterfront to Natural Bridges, a road winds above the ocean for several miles. Popular for walking and jogging, the West Cliff section runs north from Lighthouse Point.

In the Santa Cruz Mountains are ancient redwood groves, sunny riverbanks, quiet little resort towns, and a rollicking steam train.

Virtually every resident of Santa Cruz County lives within walking distance of a state park or beach. A water shuttle provides seagoing transport between Santa Cruz Harbor, Santa Cruz Wharf, and Capitola Wharf.

SANTA CRUZ BEACH BOARDWALK (all ages)

400 Beach Street, Santa Cruz 95060; (831) 423–5590.

The only beachside amusement park on the West Coast. The classic 1911 carousel and the Giant Dipper roller-coaster are National Historic Landmarks. You'll need a whole afternoon for the twenty-five rides, an old-time arcade, shops, and restaurants. At Neptune's Kingdom on the indoor minigolf course, volcanoes erupt, pirates threaten, and cannons fire. If you hear screaming, it's probably coming from the $5 million roller-coaster, the Hurricane. The Astro Canyon Virtual Coaster is not for sissies. Video arcade, pool tables, air hockey, laser tag, virtual reality, shooting gallery.

SANTA CRUZ SURFING MUSEUM (all ages)

Mark Abbott Memorial Lighthouse, on West Cliff Drive, Santa Cruz; (831) 429–3429.

The only surfing museum in the world exhibits a hundred years of surfing history, including the famous "Shark Attack" surfboard. Almost every day you will see surfers on the curls of "Steamers Lane" below.

CLUB ED SURF SCHOOL (ages 10 and up)

Cowell Beach, in front of Dream Inn, Santa Cruz; (831) 462–6083; www.clubed.com.

This is the place for lessons, board rentals, surf camp. Rent and buy kayaks, sailboards, and more beach stuff.

BOOKSHOP SANTA CRUZ (all ages)

Pacific and Front Streets, Santa Cruz 95060; (831) 423–0900.

One of the largest bookstores in Northern California, a gathering place for locals and visitors. Throughout the store are benches, stools, and armchairs, comfortable spots to peruse the books and the huge variety of domestic and international magazines and newspapers. The children's books department is comfortable, and the store offers a cafe.

PACIFIC WAVE (ages 10 and up)

Corner of Pacific Avenue and Cooper Street, Santa Cruz 95060; (831) 458–9283.

Headquarters for surfboards, skateboards, and all the cool accessories and clothing to go with them.

*S*anta Cruz Beaches

Cowell Beach. *Beach Street, Santa Cruz; (831) 429-3747.* The main Santa Cruz beach at the boardwalk and the pier. A popular piece of sand for sunning, swimming, and volleyball. A special beachgoing wheelchair is available from the lifeguard. Restrooms.

Santa Cruz Yacht Harbor and Beach. *End of Fifth Avenue and East Cliff Drive, Santa Cruz; (831) 475-6161.* Kayak and sail, sunbathe, and watch more than 1,200 boats go in and out of the harbor. RV parking, restrooms, restaurants.

Twin Lakes State Beach. *Below East Cliff Drive at Seventh Avenue, Santa Cruz; (831) 688-3241.* Where the windsurfers go. There are fire rings here, outdoor showers, restrooms, and a wild bird sanctuary at Schwan Lagoon and Schwan Lake. You can kayak and canoe on the lake.

Seacliff State Beach. *State Park Drive off Highway 1, Aptos; (831) 688-7146.* Two miles of shoreline backed by steep sandstone cliffs. A 500-foot wooden pier and the wreck of a concrete ship are roosting spots for birds, and you can fish off the pier. There are a campground and a small visitor center where you can sign up for walking tours to see the fossilized remains of multimillion-year-old sea creatures lodged in the cliffsides. On the inland edge of the beach is a paved pathway frequented by joggers, parents with strollers, and skateboarders.

Rio Del Mar Beach. *Just south of Capitola at Aptos; (831) 688-3241.* A wide stretch of sand with a jetty and lifeguards. Shopping and restaurants are within walking distance.

 FOREST OF NISENE MARKS STATE PARK (all ages)
Aptos Creek Road, Aptos; (831) 724-1266.

 A cool, green place to take a walk in the highlands inland of Santa Cruz. This densely forested, 10,000-acre wilderness on Aptos Creek is popular with runners, bikers, horseback riders, hikers, and picnickers. In elevations from 100 to 2,600 feet, unpaved roads and trails lead to a wide variety of mixed evergreen woods and creekside willows and ferns. Walk-in camping is permitted, as is horseback riding.

CAPITOLA-BY-THE-SEA (all ages)

Three miles south of Santa Cruz, off Highway 1; (831) 475–6522.

Located on the edge of a small, protected beach where Soquel Creek enters the sea, Capitola is a few short blocks of boutiques, art galleries, and beachwear shops, a quaint art colony that has welcomed vacationers since 1861. Sheltered by two high cliffs, the beach sports a small fishing pier. Fishing licenses are not required for fishing off the pier, and a bait and tackle shop is here. Capitola Beach and most other public beaches in the area are cleaned nightly. Even in the summer they start out trash-free and pearly-white every day.

Restaurants with outdoor patios are lined up on the waterfront. The shops and galleries are touristy but fun.

NATURAL BRIDGES STATE BEACH (all ages)

A few minutes north of Santa Cruz, 2531 West Cliff Drive, Santa Cruz 95060; (831) 425–4609.

Named for dramatic sandstone arches, this beautiful beach has tidepools rich with sea life. Guided tidepool tours are available. A short boardwalk from the beach parking lot leads through a eucalyptus forest to the California Monarch Butterfly Preserve. Depending on the time of year—early October through March is best—you'll see hundreds of thousands of butterflies hanging in the trees and moving about in great golden clouds. A 0.75-mile self-guided nature walk begins at the Monarch Trail and heads for Secret Lagoon, where blue herons, mallard ducks, and more freshwater and seagoing birds live.

LONG MARINE LABORATORY AND AQUARIUM (all ages)

100 Shaffer Road, Santa Cruz, near Natural Bridges 95060; (831) 459–2883.

A University of Santa Cruz research facility, open to the public. In addition to the aquarium are an 85-foot blue whale skeleton and "touch tanks" where kids can pick up sea animals. Docents take you behind the scenes where scientists do research.

WILDER RANCH STATE PARK (all ages)

1401 Coast Road, 2 miles north of Santa Cruz; (831) 426–0505.

A 6,000-acre working ranch since the 1800s. Stroll in and out of the old barns, homes, and gardens. A fern grotto is chiseled into the beachfront cliffs. Somoe 2,300 adjoining acres were recently purchased by the

11

Family Hosteling
Golden Gate Council Hosteling International information: www.norcalhostels.org. For a brochure describing all Northern California hostels, call (415) 863–1444 (fax: 415–863–3865). Hostels are not just for the young and footloose anymore. Many American hostels have private rooms and cabins for families and small groups. The advantages are cost (as low as $10 per person; a few dollars higher in big cities), location (nearby natural and cultural attractions that families want to see and explore), and the chance to meet travelers from all over the world.

You cook your own meals in a fully equipped common kitchen and socialize with other hostelers in a common living room. Clean beds are provided (bring your own linens/sleeping bags), as are laundry facilities and common bathrooms with showers. Some hostels ask you to do brief chores. On the coast of California are several hostels that are perfect for vacationing families. They are popular, so reserve well in advance.

- **Pigeon Point Lighthouse Hostel.** *210 Pigeon Point Road at Highway 1, Pescadero 94060; (650) 879–0633.* Four family houses, each with a fully equipped kitchen, clustered around one of the tallest lighthouses in the United States. An incredible location on a dazzling stretch of coastline, near state parks, tidepools, beaches, redwood forests, and the famous Ano Nuevo State Reserve, where hundreds of elephant seals are a sight to behold.

- **Point Montara Lighthouse Hostel.** *Twenty-five miles south of San Francisco on Highway 1, P.O. Box 737, Montara 94037; (650) 728–7177.* The 1875 Point Montara Fog Signal and Light Station became a hostel in 1980. Family rooms; fireplace in community room; great location near beaches, boat harbors, Half Moon Bay.

- **Hidden Villa Ranch Hostel.** *Forty-five miles south of San Francisco and 15 miles north of San Jose, 26870 Moody Road, Los Altos Hills 94022; (408) 949–8648.* On a 1,600-acre ranch in the foothills of the Santa Cruz Mountains, the first hostel in California, established in 1937. Rustic, heated cabins, plus a fireplace and piano in the common room. This is a working farm with organic gardens. Nearby are hiking trails and parks.

- **Santa Cruz Hostel.** *P.O. Box 1241, Santa Cruz 95060; (831) 423–8304.* Newly renovated cottages close to downtown and the beach.

Save the Redwoods League and given to the state for Wilder Ranch, adding miles of hiking and mountain-biking trails.

DAVENPORT (all ages)

About 9 miles north up the coast from Santa Cruz on Highway 1.

The hamlet of Davenport makes a nice half-day trip from Santa Cruz. On the bluff, the Davenport Overlook is a perfect vantage point from which to see California gray whales on their annual trips to and from Mexico. The beach here is less crowded than others and a favorite of windsurfers. On the highway, the New Davenport Cash Store and Restaurant is definitely worth the drive for grilled chicken sandwiches, homemade soup, omelets with homemade chorizo, and big killer brownies in a wood-floored, sunny cafe; it's popular for weekend break-fast. The gift shop sells guidebooks, masses of jewelry, and a surprising array of African trinkets and crafts.

HENRY COWELL REDWOODS STATE PARK (all ages)

101 North Big Trees Park Road, Felton 95018; (831) 335–4598.

A rare opportunity to see first-growth redwoods in 1,800 acres of stream canyons, meadows, forests, and chaparral-covered ridges along the meandering river and Eagle Creek. An observation deck overlooks the Monterey/Santa Cruz coastlines and the mountains. A lovely shaded picnic grove on the river has barbecues and water. Take the short, easy Redwood Grove Nature Trail to the Big Trees Grove.

The redwood-dotted campground in the park contains more than a hundred tent and RV sites, for vehicles up to 24 feet, with no hookups (831–438–2396).

Nearby is a photo op at the Felton Covered Bridge. Built in 1892, this is the tallest bridge of its kind in the country and one of the few left in the state.

BIG BASIN REDWOODS STATE PARK (all ages)

From Boulder Creek on Highway 9, go 9 miles west on Highway 236 to the park entrance; (831) 338–8861. Store, snack bar, shop, restrooms. Camping in RV and tent sites, walk-in sites, tent cabins, hike and bike sites. The fee is $6.00 per vehicle.

California's first state park comprises 18,000 acres of 1,000-year-old redwood groves, fern canyons, waterfalls, and 80 miles of trails, a lush, green world for hiking, camping, picnicking, horseback riding, and mountain biking. The Sea Trail drops 11 miles from high mountain ridges through dense woodlands, past waterfalls and zowie sea and mountain views all the way down to Waddell State Beach.

The easiest and most popular trail, the Redwood Nature Trail opposite the headquarters, is a 0.6-mile loop, a tour of redwoods and Opal Creek. You'll see the Chimney Tree, the Mother of the Forest—329 feet tall—and the Father of the Forest, a really, *really* big-around redwood.

ROARING CAMP AND BIG TREES RAILROAD (all ages)

Just south of Felton on Graham Hill Road in the Santa Cruz Mountains; (831) 335–4484; www.roaringcamp.com.

Tops on kids' favorite places in the Santa Cruz Mountains, a recreation of an 1880s logging town, complete with a covered bridge, a general store, and a wonderful narrow-gauge steam train to ride up through forests of giant redwoods to the summit of Bear Mountain on the steepest railroad grade in North America. A second route runs along the San Lorenzo River down to Santa Cruz beaches. A chuckwagon barbecue serves charcoal-broiled steak and chicken burgers in a forest glade, or you can have your own picnic on the mountain.

Annual events are eagerly awaited by kids who love Roaring Camp. In April 10,000 eggs are hidden at the Amazing Egg Hunt, and Civil War battles and camp life are reenacted at the largest encampment in the United States. The Jumpin' Frog Contest happens in July, as does a Harvest Fair in October, with 1880s crafts, demonstrations, pumpkin carving, and **Free** pumpkins.

Where to Eat

Zachary's. *849 Pacific Avenue, Santa Cruz 95060; (408) 427–0646.* Voted Best Breakfast in Santa Cruz, sourdough pancakes, scones, corn bread, and much more. Breakfast, lunch, brunch. $

Gayle's Bakery and Rosticcerias. *504 Bay Avenue, on the corner of Bay and Capitola Avenues, Capitola 95010; (408) 462– 1127.* The heated patio is comfortable summer and winter. Besides pies, cheesecake, and pastries, Gayle's is famous for homemade pasta, pizza, and spit-roasted meats. $

Sea Food Mama's. *820 Bay Avenue, above town at the Crossroads Center, Capitola 95010; (408) 476–5976.* The menu is printed every day with a huge variety of what's fresh in seafood. This is a casual, fun place with a jukebox. $

Broken Egg and Crepe Cafe. *7887 Soquel Drive, Aptos 95001; (408) 688–*

4322. Indoor and outdoor breakfast, lunch, and dinner, a favorite for more than two decades. $

El Palomar Restaurant Taco Bar. *Pacific Garden Mall, Santa Cruz 95060; (831) 425–7575.* The best tacos in town, maybe in the world. Try the fresh seafood versions and the guacamole taco, while watching cable TV sports. $

Tony and Alba's Pizza and Italian Food. *817 Soquel Avenue; Santa Cruz 95060; (831) 425–8669.* A favorite family place for wonderful brick oven pizza. Also in Capitola and Scotts Valley. $

Crow's Nest. *2218 East Cliff Drive at the Santa Cruz Harbor 95060; (831) 476–4560; www.crowsnest-santacruz.com.* A casual, multilevel restaurant overlooking the busy harbor, with a heated, glassed-in deck. The food is not gourmet, but it's good, with plenty of fresh seafood and good choices for children. $–$$

Where to Stay

Seascape Resort. *1 Seascape Resort Drive off San Andreas, Aptos, 9 miles south of Santa Cruz; (800) 929–7727 or (831) 688–6800; www.seascaperesort.com.* Studio, one- and two-bedroom condos, and villas for up to eight people, all with ocean views, fireplaces, equipped kitchens; restaurant with a bay view. Olympic swimming pool, golf course, sandy beach, tennis courts, gym.

Kids' Club includes supervised recreation for 5- to 10-year-olds, from hikes to beach games and nightly video parties. Discounted tickets to area attractions, kids' beach kits.

A unique amenity at Seascape is "Fires-to-Go": A bellhop arrives with firewood and snacks for a beach bonfire, and drives your family to the private beach, where he or she builds and lights the fire! $$$–$$$$

Capitola Venetian Hotel. *1500 Wharf Road, Capitola 95010; (800) 528–1234; www.capitolavenetian.com.* Historical landmark on the beach, a 1920s Mediterranean pink stucco motel, unassuming eclectic/eccentric decor, kitchenettes, some fireplaces, no pets. Reasonable rates for families and groups. $–$$

Griffin's Fern River Resort. *Near Roaring Camp, 5250 Highway 9, Felton 95018; (408) 335–4412; www.gdl.net/ fernriver.* A nice, small, rustic resort with little red housekeeping cabins, some fireplaces, a private sandy river beach, and four acres of lawns, trees, and fern gardens. Fireplaces, kitchenettes, no pets. $–$$

Villa Vista. *2–2800 East Cliff Drive, ten minutes from downtown Santa Cruz 95060; (408) 866–2626; www.villavista.com.* Two perfectly wonderful condo units, each contains three master bedrooms with baths, gourmet kitchen, sea-view patio, home entertainment center, laundry facilities. Great for several couples or a large family. $$$$

Holiday Inn Express. *600 Riverside Avenue, Santa Cruz 95060; (800) 527–3833.* A nice chain motel, 4 blocks from the beach and downtown, with swimming pool, complimentary continental breakfast, and rooms with two queens. $$–$$$

Santa Cruz KOA Kampground.
1186 San Andreas Road off Highway 1,
Watsonville, just south of Santa Cruz 94076;
(831) 722–0551. A nicely kept, large
facility near beaches, with tent and RV
sites and air-conditioned log cabins, a
pool, a store, and a very lively atmosphere. $

Tyrolean Inn and Cottages. *9600*
Highway 9, Ben Lomond 95005; (831)
336–5188. Seven simple cottages
within walking distance to town and
the river, fireplaces, kitchenettes, no
pets. German/American restaurant on-
site. $–$$

For More Information

Santa Cruz Visitors Bureau. *701*
Front Street, Santa Cruz 95060; (831)

425–1234 or (800) 833–3494; www.
scccvc.org.

Monterey

A Portuguese navigator sailed into Monterey Bay in the mid-1500s, and the
Spanish landed here in 1602, beginning a 200-year occupation. A rich architectural heritage remains today. Gnarled old olive trees and courtyard gardens
surround graceful tile-roofed adobes and haciendas built by the early conquistadors—the town looks like old Spain. A "Path of History" wanders between
historic buildings and museums.

You're likely to spend much of your time on Monterey's waterfront on the
edge of the miraculous Monterey Bay, on Fisherman's Wharf, at Cannery Row,
and on the seaside walking trail. Seals, sea lions, and otters provide **Free**
entertainment.

Most sights and amusements are within walking distance of downtown.
Get a self-guided-tour map at the visitors bureau at 380 Alvarado Street
(831–649–1770) and hop on and off the "WAVE" shuttle bus.

The annual Whalefest in January is a multifaceted, several-day event that
families love. Attractions include mural painting, whale watch cruises, free
entertainment, special exhibits and tours, puppets, and a free day at the
aquarium.

On Tuesdays in the late afternoons and early evenings all year, the Old
Monterey Market Place downtown features nearly 150 vendors of prepared
foods and produce, arts, crafts, and lots of music and free fun.

MONTEREY STATE HISTORIC PARK "PATH OF HISTORY"

A district roughly from Fisherman's Wharf south to Pacific and Madison and east to Camino El Estero; (831) 649–7118, www.mbay.net/~mshp. Tickets for all forty Path of History buildings: adults $5.00, youth $3.00, children $2.00; purchase them at all buildings open to the public.

In the oldest part of the city, historic buildings and museums are close together in a pleasant, garden-y network of streets. Plan on a leisurely half-day's exploration to do the complete 2-mile walk, with plenty of time for rest stops at little parks along the way.

Children particularly enjoy the Colton Hall Museum at Madison and Pacific, a century-old school on a grassy knoll, with little wooden desks and photos of the pupils from days gone by. Behind the school and around this part of town are small adobes, some of the first homes built in California. Every April, you can take a narrated tour of more than twenty-five adobes and see courtyard gardens inhabited by docents in period costumes.

The Cooper Store at Munras and Alvarado Streets sells antique toys, postcards, and souvenirs. Walk through the store to another museum and to gardens beneath a huge cypress tree.

In the oldest part of the city, historic buildings and museums are close together in a pleasant, gardeny network of streets. Plan on a leisurely half-day's exploration to do the complete 2-mile walk, with plenty of time for rest stops at little parks along the way.

*B*est Whalewatching Sites in Monterey County

- **Point Sur Light Station.** 19 miles south of Carmel on Highway 1, 1.5 miles south of the Little Sur River.

- **Ocean View Park Boulevard.** At the west end of Lighthouse Avenue, Pacific Grove, near the Point Pinos Light Station.

- **Monterey Bay.** Take a whalewatching cruise from Fisherman's Wharf (Monterey Bay Whale and Nature Cruises, 408–372–0671).

- **Point Lobos State Reserve.** Four miles south of Carmel on Highway 1

MONTEREY MUSEUM OF ART (all ages)

559 Pacific Street, Monterey 93942; (831) 372–5477.

Called the "Best Small-Town Museum in the United States," with a wide variety of ethnic, American, and folk art.

FISHERMAN'S WHARF AND WHARF #2

Del Monte Avenue and Washington Street; (831) 649–1770; www.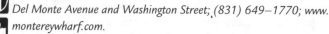

montereywharf.com.

Side by side stretching into Monterey Harbor, Wharf #2 is the home of the commercial fishing fleet and several seafood restaurants, while Fisherman's Wharf is a breezy boardwalk, delightfully weather-worn and smelling of salt spray and caramel corn and crowded with cafes and souvenir shops, fish markets, galleries, and sightseeing and tour companies. From here you can rent kayaks, go whale watching, and take a bike ride or a walk around the edge of the bay. One of the most fun things to do is to rent an overgrown bicycle, which is powered by two adults in back, with room for two little kids to ride in front.

Across from the entrance to Fisherman's Wharf, Custom House Plaza is the site of festivals and special events, terraced lawns, fountains, and bocci courts.

MONTEREY PENINSULA RECREATIONAL TRAIL

The paved path from Cannery Row, past Fisherman's Wharf, to Asilomar State Beach is part of an 18-mile hiking and walking trail connecting the greenbelts and parks on the coast. Along the way are historic landmarks, drinking fountains, benches, picnic sites, restrooms, and bike racks. It's fun to dodge brown pelicans and watch sea lions barking to get your attention. Binoculars are great to have, for spying otters floating on their backs in the kelp beds offshore, knock-knocking on abalone shells; children are drawn to the friendly-looking, inquisitive faces of the hairy little animals. Point Piños Lighthouse and Lovers' Point playground are two stops to make. Pets must be leashed, and skateboards are allowed only in designated areas.

MARITIME MUSEUM OF MONTEREY (all ages)

5 Custom House Plaza, Monterey 93942; (831) 373–2469.

Some 18,000 feet of exhibits focused on the Monterey Peninsula's long seagoing history. Priceless marine artifacts include the 16-foot-tall, 10,000-pound lens that once operated atop the Point Sur Lighthouse.

When everyone in the family is ready for a twenty-minute rest, take in the historical film here—it's **Free**.

KAYAKING MONTEREY BAY (ages 8 and up)

Monterey Bay Kayaks (693 Del Monte Avenue, Monterey 93942; (831–373–KELP) or Sea Kayak Monterey Bay (32 Cannery Row and 645 Cannery Row, Monterey 93942; 831–647–0147). They also have bike, Rollerblade, and boat rentals.

Join the otters and sea lions in their watery living room by paddling around the bay. It's much easier than you might think. A child must be 4½ feet tall and weigh eighty pounds, and can share a double kayak with a parent.

MONTEREY BAY AQUARIUM (all ages)

886 Cannery Row, Monterey 93942; (831) 648–4888; www.montereybay aquarium.org. Tickets are about $16.00 for adults, $13.00 for seniors and youths, and $8.00 for kids under 13. On weekends and holidays, arrive when the building opens, at 10:00 A.M. (9:00 A.M. in summer); otherwise, you may stand in a long line. Advance tickets are strongly recommended; purchase online www.mbayaq.org; at BASS ticket outlets, or by phone, (510) 762–BASS.

Restored smokestacks and boilers on a behemoth of a building create a cross between an old sardine cannery and a contemporary architectural masterpiece. More than 6,000 sea creatures reside here in giant tanks. Their natural habitat is one of the most biodiverse marine environments in the world, the Monterey Bay, encompassing 4,000 nautical square miles of kelp forests and rocky reefs. You'll see an amazing variety of creatures in the 90-foot-long Monterey Bay Habitat—leopard sharks, brightly colored nudibranchs, anemones, eels, otters, dolphins, whales, sharks, and hundreds more species.

The three-story Kelp Forest is the world's tallest aquarium exhibit. Playful sea otters and bat rays have their own glassed-in homes, and it's enjoyable to watch their feeding time.

When your feet wear out, sit down to watch live videos from an unmanned research submarine prowling Monterey Bay, as deep as 3,000 feet. From the aquarium's decks overlooking the harbor, you can peer down and watch otters and seals peering back at you.

Popular recent additions are the Outer Bay, containing open ocean species such as 10-foot-tall, one-and-a-half ton sunfish, huge stingrays, green sea turtles as big as dining room tables, vast schools of yellowfin tuna, and species of sharks too big for aquariums—until now. The

Drifters gallery contains the largest scale jellies exhibit in the world. Otherworldly music and a dreamlike design for the jellies venue transfix viewers before the pulsing, drifting, rainbow-hued beings.

In the new Splash Zone, young kids can stand inside a simulated penguin home, crawl into a "coral tunnel," touch sea creatures, enjoy entertainment, and play in a supervised area. There is even a play area for babies and toddlers.

Allow at least three hours for the aquarium; it can be crowded and sometimes overwhelming for little kids, so take breathers on the outdoor terrace, where salty breezes and the passing scene of watercraft will revive the spirits of even the crabbiest toddler.

The Invasion of the Butterflies

Millions of bright orange and black monarch butterflies escape winter cold and fly thousands of miles, returning to the same groves of eucalyptus, pine, and cypress on the California coast each year between October and March—a phenomenon occurring in a handful of places in the world. The city of Pacific Grove calls itself Butterfly Town USA and holds an annual children's parade to welcome the monarchs.

These are the most accessible places to see the unusual sight of the butterfly invasion:

- **Monarch Grove Sanctuary.** *Ridge Road off Lighthouse Avenue, Pacific Grove; (831) 373–3304; www.pacificgrove.com.* Self-guided or interpretive tours.

- **Butterfly Parade and Bazaar.** *October, in downtown Pacific Grove; (831) 646–6540.* Elementary school bands and children in butterfly costumes march to welcome the monarch's return to its winter home in Pacific Grove. A charming, beautiful hometown event.

- **Natural Bridges State Beach.** *Off West Cliff Drive, Santa Cruz; (831) 423–4609; gate.cruizio.com/law/natbr/.* Boardwalk and wheelchair-accessible observation area. Self-guided or interpretive tours. In February a Migration Festival is held to welcome the butterflies.

- **Point Lobos State Reserve.** *Three miles south of Carmel, on Highway 1; (831) 624–4909; www.pt-lobos.parks.state.ca.us/.* At the park entrance ask the ranger where to find the butterflies.

- **Butterfly Trees of Pismo Beach.** *Pismo State Beach, 2 miles south of Pismo Beach, south of San Luis Obispo; (831) 489–1869.* Guided tours offered.

17-MILE DRIVE (all ages)

Accessed at Spanish Bay at Asilomar and in the village of Carmel. Entry fee is $7.00 per car; (831) 649–1770.

Well worth the fee, even on a foggy day. The ghostly cypresses of Del Monte Forest and red lichen-painted rocks frame many vista points where you can stop, take photos, and explore the small beaches and tidepools. Golfers in the family will enjoy the chance to see several holes of some of the most famous and most difficult courses in the world: Pebble Beach Golf Links, the Links at Spanish Bay, and Cypress Point. Watch for erratic traffic; everyone slows down to ogle the mansions and seaside estates.

ASILOMAR CONFERENCE CENTER (all ages)

 800 Asilomar Road, Pacific Grove 93950; (888) 733–9005 or (831) 372–8016, www.asilomarcenter.com.

Unknown to most tourists, this secluded, rustic, historic resort hides in a pine and oak forest above beautiful Asilomar State Beach. Conference attendees sometimes fill up the place, but, when space is available, individuals and families rent rooms and suites here at very reasonable rates that include a bountiful, full breakfast buffet in a bright, pleasant dining room (dinner is available, too). There is a heated pool, volleyball, a game room, some rooms with fireplaces or kitchens, and easy accessibility to the wonderful tidepools and the wide, sandy beach, which is unsuitable for swimming or wading. Sixty acres of dunes are traversed by a 1-mile-long boardwalk, and a trail leads to wildflowery clifftops and stunning sea views. $–$$

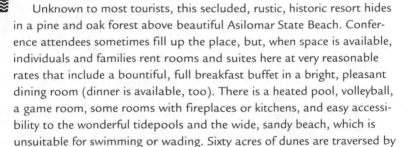DENNIS THE MENACE PLAYGROUND

On Pearl Street next to the El Estero Ballpark, Monterey; (831) 646–3866.

For little kids who can use some respite from sightseeing, a unique park designed by Hank Ketcham, the cartoonist who created Dennis, with fantastic structures such as a steam locomotive, a giant swing ride, a roller slide, and a special play area for the handicapped.

EDGEWATER FAMILY FUN CENTER (ages 5–12)

650 Wave Street, Monterey 93942; (831) 659–1899.

Over 100 video, pinball, and other games, and a 1905 carousel.

MONTEREY COUNTY YOUTH MUSEUM (ages 4–13)
601 Wave Street, Monterey 93942; (831) 649–6444; www.mymuseum.org.
A new hands-on learning center and museum, with sound experiments, a "creation station," hi-tech communications venues and changing exhibits.

 WILD THINGS (all ages)
Vision Quest Ranch, 400 River Road, Salinas 93908; (831) 455–1901; www.wildthingsinc.com. **Free** *admission.*
A unique opportunity to get close to exotic and wild animals, where they are trained for film, TV, and other productions. No reservations needed, just show up at 1:00 P.M. any day for a one-hour tour to see an African lion, a Bengal tiger, and more than 100 animals.

  ELKHORN SLOUGH AT MOSS LANDING (all ages)
Off Highway 1 between Santa Cruz and Monterey; (831) 633–2133.
A nice day-trip destination to view wetlands wildlife, Elkhorn Slough is home to thousands of sea- and shorebirds and animals. You can walk on 4 miles of easy trails in the mudflats and salt marshes and visit the Moss Landing Marine Laboratory, which is operated by nine California state universities (831–728–2822). A California record was set here for the most bird species seen in a day. You are likely to see herons, teal, plovers, golden eagles, terns, peregrine falcons, and dozens more wading and flying birds. Guided kayak and pontoon boat tours with natural history narration are the best ways to see wildlife. Try Slough Safari (408–424–3939), Venture Quest (408–427–2267), Kayak Connections (831–724–5692; www.cruzio.com), and Monterey Bay Kayaks (800–649– 5357, www.kayakelkhornslough.com). Boat tours are scheduled to take advantage of the tides, and the guides know where to find leopard sharks, bat rays, seals, otters, and other creatures.

Here at Moss Landing, there is a block or so of old store buildings devoted to antiques and "junque" shops. In July a big antiques and flea market takes place. Have a seafood lunch at Phil's Fish Market and Eatery, or yummy Mexican food at The Whole Enchilada.

Where to Eat

Pasta Mia. *481 Lighthouse Avenue, Pacific Grove 93950; (831) 375–7709.* Voted "Best Italian Restaurant"; homemade pasta, veal, grilled fish; country chic decor. $$

The Fishwife. *Near the Asilomar entrance to the 17-Mile Drive, 1996½ Sunset Drive, Pacific Grove 93950; (831) 375–7107.* A casual, popular, reasonably priced cafe with specialties such as Cajun blackened snapper, salmon alfredo, and Key lime pie. Reservations are essential; sunset views are legendary. Lunch, dinner, Sunday brunch. $–$$

Bubba Gump Shrimp Company. *720 Cannery Row, Monterey 93942; (831) 373–1884.* Fresh shrimp in dozens of dishes, fresh fish, steak; informal and fun. Yes, this is *Gump* as in *Forrest Gump.* $$

Fandango. *223 Seventeenth Street, Pacific Grove 93950; (831) 372–3456.* By the fire in the dining room, on the glass-domed terrace, or on the garden patio, European country style cuisine in a Mediterranean setting. Woodburning grill, pasta, paella, seafood, cassoulet. Full bar, exceptional wine list. $$

Abalonetti's. *57 Fisherman's Wharf, Monterey 93942; (831) 373–1851.* A family-operated restaurant on the wharf for over forty years, with an outdoor deck and indoor cafe, and comfortable spots for watching the gulls fly. Enjoy the freshest seafood in town, plus pizza and pasta. $–$$

Old Monterey Cafe. *489 Alvarado Street, Monterey 93942; (831) 646–1021; www.cafemonterey.com.* Voted "Best Breakfast" in the county. Try the buckwheat pancakes, huge omelets, and great salads and soups for lunch. $

Where to Stay

Lighthouse Lodge. *1150 Lighthouse Avenue, Pacific Grove 93950; (831) 858–1249 or (800) 858–1249.* On the seaside at Point Piños, twenty-nine suites with ocean views, fireplaces, Jacuzzi tubs. Full breakfast, afternoon refreshments. Casual, with space to run and play, popular with families. $$

Lone Oak Motel. *2221 North Fremont Street, Monterey 93942; (831) 372–4924.* A "best kept secret" for inexpensive family lodgings. Rooms, suites, kitchenettes, some fireplaces, sauna. $

Pajaro Dunes on Monterey Bay. *2661 Beach Road, Watsonville, between Monterey and Santa Cruz 94076; (831) 722–4671 or (800) 564–1771; www.pajarodunes.com.* Private beach community with rental homes, townhouses, and condos on 1.5 miles of private beach; 19 tennis courts; no pets. $$$–$$$$

Monterey Bay Inn. *242 Cannery Row, Monterey 93940; (800) 424–6242 or (831) 373–6242; www.montereybayinn.com.* A small, upscale seaside hotel;

each room has a king-size bed and oversized double sofa bed, a refrigerator, game table, and a pair of binoculars to watch the sea from your private balcony! Continental breakfast on the sunny garden patio is **Free**, and there is a private path to a small beach. $$$

Bay Lodging Reservations. *(831) 647–1107.*

Monterey Peninsula Reservations. *(888) 655–3424; www.montereyreservations.com.*

Monterey Getaway. *(800) 555–WAVE; www.timetocoast.com.*

For More Information

Monterey Visitor's Bureau. *P.O. Box 1770, Camino El Estero at the foot of Franklin Street, between Fremont and Del Monte Avenues, Monterey 93942; (831) 649–1770.*

Monterey Peninsula Visitors and Convention Bureau. *380 Alvarado Street, Monterey 93942–1770; (831) 649–1770; www.monterey.com.*

National Steinbeck Center

National Steinbeck Center *371 Main Street, Salinas, CA 93901; (831) 796–3833; www.steinbeck.org. Admission is $7.95 for adults, $5.95 for students and ages 13 to 17, $3.95 for ages 6 to 12.* **Free** *for under 5.* Some time during their schooling, most American youngsters read John Steinbeck's *East of Eden, Of Mice and Men* and *The Grapes of Wrath*. If your family's trip to the Monterey area coincides with your child's interest in Steinbeck, make the 20 mile drive inland from Monterey. The 37,000 square-foot museum is uniquely child-friendly, with interactive displays of the author's book and the time and place in which he lived. You can open a drawer to see his childhood treasures; feel the chill of an "ice packed" boxcar filled with lettuce; experience the smells and the sounds of "Doc" Rickett's science lab on Cannery Row; and learn of migrant life in the Salinas Valley. There are vintage photos, ongoing videos and movies, doors and windows that open into historic vignettes, and Steinbeck's charming camper truck in which he motored with his dog and wrote *Travels with Charley*.

The cafe here is light and airy, with a sunny patio and reasonably priced snacks and lunches.

A few blocks away, Steinbeck's boyhood home is a beautifully restored, elaborately decorated Victorian loaded with memorabilia (132 Central Avenue; 831–424–2745). You can have lunch here, although it's a rather stuffy atmosphere for kids.

Carmel

A one-square-mile village of rustic country cottages and shingled beach houses, Carmel—the queen of quaint—nestles in an idyllic pine forest above a white-sand beach. Wandering the lanes off Ocean Avenue, the main street, you will see peaked-roofed doll's houses side by side with miniature castles and small summer cabins built in the 1920s and 1930s.

Shopping, shopping, shopping happens in hundreds of boutiques on Ocean Avenue and nearby streets, tucked into garden courtyards and in Carmel Plaza. Originally a Bohemian artists' and writers' colony, Carmel has more than seventy-five art and photography galleries.

There are kid-friendly shops, restaurants that welcome families, inland and coastal parks, beaches, and a fascinating California mission to explore.

Carmel is particularly dog-friendly. Dogs are allowed on leashes throughout the town and can run free on Carmel Beach. Some lodgings and even some restaurants make special accommodation for canine family members.

MISSION SAN CARLOS BORROMEO DEL RIO CARMEL (all ages)

Rio Road, on the south side of town near the beach, Carmel; (831) 624–1271.

The second mission founded by Father Junipero Serra, a glorious Spanish-Moorish cathedral surrounded by lovely gardens. Inside, the church is sienna, burnt umber, and gold, with soaring ceilings and star-shaped stained-glass windows. On a warm summer's day, walk beneath shady colonnades and sit beside a trickling fountain.

A warren of thick-walled rooms, restored from original mission buildings, hold a magnificent museum collection of Native American, religious, and early California artifacts. In September, the Carmel Mission Fiesta is a family affair.

On Rio Road across from the Mission (or at Mountain View and Crespi, or Eleventh Street and Junipero), you can access Mission Trail Park, 35 acres of cypress and pine forest and native vegetation, with 5 miles of easy walking trails.

CARMEL BEACH

At the bottom of Ocean Avenue, the main street of Carmel; (831) 624–3543.

Offering fine, soft, white granite and quartz sand, a popular place to watch the sun sink into the ocean. A kite-flying contest takes place here in May. A big annual event is the Sand Castle Contest in fall, when architects and amateurs vie for the biggest, best, sand structure.

*S*hopping with Kids in Carmel

- **Carmel Doll Shop.** *Court of the Golden Eagle, Carmel; (831) 624–2607.* A fairyland of antique European dolls, teddy bears, and Victorian gewgaws.

- **Come Fly a Kite.** *Carmel Plaza, corner of Ocean Avenue and Mission, Carmel; (831) 624–3422.* A must stop before the beach.

- **Cottage of Sweets.** *Ocean Avenue between Monte Verde and Lincoln; (831) 624–5170.* British sweets, homemade fudge, gummies, old-fashioned American "penny candy."

- **Toys in the Attic.** *Carmel Plaza; (831) 622–9011.* Collectibles, classic toys, Madame Alexander dolls, Steiff animals, Beanies, and more.

- **Total Dog,** *26366 Carmel Rancho Lane across from the Barnyard, Carmel; (831) 624–5553.* Dog raincoats and boots, dog jewelry, books and toys, figurines, plush doggie beds and treats.

- **Gibson Gallery of Animation.** *San Carlos and Seventh, Carmel; (831) 624–9296.* From Disney and other animation studios, a fabulous, changing collection of original animation cels and vintage cels. Provides a fascinating look at how animated movies are made.

- **Thinker Toys.** *Seventh and San Carlos Streets, Carmel; (408) 624–0441.* One of the world's greatest toy and game emporiums.

- **The Mischievous Rabbit.** *Lincoln between Ocean and Seventh, Carmel; (408) 624–6854.* A warren of Peter Rabbit–inspired treasures—hand-painted baby clothing, rabbit videos and books, carrot surprises.

CARMEL RIVER STATE BEACH (all ages)
Highway 1, just south of Carmel; (831) 624–4909.

Adjacent to Monastery Beach and the Carmel River Bird Sanctuary, frequented by a wide variety of waterfowl and shorebirds, a place to wander the dunes and pick up driftwood and shells, or make a 2-mile round-trip run or walk. You may see scuba divers getting ready to descend into the kelp forests of the Carmel Bay Ecological Reserve offshore. Restrooms, picnic sites.

POINT LOBOS STATE RESERVE (all ages)

Four miles south of Carmel, on Highway 1; (831) 624–4909.

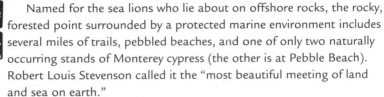

Named for the sea lions who lie about on offshore rocks, the rocky, forested point surrounded by a protected marine environment includes several miles of trails, pebbled beaches, and one of only two naturally occurring stands of Monterey cypress (the other is at Pebble Beach). Robert Louis Stevenson called it the "most beautiful meeting of land and sea on earth."

From 6 miles of coastline in the park, visitors often see whales, harbor seals, otters, scuba divers, and storms of pelicans, gulls, and cormorants. In the meadows mule deer tiptoe through purple needlegrass and wild lilac. Point Lobos is completely protected: the land, the marine life on the beach and in the tidepools, and underwater. Not a thing may be removed or disturbed; dogs are not allowed; and visitors are required to stay on hiking trails or beaches. Kids particularly like Sea Lion Point, accessed by an easy half-hour walk to Headland Cove, where sea lions bark and you can see the otters. It will take a half-day to enjoy the sights of Point Lobos, and you are advised to come early on weekends. Guided interpretive walks are conducted by park rangers.

Where to Eat

Katy's Place. *Mission Street between Fifth and Sixth, Carmel 93921; (831) 624–0199.* French toast with strawberries, nine kinds of eggs Benedict, and a million omelets. A locals' favorite, serving breakfast and lunch like grandma used to make. $

General Store and Forge in the Forest. *Corner of Fifth and Junipero, Carmel 93921; (831) 624–2233.* At an umbrella table under the oaks, on a heated patio, or inside by the fireplace, fresh fish, burgers, and salads are the best. $$

Village Corner. *Corner of Sixth and Dolores, Carmel 93921; (831) 624–3588.* Inside and on the sunny patio, sandwiches, salads, and lower prices than at most such places in Carmel. This is a locals' hangout. I often lunched here with my mom, while she commiserated with her neighbors about how Carmel wasn't like it had been before the tour buses came to town. Breakfast, lunch, and dinner. $

Carmel Mission Ranch. *26270 Dolores Street, Carmel 93921; (831) 624–3824.* Overlooking the Carmel River with views of Carmel Bay and Point Lobos, cowboys and cowgirls kick back and eat steak, local fresh fish, and California cuisine in casual surroundings. Plush, pricey rooms here are in charming former ranch buildings and can be great for family groups; some accommodations have several bedrooms, fireplaces, living rooms, and memorabilia from Clint Eastwood's movies (he owns the place). $$

Caffe Napoli. *Ocean between Dolores and Lincoln, Carmel; (831) 625–4033.* Pizza, pasta, and bruschetta on checkered tablecloths. $

Bruno's Market and Deli. *Sixth and Junipero, Carmel; (831) 624–3821.* Voted "Best Grocery Store" in the county. Wonderful gourmet sandwiches and salads, ready-made entrees, sushi, barbecued chicken and meats, beautiful produce. $

Where to Stay

Carmel River Inn. *2660 Oliver Road, Carmel 93921; (831) 624–1575.* On the south end of Carmel at the Carmel River bridge overlooking the river, with a swimming pool and simple rooms and cottages; some have fireplaces, two bedrooms, kitchenettes and refrigerators. $$–$$$

Carmel Village Inn. *Ocean Avenue and Junipero Streets, Carmel; (831) 624–3864.*

Lovely landscaped grounds with thirty-four rooms, some with microwaves and refrigerators; some studio apartments with kitchens and fireplaces. $$$

Carmel Wayfarer Inn. *Fourth and Mission Streets, Carmel; (831) 624–2711.* Small rooms, some with fireplaces and kitchenettes; two units with sleeper sofas in living room. $$$

For More Information

Carmel Business Association (visitor bureau). *San Carlos between Fifth and Sixth, P.O. Box 4444, Carmel 93921; (831) 624–2522; www.chamber.carmel.ca.us.* Upstairs in the Eastwood Building, you can pick up a walking-tour map and brochures.

Carmel Valley

A few miles inland from Carmel, the Carmel River runs along between two small mountain ranges through horse farms and farmland. The tawny climate is warm and dry when fog blankets the coastline. Near tiny Carmel Valley Village, 11.5 miles from Highway 1, are a few small ranch resorts and not much else except horseback-riding and hiking trails, tennis courts, and swimming pools. Inexpensive lodgings, fewer people, and good weather make the valley a great headquarters for family trips to the Monterey and Carmel areas.

Shopping is one of the primary activities in the town of Carmel, but dragging young kids through quaint shops can quickly turn into a family disaster. One of the easiest and most fun places I've ever seen for shopping with kids is the Barnyard, at the entrance to Carmel Valley.

THE BARNYARD

At the intersection of Highway 1 and Carmel Valley Road, 5 minutes south of Carmel; (831) 624–8886.

A rambling complex of shops and restaurants in contemporary barn buildings where kids can run around outside on terraces among a riot of blooming plants and flowers, or sit on a bench with a book or a game while parents browse. Several restaurants in the Barnyard include a crumpet cafe, an English pub, a Chinese place, and a pizzeria.

THUNDERBIRD BOOKSHOP AND RESTAURANT

The Barnyard; (831) 624–1803. Open daily 10:00 A.M. to 8:00 P.M.

For a leisurely lunch indoors or out—and by the fireplace in wintertime—let the children select books to read (it's allowed) while they eat healthy salads, grilled sandwiches, homemade soups, and monster desserts. $

SANDCASTLE-BY-THE-SEA

The Barnyard; (831) 626–8361.

Wooden toys, games, kits, costumes—well-made, sturdy things that parents feel good about.

FRIENDS OF THE SEA OTTER

The Barnyard; (831) 625–3290.

Unique in the world, the complete sea otter store and education center.

GARLAND RANCH REGIONAL PARK (all ages)

About 8.6 miles east of Highway 1, on Carmel Valley Road, Carmel Valley; (831) 659–4488.

The primary public venue for outdoor recreation in the valley, the park runs along the river and up onto the ridges in oak forests—5,000 acres of wilderness crisscrossed by trails. The most popular paths are the easy Lupine Loop, the Buckeye, and the Waterfall Trail to the mesa. In springtime wildflowers explode in great colorful clouds, water rushes over the falls, and lush grass surrounds the pond on the mesa. Up here views of the entire valley are mesmerizing.

Near the parking lot, picnic sites beside the river are pleasant on hot days. John Steinbeck wrote in *Cannery Row*, "The Carmel [River] crackles among round boulders, wanders lazily under sycamores, spills into pools, drops in against banks where crayfish live . . . frogs blink from its banks and the deep ferns grow beside it. It's everything a river should be."

Where to Eat

Rio Grill. *101 Crossroads Boulevard, Carmel 93923, in a shopping center near Highway 1 and Carmel Valley Road; (831) 625–5436.* Santa Fe–style decor, butcher-paper-covered tables with crayons for the creative, and tons of awards, such as Best Restaurant in Monterey County, make this a top choice for Southwestern-style food. A woodburning grill and an oakwood smoker produce fresh fish, meat, and poultry specialties. $$

Bon Appetit. *7 Delfino Place, Carmel Valley Village 93921; (831) 659–3559.* Sit outdoors under an umbrella, watch the passing scene of the village, and enjoy bouillabaisse, paella, mesquite-grilled fresh fish, gourmet pizzas, and a notable wine list. $$

Wills Fargo. *Carmel Valley Road and El Caminito, Carmel Valley Village 93921; (831) 659–2774.* Steak by the pound, casual western atmosphere, dependably good, and fun for years and years. $$

Where to Stay

Riverside RV Park and Saddle Mountain RV Park. *A mile off Carmel Valley Road on Schulte Road, Carmel Valley 93923; (831) 624–9329.* Tree-shaded RV sites, most with nice views of the valley. Large, attractive swimming-pool terrace, with picnic tables under oak trees. Day use is available for the pool and barbecues. $

Valley Lodge. *8 Ford Road, Carmel Valley 93923; (800) 641–4646.* Small,

quiet, reasonably priced, with pretty patio rooms and fireplace cottages, a heated pool, and a sauna; continental breakfast included. $$

Blue Sky Lodge. *Carmel Valley Road at Flight Road, P.O. Box 233, Carmel Valley 93923; (831) 659–2256.* Large family units, living rooms and fireplaces, heated pool. Pets welcome. Walk to the village. $$

For More Information

Carmel Valley Chamber of Commerce. *Oak Building, Carmel Valley Road, Carmel Valley 93923; (831) 659–4000.*

Big Sur

Beginning just south of Carmel along Highway 1, Big Sur is a sparsely developed stretch of coastal wilderness that runs 90 miles south to San Simeon. High cliffs and river valleys are hemmed in by the rugged Santa Lucia Mountains on one side and a largely inaccessible seacoast on the other, with sheer 1,000-foot drops to beaches below. Offshore are natural arches and sea stacks, rocky remnants of ancient shores. The two-lane highway is crossed by nearly thirty bridges over wild canyons, deep valleys, and creeks that rush down mountains into ferocious ocean surf—a scenic drive but rather unrelentingly curvy for younger children if you drive more than a half-hour or so at a time. Fortunately, there are many stops to make for walks in forest parks, beach explorations, and lunches and snacks at a few—just a few—cafes.

Big Sur is a banana belt, with higher temperatures than Carmel and Monterey, receiving more rain but also more sunny days. In winter you'll often find clear, blue skies here when it's drippy just a few miles north. In several river and forest parks, including the Los Padres National Forest, are good campgrounds and walking and hiking trails.

Be aware there are only a handful of gas stations and grocery stores on the Big Sur highway, and prices are astronomical.

POINT SUR LIGHT STATION (all ages)

Nineteen miles south of Rio Road in Carmel on Highway 1; (831) 625–4419; www.lighthouse-pointsur-ca.org.

A historic 1889 stone lighthouse, several buildings, and an interpretive center are open for guided tours, with reservations required. The two- to three-hour tour includes a 0.5-mile walk with a 300-foot gradual climb to the lighthouse, located on a dramatic promontory over the sea. Wildflowers and whales are frequent rewards.

ANDREW MOLERA STATE PARK (all ages)

Twenty-two miles south of Carmel, on Highway 1 (access not suitable for RVs); (831) 667–2315.

The Big Sur River flows down from the Santa Lucias through 4,800-acre Molera State Park, falling into the sea at a long sandy beach. One of many hiking trails runs along the river through a eucalyptus grove where monarch butterflies overwinter, to the river mouth, where you can see a variety of sea- and shorebirds. Besides ancient redwoods, you will encounter the Santa Lucia fir, found only here, and possibly the endangered peregrine falcon and bald eagles.

Reservations are not accepted for the walk-in tent campground in a meadow; the facility has picnic sites, a horseback-riding concession, biking trails, and restrooms. For trail maps and information, write in advance to the U.S. Forest Service, 406 South Mildred, King City 93930 (408–385–5434).

One of the most unforgettable ways to see Big Sur is on horseback. Molera Trail Rides offers daily two-hour rides in the park, each featuring a different perspective, such as the beach, redwood groves, mountain ridges, and sunset excursions (831–625–5486 or 800–942–5486).

PFEIFFER BIG SUR STATE PARK (all ages)

Twenty-six miles south of Carmel, on Highway 1; (831) 667–2171 or (831) 667–2315.

The most popular, easily accessible, and family-friendly park in the area, a place to hike, picnic, and fish on the Big Sur River. A system of short trails around the campground leads to giant redwoods, a waterfall, river boulders, and pools. A 1.8-mile creekside loop brings you to 60-foot Pfeiffer Falls in a fern canyon and to dazzling ridgetop views. Docent-led nature walks to Pfeiffer Beach are given in summer.

More than 200 developed, tree-shaded campsites offer fire rings, toilets, motel/cabins, a lodge, picnic areas, a restaurant, a gift shop, a Laundromat, restrooms, and showers. Next to the park at Big Sur Station, park rangers hand out trail maps and give advice on trail conditions.

NEPENTHE

Twenty-nine miles south of Carmel, on Highway 1; (831) 667–2345.

For decades a favorite destination for visitors in the Big Sur area, the restaurant features stone patios perched over the sea that offer a long and magical view of a spectacular shoreline. Try the ambrosia burger or the fresh fish, and plan to spend a leisurely lunchtime. $$

JULIA PFEIFFER BURNS STATE PARK (all ages)

Thirty-seven miles south of Carmel, on Highway 1; (831) 667–2315.

A glowing jewel of forest and coastline on 3,600 acres of undeveloped wilderness. A 0.5-mile, easy trail along McWay Creek leads to a waterfall that plunges over an 80-foot cliff into the ocean. The Partington Creek Trail goes through a canyon and a 100-foot rock tunnel to Partington Cove Beach, where sea otters play in the kelp beds.

About halfway to San Simeon, Jade Cove is actually a string of coves, where Monterey jade is found at low tide and following storms.

On Highway 1 along the entire Big Sur coastline, deer and other wildlife frequently wander onto the road, especially at night, so it is best to drive slowly and enjoy the views, safely!

Where to Eat

Ripplewood Resort. *Twenty-four miles south of Carmel on Highway 1, Big Sur Valley; (831) 667–2242.* Good for breakfast, lunch, and Mexican dinners. $

Rocky Point. *Ten miles south of Carmel on Highway 1; (831) 624–2933; www.*

rocky-point.com. Spectacular views of the coast from the dining room and the terrace make breakfast, lunch, and dinner memorable experiences. Try the enchiladas, the crab salad, or one of the fabulous steaks. $$

Where to Stay

Ventana Big Sur Campground. *Thirty miles south of Carmel, on Highway 1; (831) 667–2331.* A lovely private campground in a 40-acre redwood grove. $

Big Sur Lodge. *Just inside the entrance to Pfeiffer Big Sur State Park, P.O. Box 190, Big Sur 93920; (831) 667–2171 or (800) 424–4787; www.bigsurlodge.com.* Cozy, simple cottages in a forest; kitchens, fireplaces; lovely views; pool. The casual family-oriented restaurant serves California cuisine, pasta, local seafood, and stuff kids like; the patio overlooks the Big Sur River—heavenly. $$

Deetjen's Big Sur Inn. *Thirty-one miles south of Carmel, on Highway 1; (831) 667–2377.* Quaint, rustic, Norwegian-style inn in a redwood grove, twenty simple

cottages, fireplaces or woodburning stoves, down comforters. Each cottage has two or three separate guest rooms with shared bath (choose your unit carefully, as some can be noisy). The restaurant serves good American food. $$

River Inn. *Pheneger Creek, Big Sur 93920; (800) 328–2884.* Eighteen queen rooms and family suites with balconies overlooking the river; simple, rustic accommodations. Restaurant and bar, swimming pool, general store; near state parks. $

Riverside Campground and Cabins. *Twenty-five miles south of Carmel, P.O. Box 3, Big Sur 93920; (831) 667 -2414.* Campsites, RV sites, communal bathhouse. $

For More Information

Big Sur Chamber of Commerce. *P.O. Box 87, Big Sur, CA 93920; (831) 667–2100; www.bigsurcalifornia.org.*

Big Sur Reservations. *(831) 667–2929. A variety of lodgings.*

The Big Valley

alifornia's rich agricultural heartland rolls for hundreds of miles between the Sierra Nevada Range and the Coastal Range. Freshened with many lakes and reservoirs, almost a dozen rivers, and 1,000 miles of inland Delta waterways, a string of verdant valleys—the Sacramento, the Santa Clara, and the San Joaquin—is paradise for families who love to fish, water-ski, houseboat, play outdoors, and camp.

The state capitol and three good-size towns along the north–south valley route, Highway 99, are gateways to the central and southern Sierras, three national parks, and several national forests. And a tiny inland village, founded by the Spanish and the original Native American residents, is a side trip not to be missed.

Sacramento

The mighty **Sacramento River**—wide, cool, and green; fringed with overhanging trees; and loaded with fish—nourishes a valley that feeds the world. Astride the river the state capitol, Sacramento, was a simple homesteader's fort that became a boomtown during the Gold Rush in the mid-1800s and was the western terminus for the Pony Express and the Transcontinental Railroad. The main historic and recreational attractions for families are the California State Capitol, Old Town Sacramento, the State Railroad Museum, and the river itself. Several excellent marinas, with outdoor restaurants and boat tie-ups, are found along the Garden Highway on the northern edge of the city. Thousands of magnificent old trees and glorious Victorian mansions line the downtown streets. Beautiful homes are found from Seventh to Sixteenth Streets, and from E to I Streets; don't miss the Heilbron home at 740 O Street and the Stanford home at 800 N Street.

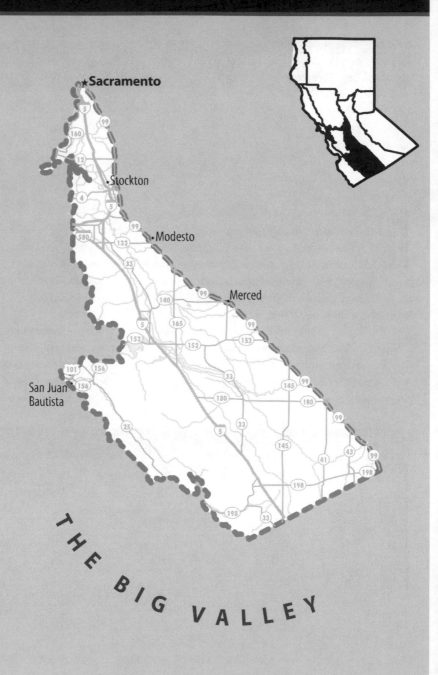

THE BIG VALLEY

The sports fans in your family will enjoy exciting home games of the NBA Kings and the WNBA Monarchs. A Triple-A baseball team, the River Cats, play in a new stadium in Old Sacramento.

Summer days average temperatures in the nineties, with many days topping hundred-degree temperatures, but this is a city of more than a million trees, as well as access to the water, so relief is never far away.

South from Sacramento along Highway 160, ramshackle fishing villages and small resorts are scattered on the banks of the river and throughout a vast delta. The tiny town of Locke is the state's only surviving rural Chinese community from the turn of the century. Boats and ferries, sailboards, houseboats, and skiffs ply miles of meandering waterways.

 ### CALIFORNIA STATE CAPITOL (all ages)

Tenth Street and Capitol Mall, Sacramento; (916) 324–0333.

 The circa 1870, double-domed capitol is surrounded by forty acres of Capitol Park, a century-old botanical garden that explodes into pink and white clouds of camellias, azaleas, dogwood, and tulips every spring. You can take a guided tour of the gardens or stroll around on your own.

With toddlers and little kids, take a self-guided tour and let them meander up and down the marble hallways while you peek in at the museum displays. You'll see magnificent carved staircases, elaborate crystal chandeliers, marble parquet floors, and historic artwork. You might even be able to sit in on a legislative session. With children about 8 years old and older, take the guided historic tour, where you'll hear stories of California's colorful politicos (call ahead to reserve). **Free**.

 ### OLD TOWN SACRAMENTO (all ages)

Between I Street, Capitol Mall, the Sacramento River and Highway 5; (916) 264–7777 or (916) 442–7644; www.oldsacramento.com.

  Early in the morning when the mist hangs low on the Sacramento River, footsteps echo on the boardwalks of Old Town, and you can imagine the rollicking port during the California Gold Rush, when as many as 800 sailing vessels tied up here at the docks. Reeling from months of sailing around the Horn, gold seekers raced down the gang-planks, bargained for provisions and livestock, then rode away in wagons and on horseback to seek their fortunes in the Sierra foothills. "Forty-niner" days are still alive in the restored wooden false-front saloons, firehouses, dining halls, and emporiums of Old Town Sacramento, a National Historical Monument.

Browsing the 100 boutique shops, more than 20 restaurants, and museums and historical sites will take a full day or two. Annual events in Old Town include the Festival de la Familia, with hundreds of vendors and **Free** entertainment, such as Latin, Caribbean, and Native American music; the Pacific Rim Festival; and the huge Jazz Jubilee.

From spring to fall, a bright yellow water taxi runs from the L Street landing to three marinas along the river, where you can stop and dine at waterfront restaurants.

The Great Outdoors Near Sacramento

- **Folsom Lake Recreation Area.** *Twenty-five miles east of Sacramento off Highway 50, between Folsom and Auburn; (800) 444–7275.* Extending 15 miles up the canyon of the North Fork of the American River, an 18,000-acre lake that's great for camping, boating, swimming, hiking, and fishing. You can rent horses and bikes here for exploring more than 80 miles of trails. At the marina, reserve a campsite at one of the tent and RV camps, bike camps, or equestrian camps (916–988–0205). Windsurfing is popular, especially in April and May.

- **Brannan Island State Recreation Area.** *Highway 160, 3 miles south of Rio Vista; (916) 777–7701.* Another windsurfing paradise is Windy Cove, right in the middle of the Delta on the Sacramento River. Windy Cove was developed by local surfing fanatics and is one of the primo spots in the state.

- **Grizzly Island.** *Take Highway 12 toward Rio Vista, go south on Grizzly Island Road at the Sunset Shopping Center, then proceed 9 miles to the wildlife preserve; (707) 425–3828. The entrance fee is $2.50 per adult.* You'll see river otters, turtles, tule elk, egrets, herons, coots, wigeons, grebes, and many more animals and birds in this 8,600-acre wildlife preserve in the Sacramento Delta. A relaxing place to take an outdoor break between Sacramento and the Bay Area, Grizzly Island is best in winter, when thousands of migratory waterfowl stop to feed and rest in the Suisun Marsh surrounding the island (avoid October through mid-January, which is duck-hunting season).

SOUTHERN RAILROAD EXCURSIONS (all ages)

Front Street in Old Sacramento at the railroad depot; (916) 446–6645, www. csrmf.org. Admission for adults $6.00, ages 6 to 12 $3.00, and under 6 go free.

Tuckered from sightseeing in Old Sacramento? Pile everyone aboard a vintage passenger coach or an open-air gondola for a forty-minute, 6-mile ride along the river, pulled by a steam locomotive. The whistle blasts, the steam pours out, and the river breezes blow! Definitely worth the price.

CALIFORNIA STATE RAILROAD MUSEUM (all ages)

North side of Old Town Sacramento; (916) 445–7387 or (916) 445–6645; www.csrmf-org. Admission for adults $6.00, ages 6 to 12 $3.00, under 5 go free.

A 100,000-square-foot display of three dozen antique locomotives and railcars in pristine condition, the museum is a dream come true for kids fascinated by rail travel. You can hop aboard a real sleeping car that rocks back and forth and sounds as if it's rolling along. Retired conductors spin tales of the rails. One of the magnificent engines weighs a mere million pounds. On the second level a wonderful toy train runs through tiny towns and over bridges. Children can climb around several cars indoors and outdoors and take a short train ride up and down the river. Next to the museum the Railroad Museum Gift Shop sells myriad toy trains, books, and railroad-related souvenirs. The annual California Railroad Festival is held here in June (916-445-7387).

FANNY ANN'S (all ages)

1023 Second Street, Old Town Sacramento 95814; (916) 441–0505.

Five floors of a crazily antiques-crammed restaurant and bar, a fun place to take the kids during the day; an adult crowd gathers at night. Play pinball while you wait for American food, burgers and fries, salads, and sandwiches. $$

STICKY FINGERS (all ages)

1027 Second Street, Old Town Sacramento 95814; (916) 443–4075.

On the second floor of a vintage building, dig into ribs, chicken, and seafood. A live Dixieland combo often plays on the veranda. $$

MIKE'S PUZZLE STORE

1009 Second Street, Old Town Sacramento 95814; (916) 444–0446.
Hundreds—maybe thousands—of puzzles.

ROCKY MOUNTAIN CHOCOLATE FACTORY (all ages)

1039 Second Street, Old Town Sacramento 95814; (916) 448–8801.
Hand-dipped ice cream bars, caramel apples, chocolate-covered strawberries, and fresh, homemade candy. You could be in trouble here.

DISCOVERY MUSEUM HISTORY CENTER (all ages)

101 I Street, Old Town Sacramento 95814; (916) 264–7057; www.thediscovery. org. Admission for adults $5.00, ages 13 to 17 $4.00, ages 6 to 12 $3.00, under 6 go Free.

I had a hard time getting my granddaughters out of here. Besides permanent hands-on history, science, and technology exhibits, there are temporary interactive presentations of geography puzzles, science carnivals, games, and demonstrations and California's largest gold collection.

DISCOVERY MUSEUM SCIENCE AND SPACE CENTER/
CHALLENGER LEARNING CENTER (all ages)

3615 Auburn Boulevard, Sacramento 95821; (916) 575–3941, www.thediscovery. org. Admission for adults $5.00, ages 13 to 17 $4.00, ages 6 to 12 $3.00, under 6 go Free.

Take a break at the relaxing planetarium show, and explore space, wildlife, and science exhibits; there is also a short nature trail. The terrific shop here sells science-related books, toys, and games. Make reservations for the monthly simulated space missions (916-485-8836).

GOLFLAND/SUNSPLASH (ages 5–18)

1893 Taylor Road, 15 minutes south of Sacramento on Highway 80, Roseville, 95661; (916) 784–1273, www.Golfland-SunSplash.com.

On a 100-degree day (nearly every day in midsummer), stop here to cool off in the water slides and wave pool, plus two mini-golf courses, a laser tag arena, and zillions of arcade games.

TOWE FORD MUSEUM (all ages)

2200 Front Street, Old Town Sacramento 95814; (916) 442–6802.
Crazy for cars? Visit this cache of almost 200 antique and classic cars and trucks, including every Ford car from 1903 to 1953.

JEDEDIAH SMITH MEMORIAL BICYCLE TRAIL/AMERICAN RIVER PARKWAY (all ages)

A paved biking and walking path follows the river for 23 miles, from Old Town to Folsom Lake, in the foothills of Gold Country. Guided walks on the parkway are available through the **Effie Yeaw Nature Center** (916–489–4918). For a trail map contact the Parks Department (916–875–6961). Summer temperatures on the trail are often one hundred degrees or higher, with balmy evenings.

SACRAMENTO JAZZ JUBILEE (all ages)

Old Sacramento and venues around the city; (916) 372–5277; www.sacjazz.com. Tickets are $15 to $85.

Jazz fans assemble in droves on Memorial Day weekend to hear the top Dixieland bands in the world, and Latin jazz and Big Band music. This is definitely a family affair during the day—you will see kids kicking up their heels with moms, dads, and grandparents. On the **Free** kids' stage on the grass at the north end of Old Sacramento, youngsters blow kazoos, crash around on drums, and have a ball. There is a "Trainyard for Kids" play area and a children's parade on three mornings in a row! The main Jubilee Parade downtown is on Friday. Reserve lodgings well in advance.

SACRAMENTO ZOO (all ages)

3930 West Lane Park Drive in William Land Park, Sacramento 95814; (916) 264–5885. Admission is $4.50 for persons ages 13 and up and $3.00 for kids ages 3 to 12.

Recently remodeled and expanded, with national recognition for the rare cat, primate, and bird collections, and the red panda exhibit.

Across the street from the zoo, **Fairytale Town** is heaven for the littlest angels, with play structures themed to Mother Goose, puppet shows, and more. Also here is **Funderland,** an amusement park with rides for kids of elementary school age. **William Land Park** is a large city park, with playgrounds, picnic areas, and a duck pond.

Where to Eat

Crawdads River Cantina. *1375 Garden Highway, Sacramento; (916) 929–2269.* Try the Cajun popcorn (shrimp fried in beer batter) and watch the river roll by; children's menu, festive American food. $$

Ford's Real Hamburgers. *1948 Sutterville Road, near William Land Park, Sacramento 95814; (916) 452–6979.* The real thing, reasonably priced. $

Vic's. *3199 Riverside Boulevard, near Land Park, Sacramento 95814; (916) 448–0892.* Old-fashioned soda fountain, sandwiches, thick shakes, homemade ice cream. $

Max's Opera Cafe. *1725 Arden Way at Arden Fair Mall, Sacramento 95814; (916) 927–6297.* As good as the famous Max's in San Francisco, this New York-style upscale deli serves fabulous sandwiches, burgers, pasta, and salads, followed by legendary mile-high pieces of pie and cake. At night, the staff sings opera and show tunes. $$

Old Spaghetti Factory. *1910 J Street, Sacramento 95814(also in Roseville and Rancho Cordova); (915) 443–2862.* Sit in the trolley car or at a wooden table under the stained-glass chandeliers, in a bright, Old Town environment. The good, traditional Italian food is inexpensive, especially at lunch, and the children's menu features the simpler items that kids prefer. $

Al the Wop's. *On the blocklong main street of the Chinese town of Locke, near Walnut Grove 95690; (916) 776–1800.* Thousands of dollar bills are tacked to the ceiling, peanut butter and jelly sit on the tables, and the steak sandwiches and burgers are legendary in this atmospheric remnant of the little old town where Chinese fishermen lived. After lunch, take a peek into the Dai Loy Museum and the "junque" shop Locke Ness. $

Where to Stay

Radisson Hotel Sacramento. *500 Leisure Lane, Sacramento 95814; (916) 922–2020 or (800) 333–3333.* Five minutes' drive from Old Town, a comfortable oasis, with swimming pools, par course, bike rentals, gardens around a small lake, and several restaurants. Each room or suite has a balcony or patio overlooking eighteen acres of gardens. $$

Best Western Sutter House. *1100 H Street, Sacramento 95814; (916) 441–1314 or (800) 830–1314; www.thesutterhouse. com.* Good value and convenient to downtown and Old Town Sacramento. Ask for a room on the pool courtyard. Simple rooms; continental breakfast included. $–$$

For More Information

Sacramento Convention and Visitor's Bureau. *1303 J Street, Sacramento 95814; (916) 264–7777; www.sacramentocvb.org.*

Visitor Information Center. *1101 Second Street, Old Sacramento 95814; (916) 442–7644.*

California Division of Tourism. *801 K Street, Sacramento 95814; (800) 862–2543; www.gocalif.ca.gov.* Information and brochures for travel statewide.

Stockton

The largest of the Delta towns, Stockton is a deep-water port anchoring hundreds of miles of inland waterways. If your family likes to fish and mess about in boats, the Stockton area has it all.

Fed by the Sacramento River, the San Joaquin, and five more rivers with origins in the snowpack of the Sierras, the Delta is one of the largest recreation areas in the country. Exploring this enormous labyrinth of sloughs, canals, and meandering rivers can be on foot on a shady path, or slow, sweet days motoring about on a houseboat, or making waves on water skis behind a speedboat. For the locations of launching ramps and marinas and to find out what's biting, call or stop in at a local sports equipment store.

In town are a few bright spots, including a lovely historic district and a fairyland amusement park. A big annual family-oriented event is the **Great Italian Street Painting Festival** in May, when you can stroll the artfully decorated sidewalks. Kids can get into the act, too.

Just north of Stockton the last undammed river flowing from the Sierras through the Central Valley—the Consumnes—provides unparalleled wildlife viewing. The Nature Conservancy preserve on the river has easy trails through wetlands and forests rich with bird life.

MAGNOLIA HISTORIC DISTRICT (all ages)

A rough rectangle between Flora Street and Harding Way, and El Dorado and California. Get street maps from the Visitor's Bureau, 46 West Fremont Street, Stockton 95202; (800) 350–1987.

Take a short drive or an hour's stroll around Stockton's lovely old residential district to see homes from as early as 1860—extravagantly decorated Victorians, romantic Spanish Revival mansions, and Craftsman cottages, a rich architectural cache on tree-shaded streets.

CHILDREN'S MUSEUM OF STOCKTON (ages 2–10)

402 West Weber, Stockton 95202; (209) 465–4FUN.

Some 24,000 wonderful square feet of hands-on stuff to do and learn, with a play grocery store, hospital, and bank; a TV station; art, music, and science demonstrations and games; and a special area for toddlers.

PIXIE WOODS/LOUIS PARK (ages 1–10)

Monte Diablo and Occidental Avenue, Stockton; (209) 937–8206. Tickets are adults $1.75 and kids under 12 $1.25.

A fairyland park built decades ago, with big shade trees and lawns. Kids to about 10 years old will love riding the little train past Frontier Town, the carousel, and the steam paddlewheeler on the lagoon. Snacks and fast food available.

MICKE GROVE PARK AND ZOO (all ages)

Eight miles north of Stockton off Highway 99; take 8-Mile Road to 11793 North Micke Grove Road, Lodi; (209) 953–8800.

A great place to spend an afternoon. The zoo houses a nice variety of wild animals, plus tropical birds and endangered species exhibit. You can picnic under the oaks, try out the playground equipment, go swimming in the public pool, or take a turn on the merry-go-round at the Funderwoods amusement park, which is designed for kids ages 2 to 10. A large museum complex in the park has historic exhibits and nearly 100 tractors displayed outdoors. In the fall, maples and ginko trees are aflame in the Japanese Garden, a peaceful place with a waterfall and a stone pagoda.

HOUSEBOATING (all ages)

There is nothing like a houseboat for a real Huck Finn experience. From 28-footers to big, luxurious 50-footers, the boats are like floating apartments, furnished with every convenience for up to twelve people. You bring aboard bedding and food, and pay for the gas, about three to five gallons an hour. No experience is necessary, and the boats move at a leisurely pace, about 10 miles an hour. For day-trips try a "patio boat," a kind of small floating barge with a roof, seating areas, and not much more. They move a little faster and are fun for camping, picnicking, and fishing expeditions.

Kids especially like crawdad catching in the warm Delta waters, and some houseboat-rental companies will loan or rent you crawdad traps. May to December are the best months, and a fishing license is required. You bait the trap with dog food, drop it overboard on a line, and

Houseboat Rentals in Stockton

- **King Island Resort.** *11530 8-Mile Road; (209) 951–2188.*

- **Paradise Point Marina.** *8095 Rio Blanco Road; (209) 952–1000.*

- **Herman and Helen's Marina.** *Venice Island Ferry; (209) 951–4634.*

let it rest on the bottom overnight; you'll get anywhere from ten to fifty crawdads. Ask a Delta resident how to clean and cook them, and be sure to eat them with your fingers with a spicy dipping sauce.

Houseboating Tips for Families

- **Plan ahead:** Make reservations several months in advance for high-season weekends. Just like motels and campgrounds, houseboats "sell out" quickly.

- **It's not cheap:** A boat sleeping six to ten people in the summer and on holiday weekends will cost $1,000 to $3,000 a week, plus gas, which runs $40 or more a day.

- **A good night's sleep:** If your group of friends and family fill up the houseboat and you plan to have children sleep on the floor, consider bringing sleeping bags and maybe a tent, for sleeping on the riverside.

- **Getting around:** Don't hesitate to bring with you or rent an outboard skiff to tow behind the houseboat. You'll be glad to have it for zipping to marinas for ice and groceries, for fishing quietly, and for getting away from what may be a noisy, lively life on the houseboat.

- **Save money on food:** Shop for groceries before you get to the houseboat marina. Food and drinks are expensive once you get there.

- **Upgrades:** Consider making this a truly primo family vacation by going for upgrades such as a water slide, air-conditioning, and an extra bathroom.

TOWER PARK MARINA RESORT (all ages)

14900 West Highway 12, at the Little Potato Slough drawbridge, Lodi 95240; (209) 369–1041.

A large riverside resort with 400 RV sites, a guest marina, watercraft rentals, boat launching, a general store, picnic sites, and a beach. All tables face the water at the **Terminus Tavern** restaurant at Tower Park. An annual boat show in May, **Deltafest,** is held here; in addition to a huge show of boats in the water and ashore, live entertainment, fishing clinics, demonstrations, and food booths are part of the fun.

OAKWOOD LAKE WATERPARK AND CAMPING RESORT

 Located twenty minutes south of Stockton off Highway 99, at 874 East Woodward Avenue, Manteca 95336; (209) 239–2500.

More than twenty water slides and a sandy beach, a bungee jumping tower, and picnic areas make this the perfect spot on a hot summer day. Some 300 campsites are well maintained, with every amenity.

CONSUMNES RIVER PRESERVE (all ages)

 Twenty-six miles north of Stockton, take the Twin Cities Road exit off Highway 5; (916) 684–2816. Launch your own boat or take a guided kayak tour; (415) 456–8956.

Great numbers of migrating and resident ducks, geese, swans, and other waterfowl and land birds are found on this 5,400-acre preserve owned by the Nature Conservancy. Stop in at the interpretive center for self-guiding maps to the wetlands, riverside, and oak forest trails; on weekends you can take a guided tour. From spring through July the wildflowers are extraordinary. One-mile Lost Slough Trail has a boardwalk through marshy nesting grounds; Willow Slough Trail is an easy, 3-mile route meandering through beautiful cottonwoods along the river.

Where to Eat

On Lock Sam. *333 South Sutter, Stockton 95203; (209) 466–4561.* For more than one hundred years, the Wong family has been serving Chinese food to the Stockton community—don't miss this one. $

Ye Old Hoosier Inn. *1537 North Wilson Way, Stockton 95205; (209) 463–0271.* Families have been coming here since the 1930s. Casual and comfortable, with stained glass windows and antiques, the inn serves hearty fare, such as homemade sausage and buttermilk biscuits with cream gravy, chicken fried steak, sandwiches and burgers. Breakfast, lunch, and dinner. $–$$

Garlic Brothers. *6629 Embarcadero Drive, Village West Marina, Stockton 95207; (209) 474–5585.* Have refreshments on the deck above 14-Mile Slough, then go for the hearty meat, poultry, and seafood grilled on a wood fire or rotisserie; you can arrive by boat or car. $$

San Felipe Grill. *4601 Pacific Avenue, Stockton 95207; (209) 952–6261.* A casual spot with super-duper traditional Mexican food. Try the gigantic burritos and the San Felipe tacos—plenty of napkins are in order. $

Where to Stay

Marriott Residence Inn. *3240 West March Lane, Stockton 95219; (209) 472–9800.* New and extra nice; studios, one- and two-bedrooms, fireplaces; pool, guest laundry, continental breakfast. $$

Snug Harbor. *(916) 775–1455; www.snugharbor.net.* Take the Rio Vista Bridge or the little auto ferries onto Ryer Island, home to Snug Harbor on Steamboat Slough, a quiet inlet where waterfront RV sites, simple, fully equipped cabins, and full marina facilities are popular with vacationing families and fishermen. This is a great headquarters for exploring the delta.

For More Information

Stockton/San Joaquin Convention and Visitor's Bureau. *46 West Fremont Street, Stockton 95202; (800) 350–1987 or (209) 943–1987; www.ssjcvb.org.*

Delta Rental Houseboat Hotline. *For information and brochures call (209) 477–1840.*

Modesto

Within a short drive of the Sacramento Delta and the Sierras, Modesto—awarded the title of "All-American City"—is surrounded by vast fruit orchards and veggie fields: almonds, apricots, peaches, walnuts, and more. Spring is a glorious time in the Modesto area and throughout the Central Valley. Wildflowers—vibrant blue lupine, goldfield, poppies, mustard—cascade in great waves across the grasslands and in the riparian areas.

The town is a good jumping-off point for recreation on the Stanislaus River, where nine U.S. Army Corps of Engineers–maintained areas are located along 59 miles of the river; between Modesto and Knights Ferry are more than sixteen drive-in, boat-in, and walk-in campgrounds.

The movie *American Graffiti* was based on producer George Lucas's boyhood experiences in Modesto in the '50s and '60s, when cruising was a way of life. For a peek into the past, go to the A&W Root Beer drive-in at Fourteenth and G Streets, where carhops still cruise to your car on roller skates. Classic car shows are held in June.

MCHENRY MANSION (all ages)

Fifteenth and I Streets, Modesto 95354; (209) 577–5344. Free *admission.*

In the heart of the lovely old home district and built in 1883, a spectacular, fully furnished and decorated Victorian Italianate mansion.

 MCHENRY MUSEUM (all ages)

Near the McHenry Mansion, 1402 I Street, Modesto 95354; (209) 577–5366. Free *admission.*

In a 1912 library, displays from pioneer days through the middle-twentieth century. The grounds are shaded by magnificent oaks, elms, redwoods, palms, and magnolias.

HERSHEY CHOCOLATE USA (all ages)

120 Sierra Avenue, a few minutes from Modesto in Oakdale 95361; (209) 848–8126. Free *tours; reservations necessary.*

The chocolate lovers in your family will want to take the Free half-hour tour and tasting, from the cocoa bean to the candy bar. Tours are held weekdays 8:30 A.M. to 3:00 P.M.

Free Tastes and Tours Near Modesto

- **Blue Diamond Growers Store.** *4800 Sisk Road, Salida, 5 miles northwest of Modesto on Highway 99; (209) 545–3222.* Watch a film of a day in the life of an almond grower and watch almonds being processed. Tastings and tour are Free. Open weekdays 10:00 A.M. to 5:00 P.M.; weekends 10:00 A.M. to 4:00 P.M.

- **Hilmar Cheese Company.** *9001 North Lander Avenue, Hilmar, 18 miles south of Modesto off Highway 99; (209) 667–6076.* A wide variety of luscious cheeses are available to taste; the cheese-making process can be viewed Monday through Saturday, 8:00 A.M. to 6:00 P.M. On the premises are a deli, an ice cream parlor and a picnic area.

- **Oakdale Cheese and Specialties.** *10040 Highway 120, Oakdale, 13 miles east of Modesto on Highway 108; (209) 848–3139.* A cheese factory and European bakery operated by a couple from the Netherlands. Watch cheese-making through windows and on video, and tour the aging rooms. Open daily, 9:00 A.M. to 6:00 P.M.

- **Bloomingcamp Apple Ranch.** *10528 Highway 120, Oakdale; (209) 847–1412.* Taste and buy homemade cider, apples, dried fruits, pies, jams, and jellies. Open daily 9:30 A.M. to 5:30 P.M.

WEST BEAR CREEK (all ages)

Off Highway 165, forty minutes south of Modesto; (209) 826–3508.

In the wintertime, until mid-March, a 2-mile auto tour of the West Bear wetlands is a peaceful experience. Half a million waterfowl rest here while migrating along the Pacific Flyway. White-tailed kites and harriers wheel above, while sandhill cranes, pelicans, and a variety of ducks and geese ply the ponds. This is a small segment of the vast San Luis National Wildlife Refuge.

KNIGHTS FERRY RECREATION AREA (all ages)

On the Stanislaus River off Highway 108–12, Sonora Road, Knights Ferry; (209) 881–3517. A "Flow Fone" gives up-to-date information on water conditions (916–322–2327).

Stop in at the U.S. Army Corps of Engineers Information Center for information and maps on where to camp and fish on the Stan. Cast for big rainbow trout in the rapids, riffles, and deep pools between Goodwin Dam and Oakdale. Try for bass and catfish below Orange Blossom Bridge. Rabid river rafters put in above Knights Ferry for 4 miles of surging whitewater. Canoes and lighter-weight craft should stick to the river below Knights Ferry.

KNIGHTS FERRY BRIDGE AND TRAIL (all ages)

Twenty-five miles northeast of Modesto on the Stanislaus River off Highway 108–12, Sonora Road, Knights Ferry; (209) 881–3517.

The 355-foot-long covered bridge is the longest west of the Mississippi, crossing the river near an old gristmill. Closed to vehicles, this is a scenic spot for photos. The park here has pretty picnic areas with barbecues. At the northeast end of the bridge, a hiking trail leads to sandy beaches and to swimming and fishing holes.

SUNSHINE RIVER ADVENTURES (ages 6 and up)

P.O. Box 1445, Oakdale 95361; (800) 829–7238; www.raftadventure.com.

Guided whitewater-rafting trips on the Stanislaus, as well as canoe and raft rentals. An easy introduction to river rafting is the Knights Ferry to Orange Blossom Park Float, a self-guided, four- to five-hour trip popular with families (kids must be 6 or over). Bring a small ice chest, tennis shoes, a litter bag, bathing suits, and sunscreen. No pets. Return shuttle is provided. About $15 per person, discounts for kids. Rates include raft, paddles, life vests, and instructions. Packed lunches are $6.50.

My first river-rafting experience was on the Stan. The rafting company left my gear in the parking lot, so I lived in the same shorts, shirt, and bathing suit for three days. As soon as we hit the water, the world and my troubles disappeared. The water was cold and moving fast, rushing in my ears, the riverbanks rocky, leafy, sandy, and hot when we stopped for lunch. We saw waterfalls, river otters, snakes (harmless), an eagle, hawks, trout, wildflowers. We paddled hard; we held on tight through (what we thought were) scary rapids and over mountain-size boulders; we screamed and yelled and drank lots of water and beer; and food never tasted so good—fresh salads, bread baked in the coals, and barbecued steaks, all made on the beach by the boat people.

Where to Eat

Outback Steakhouse Restaurant. *2045 West Briggsmore Avenue, Modesto 95354; (209) 570–2410.* Steaks, ribs and chicken barbecue, pasta, burgers and the famous Bloomin' Onion. Dinner only. $

Modesto Stanislaus Firehouse Pub and Grille. *924 Fifteenth Street, near the McHenry Mansion, Modesto 95354;* *(209) 575–3473.* Home-style soup, sandwiches, burgers, ribs, pub food; 117 beers. $

Olive Garden. *220 Plaza Parkway, Modesto 95354; (209) 544–8057.* How do you feed a car full of kids for not a lot of money? Platters of Italian food here are so big you can split them. $

Where to Stay

Holiday Inn of Modesto. *1612 Sisk Road (Briggsmore exit off Highway 99), Modesto 95354; (209) 527–5074.* An indoor and an outdoor pool, a playground, a wading pool, tennis courts, a coin laundry, and a coffee shop. Simple rooms; reasonable rates. $

Big Bear Park and RV Campground. *Twelve miles east of Modesto, on Highway 132 95354; (209) 874–1984.* A water-ride and campground combo, with shaded lawns, a half-acre lake with swimming beaches, and fishing and swimming in the Tuolumne River. $

For More Information

Modesto Convention and Visitors Bureau. *1114 J Street, Modesto 95354; (800) 266–4282; www.modestocvb.org.*

Merced

Directly east of Yosemite, at the junction of Highways 99 and 140, the town of Merced is within striking distance of a plethora of things that families like to do. A half-hour east of town are two beautiful, low-elevation recreation lakes, and a world-class museum of vintage aircraft is well worth a stop.

More than a century old and designated as a "Tree City USA," Merced has wide, shady streets with Victorian mansions and miles of bike trails connecting an open-space park system.

May through October on Thursday evenings, Main Street hosts a street fair with produce booths, live music, educational demos, food, and fun.

LAKE YOSEMITE (all ages)

Five miles northeast of Merced, on North Lake Road; (209) 385–7426.

Within biking distance of town, a day-use park for picnicking, windsurfing, sailing, and fishing. Rent a rowboat! You're guaranteed to catch bass all year long. Snack bar, restrooms.

LAKE MCCLURE AND LAKE MCSWAIN (all ages)

In the Sierra Foothills, about 25 miles from Merced, off Highway 59; (800) 468–8869.

Very warm in the summertime and popular for waterskiing and houseboating, the lakes are stocked annually with trout and bass. More than 500 campsites are scattered in the oak and pine forests around the lakes.

ater Works! Best Valley Water Parks

- **Blackbeard's Family Fun Center.** *Nine miles north of Fresno off Highway 99, on Chestnut Avenue; (209) 292–4554.* Mini-golf, water slides, bumper boats, games, and rides.

- **Waterworld USA.** *1600 Exposition Boulevard, at Cal Expo, Sacramento; (916) 924–0555.* A huge wave pool, several slides, a tubing river, play venues, and a slide for kids ages 3 to 6.

- **Oakwood Lake Waterpark and Camping Resort.** *Twenty minutes south of Stockton off Highway 99, at 874 East Woodward Avenue, Manteca; (209) 239–2500.* Thirty water slides, a beach, bungee jumping, picnic areas, and a campground.

APPLEGATE PARK (all ages)

1045 West Twenty-fifth Street between M and R Streets; (209) 385–6840.

Acres of green beneath shady umbrellas of trees, with a little zoo and summertime amusement rides.

CASTLE AIR MUSEUM (all ages)

Castle Air Force Base in Atwater, 6 miles north of Merced; (209) 723–2178. Museum admission is adults $5.00 and children 12 and up $2.00.

One of the country's finest collections of World War II and Korean War aircraft, plus recent planes. It's quite impressive for children to stand beneath the wings of the black, batlike SR–71, B–29s, B–17s, big transports, helicopters, and more—a dramatic array. Indoors are the museum of wartime memorabilia, a gift shop, and a coffee shop. If would-be pilots are members of your family, try to be in Merced for the annual **West Coast Antique Fly-In** in June.

MCCONNELL STATE RECREATION AREA (all ages)

Off Highway 99 at Delhi, between Turlock and Merced; (209) 394–7755.

Swim, fish, picnic, and camp at this delightful park beside the Merced River.

Where to Eat

Main Street Cafe. *460 West Main, Merced 95340; (209) 725–1702.* All-American comfort food, sandwiches and soups, homemade pastries, ice cream. Breakfast and lunch. $

Pacifica Grill. *1700 McHenry Avenue, McHenry Village, Modesto 95350; (209) 526–9999.* A bright, colorful cafe with an inventive South-of-the-Border menu: *ceviche* tostadas; teriyaki chicken, veggie and fresh fish burritos; and simpler choices for kids. Everything is grilled, nothing fried. Try La Peninsula Caesar with green olives, pine nuts, avocado, and *Cotija* cheese. $

Where to Stay

Ramada Inn. *2000 East Childs Avenue, Merced 95340; (800) 2–RAMADA.* Rooms with sitting areas and sofa beds, coffeemakers, microwaves, and refrigerators. Large pool, access to sports club and golf course, and adjacent to a very good restaurant, the Eagle's Nest, which has a good children's menu. $$

For More Information

**Merced Convention and Visitors
Bureau.** *690 West Sixteenth Street,*

*Merced 95340; (209) 384–7092 or (800)
446–5858; www.yosemite-gateway.org.*

San Juan Bautista

A Spanish village since the late 1700s, San Juan Bautista is a perfectly preserved,
precious fragment of early California. In an agricultural setting in the Salinas
Valley between the tawny Gabilan Mountains on the east and the coastal range
of the Santa Lucias on the west, the town encompasses a large state historic
park, one of the most beautiful of the California missions, and a few charming
streets of antiques shops and Mexican restaurants shaded with pepper, mimosa,
and black walnut trees. Everything is within a few short blocks.

One of the nicest characteristics of the mission complex is the proximity of
the museum buildings to the large, grassy plaza. Children who can't bear to
look at another artifact can run around outside on the lawn while parents
soak up the history.

MISSION SAN JUAN BAUTISTA (all ages)

Second and Mariposa Streets, San Juan Bautista; (831) 623–2127.

Founded in 1787, this is one of the largest and most impressive of
all California mission churches, with three aisles and a glorious, forty-
foot-high ceiling of grayed beams in traditional viga-lattia construction.
Light floods the cathedral, making vibrant the rust and blue painted
decoration, most of it created in 1816 by a Boston sailor who worked
at the mission in exchange for room and board. Before and during the
Sunday masses, local families mingle and chat near the giant entry
doors and the soft singing voices of the congregation float out the door
into the sunshine of the plaza.

Surrounding the cathedral are a series of open rooms housing a
museum of early Indian, Spanish Colonial, and Victorian artifacts and
one of the best collections of Mission furniture in the world. You will
also see a small kitchen from which 1,200 people were fed from iron
pots in an open fireplace.

The mission gardens are cool and lovely, with old cacti, aromatic
lavender, and climbing roses. Behind the church, under ancient olive
trees, are buried 4,300 Indians and early pioneers.

SAN JUAN BAUTISTA STATE PARK (all ages)
Midtown San Juan Bautista; (831) 623–4881.

Full of carriages and wagons today, the **Plaza Stable** was headquarters for seven stage lines in the 1860s, when as many as eleven coaches a day arrived, loaded with silver and gold miners, traders, and other travelers. Dusty travelers headed first to the **Plaza Hotel** to get a beer or something stronger in the bar and to book a room for the night. The owner of the hotel, Angelo Zanetta, built himself a magnificent house on the plaza, and the structure—the Zanetta House—now contains an outstanding collection of early California furnishings and personal items. The red-tile-roofed **Castro House** was owned by a family from the Donner Party who struck it rich in the Gold Rush. Behind the house is a glorious, 150-year-old pepper tree shading beautiful gardens.

Living History Day is held in the state park on the first Saturday of each month, from noon to 4:00 P.M. Here costumed residents demonstrate making tortillas, butter, and quilts and regale visitors with tales of the old days in San Juan.

TOPS
5 Second Street, San Juan Bautista 95045; (831) 623–4441.

Kids love the rocks, flashy minerals, and semiprecious gems in this little shop that specializes in stones from all over the world.

JARDINES DE SAN JUAN
115 Third Street, San Juan Bautista 95045; (831) 623–4466; www. jardinesrestaurant.com.

A Mexican restaurant with a big, popular, Mission-style garden patio. Guitarists strum; breezes ruffle the fig and maple trees; lunches and dinners are served at umbrella tables or indoors in cool, art-filled dining rooms. On the children's menu are mildly flavored burritos, *quesadillas,* and plain rice and beans with tortillas. Parents go for the fresh red snapper Veracruz and for *pollos borrachos*—chicken cooked in sherry, an old Puebla recipe. $$

MISSION GALLERY
106 Third Street, San Juan Bautista 95045; (831) 623–2960.

Within a small circle of shops graced by a magnificent, ancient pepper tree. This is the finest gallery in town for prints and paintings of the valley, plus opulent Asian accessories for the home.

REYNA'S GALLERIAS AND AMERICAN INDIAN MUSEUM

311 Third Street, San Juan Bautista 95045; (831) 623–2379;
www.oneearthonepeople.org.

Everyone in the family will enjoy the fascinating American Indian clothing, artifacts and crafts, an eclectic array of books and cards, and monthly exhibits of local artisans' works.

AMERICAN INDIAN AND WORLD CULTURES FESTIVAL (all ages)

May, in downtown San Juan Bautista; (831) 623–2379.

Entertainment, costumes, a parade, food, children's activities and educational displays.

SAN LUIS RESERVOIR STATE RECREATION AREA (all ages)

Thirty miles east of San Juan Bautista, on Highway 152; (831) 826–1196.

Three lakes for fishing, swimming, and waterskiing. Most of the fish species found in the Sacramento Delta are found at San Luis. Windsurfing is very good from March through September.

Santa Nella R.V. Park (831–826–3105) and **Lakeview R.V. Park** (831–826–1196) are convenient places to camp near the reservoir.

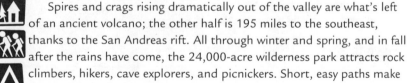

PINNACLES NATIONAL MONUMENT (all ages)

An hour south of San Juan Bautista, off Highway 25, Paicines; (831) 389–4485.

Spires and crags rising dramatically out of the valley are what's left of an ancient volcano; the other half is 195 miles to the southeast, thanks to the San Andreas rift. All through winter and spring, and in fall after the rains have come, the 24,000-acre wilderness park attracts rock climbers, hikers, cave explorers, and picnickers. Short, easy paths make ferny creeks and mountain views easily accessible.

Spring is spectacular, with riots of wildflowers, which bloom here earlier than in most parts of the state. Winters are mild, fresh, and green. Midsummer can be extremely hot and dry, with temperatures in the hundreds. A nice private campground at the entrance to the park has a swimming pool (408–389–4462).

CALIFORNIA ANTIQUE AIRCRAFT MUSEUM (all ages)

Six miles north of Gilroy in San Martin, at 12777 Murphy Avenue, across the street from the airport; (831) 683–2290.

On display are planes from 1928 to the 1950s, such as a Sopwith Pup, a Bowlus Albatross, and a Benson Gyrocopter.

Where to Eat

Felipe's Restaurant and Bar. *313 Third Street, San Juan Bautista 95045; (831) 623–2161.* Where the locals go for Mexican and Salvadoran food, with live music on weekends. Salvadoran dishes are not complete without the zippy pickled cabbage, *curtido*. Try the specialties of the house: fried plantains and fried ice cream. $

Cutting Horse. *301 Third Street, San Juan Bautista 95045; (831) 623–4549.* Steak and hearty, traditional American fare is featured here in a new, comfortable, and attractive establishment. $$

Orient Express. *35 Washington Street, San Juan Bautista 95045; (831) 623–2978.* The owner-chef trained in France and brings a delicate touch to traditional Chinese cuisine in this casual, bright, and pretty place. Lunch specials and "family dinners" are inexpensive.

Besides familiar favorites, such as sweet-and-sour pork and rice dishes, try the calamari in garlic ginger sauce, and *mu shu* shrimp. $

Mission Cafe. *300 Third Street, San Juan Bautista 95045; (831) 623–4521.* Voted by the town as the best place for breakfast, and it's true! $

Dona Esther Restaurant. *25 Franklin Street, San Juan Bautista 95045; (831) 623– 2518.* Real Mexican food in a warm, friendly atmosphere, with local art and photos decorating the walls. Inexpensive children's menu of simple dishes. Outdoor patio; live entertainment and all-you-can-eat buffet on weekends. $

Margot's Ice Cream Parlor. *211 Third Street, San Juan Bautista 95045; (831) 623–9262.* Icy delights, plus sandwiches and salads. $

Where to Stay

Mission Farm RV Park. *400 San Juan–Hollister Road on the southeast corner of town, San Juan Bautista 95045; (831) 623– 4456.* Old barns and a small store; tree-shaded sites surrounded by a walnut orchard. Sites for tents and RVs. $

San Juan Inn. *410 Alameda Street, San Juan Bautista; (831) 623–4380.* Small motel with simple rooms, some with refrigerators and microwaves; swimming pool; gardens. $–$$

For More Information

San Juan Bautista Chamber of Commerce. *402A Third Street, San Juan Bautista 95045; (831) 623–2454;* *www.sanjuanbautista.com.* Stop here for the Historic Walking Tour map.

Gold Country

The foothills of the California Gold Country stretch more than 300 miles along the western slopes of the Sierra Nevadas, all the way to the southern gate of Yosemite National Park. Fed by snowy peaks, six major rivers carve dramatic, steep-sided canyons and rush down the valleys into the heart of the state.

Along the Yuba, American, Mokelumne, Stanislaus, Tuolumne, and Merced River corridors, dozens of boomtowns exploded in population when gold was discovered in the mid-1800s, only to be abandoned by the miners and adventure seekers when the lodes were exhausted a decade later.

Still looking much as they did more than a hundred years ago, small "forty-niner" Gold Rush towns on the "Golden Chain"—Highway 49—from Nevada City in the North to Jamestown in the South are both living museums and thriving towns of today. These communities that sprang up overnight for the miners and gold panners are carefully preserved, with wooden false-front stores and saloons, board sidewalks and gas lamps, and balconied Victorian hotels.

There is so much to see and do in Gold Country, and the area so vast, that your family may want to plan several trips, combining outdoor fun—such as rafting, fishing, and hiking on rivers and lakes—with sightseeing at historical sites.

Nevada City

The sights of Nevada City and its adjacent, sister city of Grass Valley, plus historic gold mines and outdoor pleasures on the banks of the Yuba and American Rivers, add up to busy vacation days in this area. Just a few miles to the east, 1.2 million acres of wilderness afford endless hiking, camping, fishing, and cross-country skiing opportunities.

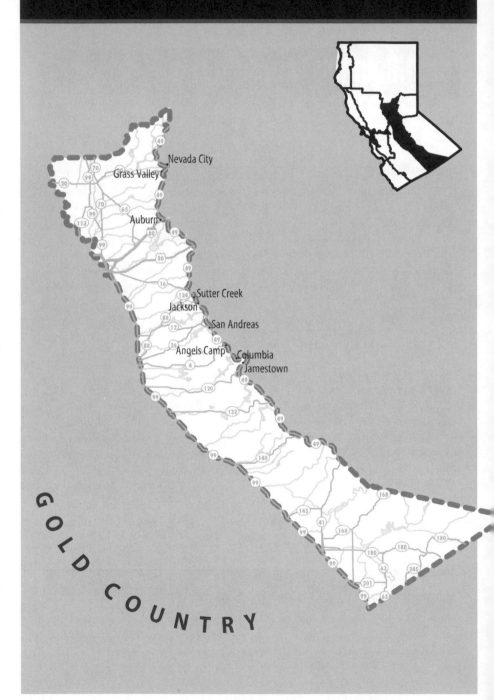

Nevada City

Grass Valley

Auburn

Sutter Creek

Jackson

San Andreas

Angels Camp

Columbia

Jamestown

GOLD COUNTRY

The most completely original Gold Rush town in the state, Nevada City has more than a hundred Victorian mansions and western saloons and hotels clustered cozily together on a radiating wheel of tree-lined streets on small hills. At an elevation of about 2,840 feet, the whole place turns red and gold in fall, when thousands of maples, aspens, and oaks turn blazing bright.

There is much to discover today within the 8-block area surrounding Broad, the main street. As soon as you cross the bridge into town, take the first right to the visitor center for a walking-tour map.

FIREHOUSE NO. 1 HISTORICAL SOCIETY MUSEUM (all ages)

214 Main Street, Nevada City, next door to the visitors center 95959; (530) 265–5468. Open daily 11:00 A.M. to 4:00 P.M. Admission is Free.

In a much-photographed building, circa 1860, with a bell tower and gingerbread trim, two floors of Gold Rush and Native American artifacts.

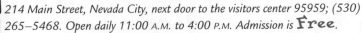 DEER CREEK MINERS TRAIL (all ages)

Broad Street, Nevada City; (530) 265–2692.

A short, easy walk along Deer Creek, with six stations that describe gold prospecting in the early days. Running through town, the creek once yielded a pound of gold a day.

NATIONAL HOTEL (all ages)

211 Broad Street, Nevada City 95959; (530) 265–4551.

Step inside the oldest continuously operating hotel west of the Rockies and take a look at the elaborate longbar, shipped around the Horn more than a hundred years ago.

FOUR WINDS

310 Broad Street, Nevada City 95959; (530) 265–9021.

A gallery of international folk art that sells inexpensive African and South American trinkets. I stock up here on small toys, dolls, and games that I save for those times in restaurants and on the road when little children get restless.

MOUNTAIN PASTIMES FUN AND GAMES

320 Spring Street, Nevada City 95959; (530) 265–6692.

Toys and games for all ages. The shop is always full of people trying out the gizmos.

NEVADA COUNTY TRACTION COMPANY (NCTC) (ages 1–12)

Behind the Northern Queen Inn, 400 Railroad Avenue, on the south end of Nevada City; (530) 265–5824. Tickets are $6.50 for adults, and $3.50 for children.

Take a short ride in a forested area on a restored narrow-gauge train, while the conductor-owner, Al Flores, talks about local history. Part of the trip entails a short walk to see Maidu grinding holes and a fascinating Chinese cemetery; in October a pumpkin farm is part of the fun. The railroad is located on the grounds of the Northern Queen Inn, one of the best family motels in the area (see below).

MALAKOFF DIGGINS STATE HISTORIC PARK

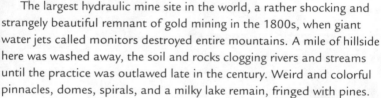

Twenty-seven miles northeast of Nevada City, on Highway 49; (530) 265–2740.

The largest hydraulic mine site in the world, a rather shocking and strangely beautiful remnant of gold mining in the 1800s, when giant water jets called monitors destroyed entire mountains. A mile of hillside here was washed away, the soil and rocks clogging rivers and streams until the practice was outlawed late in the century. Weird and colorful pinnacles, domes, spirals, and a milky lake remain, fringed with pines.

There are reconstructed buildings and hiking trails in the park, swimming at Blair Lake, and a campground. Swimming and fishing holes on the South Yuba River and a 21-mile river corridor park are accessible near the Diggins. On weekends and holidays, rangers lead **Free** gold panning tours.

LAKE SPAULDING (all ages)

Located 30 miles on Highway 20 from Nevada City, on Highway 20; (530) 527–0354.

A glacier-carved bowl of granite, at 5,000 feet, the lake, is surrounded by huge boulders and a forest. This is a great day-trip destination, with good fishing for trout, small lakeside beaches, and powerboating and sailing. A small, developed campground for tents and RVs is here too.

IMAGINARIUM (ages 2–10)

112 Nevada City Highway in Nevada City 95959; (530) 478–6400; www.ncimaginarium.org. Open weekends. Admission $3.00.

This great little hands-on, interactive science center makes a fun, one-hour stop. Kids like to pluck the two-story guitar and have a hair-raising experience with electricity, and they love to shrink their parents.

Three Easy Wilderness Hikes Near Nevada City

- **Independence Trail.** *Eight miles north of Nevada City on Highway 49, just before the arched Yuba River Bridge, watch carefully for the sign; (530) 477–4788.* My favorite Gold Country trail, because it's easy for all ages and abilities, and you get into eye-popping scenery within a minute, on 7 miles of packed dirt paths and boardwalk that is wheelchair and stroller accessible. The trail meanders through forests and at times is dramatically suspended over the Yuba River Canyon. Along the way there are picnic platforms as well as ramps leading to fishing holes.

- **Sierra Discovery Trail.** *From Highway 20 take Bowman Lake Road 0.6 mile to the parking lot; (530) 386–5164.* A delightful loop along the Bear River, this 1-mile, easy trail is popular, for good reason. The partly paved, partly gravel, partly boardwalk path is accessible to wheelchairs and strollers as it winds through a pine and cedar forest. Meadows are awash with wildflowers, and a small waterfall rushes year-round. Watch for water ouzels at the waterfall—they are the only American songbirds that dive into the water.

- **Bullards Bar Trail.** *North from Nevada City on Highway 49 to Marysville Road, turn left and follow signs to Dark Day Picnic Area; turn right for 0.5 mile; then take left fork to trailhead; (530) 288–3231.* Along the edge of Bullards Bar Reservoir, a flat, scenic trail. Stop and take a swim, catch a fish, and enjoy a picnic under a giant ponderosa pine.

Where to Eat

Posh Nosh. *318 Broad Street, Nevada City 95959; (530) 265–6064.* On a tree-shaded patio, sandwiches, pasta, salads, and homemade desserts are memorable. $

Apple Fare. *307 Broad Street, Nevada City 95959; (530) 265–5458.* Where the locals go for breakfast and for pie. Try to get seats at the big round table and listen in on the gossip. $

Creekside Cafe. *101 Broad Street, Nevada City 95959; (530) 265–3445.*
Above the rushing waters of Deer Creek, the outdoor deck is the place to be on a warm summer night. Inside are candlelit tables before a fireplace. Fresh fish, poultry, and meats in exotic sauces. $$

Gourmet To Go. *110 York Street, Nevada City 95959; (530) 265–5697.* Homemade everything—sandwiches, salads, soups, desserts. If you don't have a picnic spot in mind, ask the deli staff. $

Where to Stay

Northern Queen Inn. *400 Railroad Avenue, off Highway 49, Nevada City 95959; (530) 265–5824; www.northern queeninn.com.* Rooms are simple and spacious, and separate cottages with kitchenettes are on the creek. You'll find a swimming pool on the grounds, a good family-oriented restaurant, and restored narrow-gauge railcars. $$

Kendall House. *534 Spring Street, Nevada City 95959; (530) 265–0405.* In a quiet neighborhood 2 blocks from downtown, a B&B with a separate cottage and a swimming pool, just perfect for a small family. The cottage has a sitting room, a dining area, a fireplace, a kitchen, and a private deck. You are likely to have the swimming pool to yourselves. Extensive gardens are bright with color in the fall; cool and leafy on hot summer days. $$–$$$

For More Information

Nevada City Chamber of Commerce. *132 Main Street, Nevada City 95959; (530) 265–2692 or (800) 655–6569; www.ncgold.com.* In the stone and brick Yuba Canal Building, built in 1850 on the banks of Deer Creek.

Tahoe National Forest Information Center. *Coyote Street and Highway 49, P.O. Box 6003, Nevada City 95959; (530) 265–4531.* Maps and information on camping, fishing, lakes, and hundreds of miles of trails.

Grass Valley

Inhabited during the Gold Rush by thousands of English and Irish miners who worked five major gold mines in the area, Grass Valley is honeycombed with miles of underground tunnels and shafts. On Mill and Main Streets remain dozens of buildings constructed in the mid-1800s, when this was the richest mining town in the state.

Antiques shops are rampant up and down the main streets. A block off Main Street take a stroll on Neal and Church Streets to see rows of magnificent Victorian mansions and churches.

GRASS VALLEY MUSEUM (all ages)

Mount St. Mary's Convent, 410 South Church Street, Grass Valley 95945; (530) 272–4725. Admission is **Free**.

A restored school and orphanage exhibiting Gold Rush artifacts and domestic items, in the middle floor of the old convent house. The fascinating cemetery on the grounds dates to 1852.

Cornish Pasties

Cornish Pasties A traditional food introduced by the early settlers from Cornwall, England, who came to work in the mines, Cornish pasties are delicious, flaky, hand-size turnover pies in which savory fillings are baked, such as potato and other vegetables, ham and cheese, and fruit combinations. In forty-niner days each miner carried a three-tiered tin lunch pail every day. The bottom was filled with tea, the pasty was placed in the middle section, and a bun was placed on top. The miner lit a candle under his pail at the beginning of his shift, and by the time he ate, his meal was warm.

- **Marshall's Pasties.** *203 Mill Street, Grass Valley; (530) 272–2844.* For more than thirty years, pasties fresh from the oven all day long, to take out. You will know when you're getting close to Marshall's—the inviting aroma drifts down the sidewalk. Broccoli and cheese, apple-figgy, sausage, and many more. $

- **Mrs. Dubblebee's Pasties.** *251 South Auburn Street, Grass Valley; (530) 272–7700.* A bakery-cafe with top-notch pasties. Light lunch, early dinner. $

HOLBROOKE HOTEL (all ages)

212 West Main Street, Grass Valley 95945; (530) 273–1353.

Since 1862, the grand old lady of Grass Valley. A glance in the hotel register turns up such famous guests as Presidents Cleveland and Garfield. Families take Sunday dinner and brunch here. $$

SWENSON'S SURPLUS

105 West Main Street, Grass Valley 95945; (530) 273–7315.

We regularly get lost in here. Great buys on camping, fishing, and gold-mining equipment. Fanny packs, water bottles, camouflage clothing, winter boots, raingear, auto gear—it's all here.

NORTH STAR MINING MUSEUM (all ages)

On the south end of Mill Street, Grass Valley 95945; (530) 273–8522. Admission is Free.

A delightful, shady spot for a picnic on the lawn, beside the old powerhouse on Wolf Creek. Among the many pieces of antique equipment here are a working stamp mill and the largest Pelton wheel in the world, a waterwheel that produced power from the creek for the North Star Mine. A large collection of photos traces mining history, and there are hands-on demos for kids.

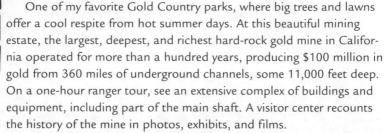

EMPIRE MINE STATE PARK (all ages)

Just south of Grass Valley off Highway 49, take the Empire Street exit; (530) 273–8522. Tickets are $3.00 for adults and $1.00 for kids ages 6 to 12.

One of my favorite Gold Country parks, where big trees and lawns offer a cool respite from hot summer days. At this beautiful mining estate, the largest, deepest, and richest hard-rock gold mine in California operated for more than a hundred years, producing $100 million in gold from 360 miles of underground channels, some 11,000 feet deep. On a one-hour ranger tour, see an extensive complex of buildings and equipment, including part of the main shaft. A visitor center recounts the history of the mine in photos, exhibits, and films.

Sweeping lawns beneath 100-foot sugar pines surround the mine owner's home, Bourne Cottage, an outstanding example of a Willis Polk–designed English country manor, with lovely gardens and a fountain pool. Also here are hiking/cycling trails and picnic areas.

BRIDGEPORT COVERED BRIDGE (all ages)

Southwest of Grass Valley, near Penn Valley; (530) 432–2546.

On the Yuba River, one of only a dozen covered bridges still standing in the state. At 256 feet it may be the longest single-span covered bridge in the world. There are nice picnic spots and wading pools among the rocks.

A lovely, easy walk runs just over a mile one-way upstream on the north side of the river, with wildflowers in the spring, beautiful views of the canyon, and access to swimming holes. On weekends and holidays, rangers lead **Free** gold panning tours.

SCOTTS FLAT LAKE (all ages)

Twenty minutes from Grass Valley off Highway 20; (530) 265–5302.

A nice day-trip for swimming, fishing, hiking, or camping lakeside in the national forest; the campground has developed tent and RV sites, sandy beaches, a store, and picnic areas.

Where to Eat

Tofanelli's. *302 West Main Street, Grass Valley 95945; (530) 272–1468.* Our favorite place to take our toddler granddaughter who lives here, because we can sit on the patio while she runs around (and around). Hearty American menu with huge plates of food, breakfast burritos, raspberry chicken. Breakfast, lunch, dinner, and Sunday brunch. $

Happy Apple Kitchen. *Ten miles from Grass Valley, 18532 Highway 174, 95945; (530) 273-2822.* A restaurant loved by families for the home-style food, including pie to die for. Every weekend in October, Bierwagen's Apple Fest and Pumpkin Patch is held in Chicago Park, adjacent to the Happy Apple. $

Flower Garden Bakery. *Next to Safeway, Neal Street, Grass Valley 95945; (530) 477-2253.* Yummy home-baked goodies, sandwiches, and salads made with healthy ingredients. Within the bakery-cafe is the Cyber Cafe, where you can play on-line while you eat lunch. $

Empire House Restaurant. *535 Mill Street, Grass Valley 95945; (530) 273-8272.* Swiss, German, and American food; lunch and dinner; casual. $

For More Information

Nevada County Chamber of Commerce. *248 Mill Street, Grass Valley 95945; (530) 273-4667; www.* *gvncchamber.org.* In the home and museum of Lola Montez, a notorious dance-hall entertainer of the 1800s.

Sutter Creek

My favorite Gold Country town, Sutter Creek is surrounded by rolling pasturelands, vineyards and orchards—a postcard-perfect settlement with white frame houses and picket fences, giving it a New England look. Clapboard houses with porches and balconies, coupled with steepled churches, look down from the hillsides over Main Street, which is riddled with antiques shops and quaint boutiques. A nice hotel here caters to families, and plenty of exploring can be done on country roads near town. Two miles north of here, Amador City is also an antiques center. The Saturday morning farmers market is the place to meet locals.

CHATTER BOX CAFE (all ages)
29 Main Street, Sutter Creek 95685; (209) 267-5935.
My favorite cafe in my favorite town, a walk back into the 1940s. It's an old-fashioned soda fountain, nostalgic with World War II posters, Big Band record covers, and a long counter where town regulars meet for burgers with homemade buns, grilled cheese sandwiches, world-class onion rings, and pies, floats, sodas, and thick shakes.

GOLD MINER CANDY SHOPPE
40 Main Street, Sutter Creek; (209) 267–1525.

Barrels of penny candy (which no longer costs a penny) line the aisles.

KNIGHT'S FOUNDRY (all ages)
Eureka Street, Sutter Creek; (209) 267–0201; www.knightsfoundry.org. Admission is $2.50 for adults and $1.50 for kids ages 6 to 18.

The only water-powered foundry still operating in the world. Call ahead for a schedule of tours and pourings.

DAFFODIL HILL
Thirteen miles east of Sutter Creek on Shake Ridge Road; (209) 296–7048. Admission is **Free**.

A lovely half-hour drive alongside a creek to see wildflowers and 300,000 daffodils and tulips bloom in a farmer's field, an entire hillside exploding with color, mid-March through early April. Picnic sites.

SUTTER GOLD MINE (ages 4 and up)
On Highway 49 between Sutter Creek and Amador City; (888) 818–7462; www.suttergold.com. Admission for adults $14.50, ages 5 to 12 $10, under 5 **Free**. *Minimum age for underground tours is 4 years.*

If your family really gets interested in gold mining and its history, this is the nicest, best-organized place to try gold panning and learn about the process. You ride in a cool "Boss Buggy" shuttle truck, go underground into a mine in your hard hats, and observe gold extraction and equipment.

ST. GEORGE HOTEL (all ages)
Near Daffodil Hill, in Volcano; (209) 296–4458.

Lunch and dinner in a charming, rather eccentrically decorated dining room where the menu depends on the chef's whim of the day. In the little burg of Volcano, a clutch of historic buildings remain. Sit on the hotel verandah and imagine the village of 1,000 people when it was the center of a rich mining area that produced over $90 million in gold; some remnants are an old jail, a brewery, and "Old Abe," a Civil War cannon. $

INDIAN GRINDING ROCK STATE HISTORIC PARK (all ages)
Pine Grove–Volcano Road, Pine Grove; (209) 296–7488. $5.00 per car.

The only state park that is primarily a monument to Native American culture. More than 1,000 grinding holes used by Miwoks are gouged out of a vast limestone surface, and you will see many petroglyphs and replicas of bark dwellings. The museum displays beautiful baskets and artifacts. Once a month Miwok elders spend time at the park, telling stories and recounting tribal history to park visitors. Nature trails and a small campground with RV sites are here too.

Where to Eat

Bellotti Inn. *53 Main Street, Sutter Creek 95685; (209) 267–5211.* Bountiful, family-style Italian dinners, in a 140-year-old hotel. $

Sutter Creek Ice Cream. *51 Main Street, Sutter Creek 95685; (209) 267–0543.* Have a root beer float or a snack in this charming old-fashioned ice-cream soda fountain. $

Caffe Via d'Oro. *36 Main Street, Sutter Creek 95685; (209) 267–0535.* A surprising Mediterranean influence emerges in unique pizzas and calzones, homemade pastas, polenta, and seasonal specials at a cafe owned by a former Chez Panisse partner. Parents like the exceptional wine list; kids are quite comfortable. $–$$

Susan's Place Wine Bar and Eatery. *15 Eureka Street, in the courtyard, Sutter Creek 95685; (209) 267–0945.* Under the arbor on the patio, cheese boards, salads, soups, and sandwiches. Lunch and dinner. $

Where to Stay

Aparicio's Sutter Creek Hotel. *271 Hanford Street, Sutter Creek 95685; (209) 267– 9177.* Spacious rooms with two queen beds or two doubles, plus two-room suites. Contemporary Victorian-style architecture. $

For More Information

Sutter Creek Business and Professional Association. *P.O. Box 600, 11-A Randolph Street, Sutter Creek 95685; (800) 400–0305 or (209) 267–1344. Sutter Creek 95685; (209) 267–5647.*

Amador County Chamber of Commerce. *At junction of Highways 49 and 88, 125 Peak Street, Jackson 95642; (800) 649–4988 or (209) 223–0350; www.cdepot.net/chamber.*

Jackson

As you approach from above on Highway 49, Jackson looks like a toy town. Picturesque streets are lined with churches and balconied houses from the mid-1800s. In my opinion, the Amador County Museum here is the premier museum of everyday life in the early days of the Gold Country. A scattering of recreational lakes are located within a short drive. Nearly eighty shops and restaurants in historic buildings line the main street.

Every year, families congregate in Calaveras County for a number of events; **Snyder's Pow Wow,** a May weekend of arts, crafts, gems, minerals, food, and fun on a working cattle ranch (209–772–1265); **Lumberjack Day,** October, featuring a parade, logging competitions, music, and food (209–293–4324); and a **Civil War Reenactment** in September (209–728–1251).

AMADOR COUNTY MUSEUM (all ages)

Above Main Street, 225 Church Street, Jackson 95642; (209) 223–6386. Admission is Free.

In a neighborhood of churches and homes from the mid-1800s, one of the oldest houses in town shelters a huge collection of artifacts and antiques. On the hottest summer day, it's cool and quiet in the house. Hundreds of photos re-create the Gold Rush, and you'll find a fine collection of Indian baskets, women's and men's fashions, furniture, and many domestic items from throughout the era. Part of the thousands who worked the mines and built western railroads, the Chinese are featured in displays of clothing, musical instruments, and tools. A working scale model shows the Kennedy Mine, whose 5,000-foot shaft was one of the world's deepest. Bring a picnic and take a rest under the trees while the kids run around on the grass.

Winter Fun Near Jackson

Bear River Lake Resort. *Forty-two miles east of Jackson, on Highway 8; (209) 295–4868.* At 5,840 feet in the Eldorado National Forest are groomed and ungroomed trails for cross-country skiers around the lake. Several snow-play hills are perfect for sleds, saucers, and inner tubes, with rentals available. A 50-mile snowmobile road loops around the lake. Also there are a general store, a snack bar, and a small resort and campground open all year.

Lakes, Fishing, and Water Sports

- **New Melones Lake.** *Just south of Angels Camp, Highway 49; (209) 536–9094; www.houseboat.com.* The result of the second largest earth-filled dam in the United States, more than 100 miles of tree-lined shore dotted with campgrounds and marinas, headquarters for fishing, sailing, waterskiing, and houseboating.

- **Pardee Lake.** *Twelve miles from Mokelumne Hill, off Highway 26; (209) 772–1472.* Popular for trout, Kokanee fishing, and sailing. Swimming, waterskiing, and Jet Skis are not allowed in the lake. Also there are a nice playground, a campground, and a swimming pool.

- **Lake Amador.** *Nine miles from Jackson, off Highway 88; (209) 274–4739.* Some 425 surface acres of warm water for fishing, sailing, and boating, plus a 1-acre swimming pond with sandy beaches, as well as a coffee shop and playgrounds. At an elevation of 500 feet in the Sierra foothills, it can be very hot and dry in midsummer and early fall. Developed campground and RV sites.

- **Lake Camanche.** *Fifteen miles southwest of Jackson, off Highway 88; (209) 772–1472.* A big stretch of water, 33 miles around, created by a dam on the Mokelumne. You'll find it all here: large campgrounds, marinas, and cottage resorts; everything from riding stables, a dance pavilion, tennis courts, bike rentals, and water slides to Jet Skis.

KENNEDY GOLD MINE (all ages)

One mile north of Jackson off Highway 49; (209) 223–9542. Admission for adults $5.00, ages 6 to 12 $3.00, under 6 Free.

One of the best places to learn about mining history. See a film, guided tours of the mine buildings, and the equipment. On the north end of Jackson, in a city park, are two of the original four giant wooden Kennedy Mine tailing wheels—58 feet in diameter—that were built in 1912 to remove more than 500 tons of mine tailings a day.

NATIONAL HOTEL (all ages)

2 Water Street, Jackson 95642; (209) 223–0500

Take a look at the lobby and public rooms of the most notorious of Gold Rush hostelries. With brass chandeliers and red velvet walls, it's still infused with a spirit of cowboy-style elegance. Across the street, the 1862 IOOF Hall once housed Wells Fargo offices, where more than $100 million in gold dust and bullion were weighed.

MOKELUMNE HILL (all ages)

Ten minutes south of Jackson, at the bottom of a canyon of the Mokelumne River.

The once lawless town of "Mok Hill" is a quiet ghost of its former rowdy self, now a village of winding streets shaded by magnificent old locust and oak trees. Have a cold drink on the verandah of the **Hotel Leger** at 8304 Main, or stay for a sumptuous Italian meal served family style—rosemary garlic chicken, calamari, polenta, and pasta at reasonable prices (209–286–1401). Across the street, take a peek into the Adams and Company Genuine Old West Saloon and Museum and Less.

CALAVERAS COUNTY MUSEUM AND ARCHIVES (all ages)

30 North Main, San Andreas 95249; (209) 754–6513.

A unique collection of Native American and mining artifacts, interesting old documents and papers, re-created miners' cabins and stores, and a Miwok teepee. The jail out back is where Black Bart, the famous stagecoach robber and poet, languished for a time.

ROARING CAMP MINING COMPANY (all ages)

Highway 88, P.O. Box 278, Pine Grove 95665; (209) 296–4100.

An old gold camp on the Mokelumne River, featuring prospectors' cabins, (modern) bathhouses, a wildlife museum, a trading post, and a snack bar. They drive you in for a four-hour tour, fishing, and swimming, and you can stay here in a simple cabin, which includes a Free Saturday-night cookout.

ANGELS CAMP (all ages)

At Highways 49 and 4; (800) 225–3764.

The site of the **Jumping Frog Jubilee** every May. Commemorating Mark Twain's famous story, "The Celebrated Jumping Frogs of Calaveras County," the popular frog competition is open to all. You can even rent a frog and try your own version of the wild gyrations necessary to make the frogs win the jumping contests.

The setting for Brett Harte's famous story "The Luck of Roaring Camp," the town of Angels Camp is a complex of historic buildings, shops, hotels, and museums, enough to fill an afternoon. In a grassy, midtown park is equipment from five mines that pulled in more than $20 million in gold between 1886 and 1920. The **City of Angels Museum** at 753 Main (209–736–2181) displays pioneer and Gold Rush antiques and artifacts, carriages, mining and farm equipment, and a steam locomotive.

River Rafting

River Rafting Wilderness rafting on one of the big rivers of the Sierra Nevada can be the highlight of a childhood, and a never-to-be-forgotten family memory. Be sure to connect with an experienced company that caters to families, choose your river and your time of year carefully, and start with a day trip. The water is high and rough in early spring, and it's cold; in the summertime, the water is warmer and the rapids calmer. The South Fork of the American River and the Merced River are the most popular choices for families with younger children and first-time rafters. The waters are warm, the rapids are exciting but not too scary, and there are plenty of quiet swimming holes.

- **Outdoor Adventure River Specialists (O.A.R.S.).** *P.O. Box 67, Angels Camp 95222; (209) 736–4677; www.oars.com.* Over thirty years in the business of guiding families on the river, with special parent-child trips and games and toys for kids ages 4 to 13, plus activities for teens.

- **Outdoor Adventures.** *P.O. Box 1149, Point Reyes Station 94956; (800) 323–4234; www.earthcom.com/Outdoor.* This well-trained and experienced group has taken many families on California rivers and throughout the West.

Where to Eat

Upstairs Restaurant. *164 Main Street, Jackson 95642; (209) 223–3342.* Upstairs is a "fern-y," art-filled environment for a sophisticated California cuisine menu; downstairs the Streetside Bistro is perfect for sandwiches and pizza lunches. Both are casual enough for kids. $

Piaggi's. *1262 South Main Street, Angels Camp 95222; (209) 736–4862.* Fresh pasta, cioppino, steaks, burgers. $

Angels Creek Café. *1246 South Main Street, Angels Camp 95222; (209) 736–2941.* Stop in for local gossip and advice on the area at this popular breakfast spot. Dig into Sue's big omelettes and platters of eggs and home fries with homemade biscuits. $

Cafe Max. *140 Main Street, Jackson 95642; (209) 223–0174.* Open early for Swiss pastries fresh out of the 1865 brick oven, and all day for sandwiches, salads, and desserts. $

Where to Stay

Amador Inn. *200 Highway 49, Jackson 95942; (209) 223–0211 or (800) 543–5221.* Nice, simple motel; pool; coffee shop. Some kitchens, fireplaces. Pets OK. Walk to downtown. $

Jackson Holiday Lodge. *About 0.5 mile west on Highway 49, Jackson 95942; (209) 223–2905.* Simple motel rooms and housekeeping cottages; pool and nice grounds. $

For More Information

Amador County Chamber of Commerce. *At the junction of Highways 49 and 88, 125 Peak Street, Jackson 95642; (800) 649–4988 or (209) 223–0350; www. cdepot.net/chamber*

Calaveras County Visitors Center. *1301 South Main Street, Angels Camp 95222; (800) 225–3764 or (209) 736–0049; www.visitcalaveras.org; frogmail@calaveras.org.*

Columbia

The most perfectly re-created Mother Lode settlement in the United States, Columbia is a State Historic Park where the 1850s are relived by costumed performers, by horse-drawn vehicles, and by sights and sounds of the past that make you feel like you've fallen back in time. When gold was discovered here, the population exploded within a month from less than 100 to 6,000 people, and 150 saloons, gambling halls, and stores opened up. Many of the western false-front and two-story brick buildings with iron shutters remain, housing the shops, restaurants, and museums of today.

The town is absolutely captivating to children, who love the costumed storekeepers and wagon drivers, the innkeepers and blacksmiths, the street musicians and itinerant actors. Musicians and performers are encountered on the street corners and in the restaurants and

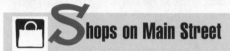

Shops on Main Street

- **Dreamwest Trading Company.** Real gold nuggets and lots of interesting rocks, guidebooks, and history books.

- **Columbia Candy Kitchen.** Four generations of the same family make fresh taffy, brittles, fudge, and penny candy.

- **Cosmos Daguerrean.** Dress up the family in the forty-niner costumes provided and have your tintypes taken.

- **Village Pharmacy.** Rows of bottles of strange remedies, plus dentist's office exhibits with scary hand drills and anything-but-painless tools for the teeth.

- **Bearcloud Gallery.** American Indian art and curios.

- **Candle and Soap Works.** In an old feed store, freshly milled soaps in clove, chocolate, lavender, and more scents, as well as candle kits and homemade candles.

theater. Horse-drawn stages clip-clop up and down the main street, which is free of auto traffic, while artisans demonstrate horseshoeing, woodcarving, and other vintage crafts. You can pan for gold in the creeks near town, take a horseback ride, and have a sarsaparilla at an old-fashioned ice cream parlor.

The town is crowded with visitors and hot during summer vacation, although pines and maples do shade the boardwalks. The mild months of spring and fall are the best times to visit. A lively schedule of festivals and special events is conducted all year in Columbia, from the Fireman's Muster in May to a "Glorious Fourth" celebration in July and the Fiddle and Banjo Contest in October.

  ### WILLIAM CAVALIER MUSEUM (all ages)
Main and State Streets, Columbia; (209) 532–0150.

The Columbia experience is enriched by "talking buttons" outside several storefronts. Push the museum buttons to hear about the museum displays in the windows. Tread the creaky floorboards within to see photos of people who lived here during the Gold Rush, as well as to eye huge chunks of ore, quartz, and semiprecious stones. At the height of Columbia's fame as the "Gem of the Southern Mines," 1.5 billion in gold was weighed on the Wells Fargo Express scales.

  ### COLUMBIA GRAMMAR SCHOOL (all ages)
On the north end of Main Street, Columbia.

In use from 1860 to 1937, with an endearing collection of antique desks, inkwells, books, and slates that children used in their schoolroom.

 ### COLUMBIA STAGE (all ages)
Catch the stage on Main Street at the Wells Fargo Express, Columbia; (209) 532–0663.

One of the greatest treats for younger children is a ride through town and into the woods and hills nearby.

  ### DOUGLASS SALOON (all ages)
Main Street, Columbia; (209) 533–2355.

Push open the swinging doors and step right into this classic western bar (children welcome) for a sarsaparilla and watch the street scene through the open shutters.

COYOTE CREEK AT NATURAL BRIDGES (all ages)
Parrott's Ferry Road, near Columbia.

A short, easy walk on a streamside nature trail. You may see people swimming here and rafting through a colorful limestone cave—not as scary as it looks.

Where to Eat

Lickskillet Cafe. *11256 State Street, Columbia 95310; (209) 536–9599.* Straightforward American home-style cooking: rosemary roasted chicken with mashed potatoes and roasted garlic gravy, rib-eye steak, Cajun meatloaf, curried chicken—bring your appetites.

Located in a vintage house; dine inside or on the porch; lunch and dinner served. $

Columbia House Restaurant. *Main Street, Columbia 95310; (209) 532–5134.* Hearty American fare for lunch and dinner. $

Underground Adventures

If your family has never toured underground caverns, you'll be fascinated by how beautiful they are. On a hot summer day in Gold Country, it's totally *cool* to see fantastic crystalline formations; gigantic, multicolored mineral towers; and stalagmites and stalagtites. Caverns are not particularly claustrophobic—believe me, I would know. Family members do need to be able to walk easily up and down stairs. Very small children should be carried in backpacks. Toddlers might be scared if/when the lights are turned off for a moment, which is sometimes done to show how dark the dark can be; ask about this possibility before you buy a ticket.

- **California Caverns.** *Eight miles east of Highway 49 off Mountain Ranch Road, San Andreas; (209) 736–2708; www.caverntours.com.* Open to the public since 1850. Eighty-minute tour groups wind through narrow passageways and limestone chambers 200 feet high.

- **Mercer Caverns.** *One mile north of Murphys, at 1667 Sheep Ranch Road; (209) 728–2101; www.mercercaverns.com. Admission $7.50.* One-hour tour featuring magnificent mineral formations.

- **Moaning Cavern.** *Parrots Ferry Road, 2 miles south of Vallecito; (209) 736–2708. Admission $6.75.* Forty-five-minute tour, featuring a 100-foot spiral staircase. For the adventurous this cavern offers a three-hour, 180-foot descent by rope in the main chamber, with equipment supplied.

Where to Stay

Trails End RV Park. *21770 Parrotts Ferry Road, Columbia 95310; (209) 533–2395.* One of several RV parks near Columbia, offering shady sites, a store, and nightly campfire gatherings. $

Marble Quarry R.V. Park. *Adjacent to Columbia State Historic Park, 11551 Yankee Hill Road, Columbia 95310; (209) 532–9539.* Wooded setting, pool, playground. $

Columbia Gem Motel. *One mile from Columbia, 22131 Parrotts Ferry Road 95310; (209) 532–4508.* Simple cottages in a pine grove. $

Columbia Inn Motel. *Adjacent to Columbia State Historic Park, 22646 Broadway Street, Columbia 95310; (209) 533–0446.* Two-bedroom units, plus suites sleeping four; simple accommodations. Pool, restaurant, and picnic area. $

For More Information

Columbia State Historic Park. *Fourteen miles south of Angels Camp, off Highway 49, Columbia 95310; (209) 532–0150.* Admission is Free.

Jamestown

Boomed and busted several times in the past 150 years, Jamestown retains an anything-can-happen Wild West atmosphere, from the days when it was just a cluster of tents on a dusty road. When the gold began to rush, saloons and dance halls were erected, then hotels and homes. Antiques and curio shops line Main Street today, and almost as many saloons and restaurants. This is one town where children enjoy the shops as much as their parents do. Most of the restaurants in town are casual and reasonably priced for family groups.

You can pan for gold near Jamestown, stay in a vintage hotel, and take a ride on a steam train. If Jamestown looks familiar to you, it may be because the movie *Butch Cassidy and the Sundance Kid* was filmed here. As in most of the Gold Country, summer temperatures are in the nineties and higher. If you have any doubt about whether there is still gold in them thar hills, a sixty-pound slab of pure gold was discovered in the Jamestown Mine in 1993.

RAILTOWN 1897 STATE HISTORIC PARK (all ages)

Fifth Avenue, Jamestown 95327; (209) 984–3953; www.pageweavers.com/ railroad/htm.

A twenty-acre exhibit of vintage steam locomotives and passenger cars, a roundhouse, shops, and a grassy picnic area in an oak grove. Plan a half-day here for all there is to see and do. Take a one-hour train ride through the foothills or a two-hour "Twilight Limited," a sort of sunset cruise with refreshments, entertainment, and a barbecue dinner at the end. Tickets for adults are $6.00 and for kids ages 6 to 12 $4.00; kids 5 and under ride **Free**.

GOLD PROSPECTING EXPEDITIONS (all ages)

18170 Main Street, Jamestown 95327; (209) 984–4653 or (800) 596–0009; www.goldprospecting.com.

When you see people panning for gold in a wooden trough on the main street, you're here. They will give you information about panning and prospecting day-trips and about rafting trips on nearby creeks and rivers. One gold-bearing creek is less than five minutes away. They run a special one-day excursion to a re-created mining camp on Wood's Creek. You will get more gold on this trip than on others because of the use of a sluice box, and you can camp there too.

GUNFIGHTER RENDEZVOUS (ages 7 and up)

April, in Jamestown; (209) 984–4616.

Six-guns are smokin' and desperadoes are swaggerin' up and down the sidewalks.

Where to Eat

Lulu's Saloon and Grill. *18201 Main Street, Jamestown 95327; (209) 984–3678.* A ceiling full of vintage lamps and chandeliers creates a fun atmosphere in this former bank, built in 1916. $

Michelangelo's. *18228 Main Street, Jamestown 95327; (209) 984–4830.* In an ultramodern, Euro-cafe atmosphere, the best in town for pizza, nouvelle Ital-ian food, pasta. The circa 1910 building served as the post office for decades. $

The Smoke Cafe. *18191 Main Street, Jamestown 95327; (209) 984–3733.* Tex-Mex specialties, Southwest decor. Lunch and dinner. Built in 1927, the building is a good example of Pueblo revival architecture popular in the twenties. $

The Willow Steakhouse. *18273 Main Street, Jamestown 95327; (209) 984–3998.* In a roadhouse built in 1862, kids eat for $5.95 and parents dig into platters of steak of every description from filet mignon to pepper steak to London broil, plus hot and cold sandwiches. Ask about the ghosts. $-$$

For More Information

Tuolumne County Visitors Bureau. *55 West Stockton Street, P.O. Box 4020, Sonora 95370; (800) 446–1333; www.mlode.com/-nsierra/visitor.*

Jamestown Visitor's Information Center. *18239 Main Street, Jamestown 95327; (209) 984–4616.*

High Sierra South

Midway in the 400-mile wave of California's great Sierra Nevada Range, Yosemite National Park is a jewel box of granite monoliths sparkling with some of the highest waterfalls on the continent. Within the 1,070-square-mile park are snowy alpine peaks, subalpine forests, and meadowlands, all crisscrossed with hundreds of miles of hiking trails.

Add to this groves of giant sequoias—the largest living things on earth—and two mighty rivers, the Merced and the Tuolumne, plus historical museums, theaters, campgrounds, and lodges, and it's no wonder that more than three million tourists visit annually. Families return year after year to sunny campgrounds along the Merced, to silent trails in the High Country, and to marvel again at El Capitan and Half Dome in Yosemite Valley. In fact, it's the most revisited national park in the country, as well as the oldest.

North of Yosemite, in a spectacular meadow at 7,200 feet, Bear Valley is surrounded by a panorama of snowcapped mountains. In summer families go mountain biking and hiking, play tennis, swim and float on the Stanislaus River, and camp and fish at eight nearby lakes. In winter a casual, reasonably priced ski resort brings families back to the valley.

A busy gateway to the south gate of Yosemite, the town of Oakhurst is a mecca for antiques lovers and for families on their way to Bass Lake and the Sierra National Forest. The small town offers family-friendly motels and restaurants, plus a few surprises. Within a few minutes' drive are a wonderful steam train, a magnificent sequoia grove, and a unique luxury resort that caters to families.

Bear Valley

YOSEMITE
NATIONAL PARK

Yosemite Village

Oakhurst   Bass Lake

HIGH SIERRA SOUTH

Bear Valley

Poised 7,200 feet high in Stanislaus National Forest, Bear Valley means good times on mountain lakes and quiet forest trails, along with laid-back Nordic and downhill skiing. Your family can spend several days here hiking the trails in Calaveras Big Trees State Park and camping and fishing on the Stanislaus River. Alpine lakes are sprinkled about nearby Ebbetts Pass and the Carson-Iceberg Wilderness area. Mountain biking and, on the river, canoeing and kayaking are popular summer sports. The midsummer Bear Valley Music Festival is a popular annual event that brings hundreds of visitors to hear big-name classical, opera and jazz performances outdoors in spectacular mountain meadow settings (800–458–1618).

Winter fun consists of skiing on one of the most extensive networks of cross-country trails in the nation, skiing downhill on **Mount Reba**, and skating on a frozen pond. Saturday nights around the ice rink are out of a storybook, with music, lights, and a bonfire.

With 450 inches of snow annually at Bear Valley, the white stuff can pile up. My children and I spent a weekend here learning to ski, and we literally climbed into and over 3 feet of snow to our cabin—which was fun . . . sort of. The next time I'll call ahead to be sure a path is cleared before we arrive. What I liked best about skiing with the kids here is that everything at the ski resort and within the village is close together and the atmosphere definitely is family-oriented and reasonably priced.

Above Bear Valley on Highway 4, 8,730-foot-high Ebbetts Pass is the road to glory in spring, when heavy snowmelt rushes off in a million waterfalls and wild-

*S***now Play** Around the valley and along Highway 4 above Bear Valley are several snow-play areas and cross-country ski trailheads, including U.S. Forest Service roads used by both skiers and snowmobilers. Besides the developed areas (listed below), watch for roadside play hills from Dorrington to Bear Valley.

Cottage Springs. *Eight miles east of Arnold, on Highway 4; (209) 795–1209.* Tube hill and rentals; sledding hill for kids to age 10.

Bear Valley Sledding Hill. *Highway 4 in Bear Valley; (209) 753–2834.* For kids 4 to 10, $6.00 including sled rental.

Lake Alpine Snow Park. *Two miles west of Bear Valley, off Highway 4; (209) 795–1381.* Sledding hill with rentals. You must buy a parking permit at the ranger station on Highway 4, near at the Mount Reba Ski Area turnoff.

flowers run riot over the meadows and beneath aromatic forests of Jeffrey pine, incense cedar, white fir, oaks, and the massive sequoias.

Just past the state park on Highway 4, on the way to Bear Valley, stop at Dorrington, a tiny former stagecoach stop, where you can take a peek in the vintage saloon and have a Northern Italian dinner at the hotel. Ask for directions to the largest Sugar pine in the world—32 feet around, 220 feet tall. Board's Crossing Road near Dorrington leads to several campgrounds on the Stanislaus River.

BEAR VALLEY VILLAGE

Forty-five miles east of Angels Camp, on Highway 4; (209) 753–2327.

Two carved wooden grizzlies greet you at the entrance to the village, a small complex anchored by Bear Valley Lodge and the Village Center, where you'll find a general store, a coffee shop, a few galleries, and places to buy sports clothing and equipment (shop for groceries and essentials on the way up here in Arnold, 20 miles south, where prices are more reasonable). Surrounded by condos that are rented by the day or the week, the village is the headquarters for the ski area and for renting summer sports equipment and boats. Most roads are not plowed in winter, giving the valley a picturesque, alpine look. Highway 4 stays open year round to about 3 miles above Bear Valley Village.

BEAR VALLEY LODGE

P.O. Box 5038, Bear Valley 95223; (209) 753–2327; www.bearvalleylodge.com.

Simple, spacious rooms in a five-story lodge, plus a pool, tennis courts, restaurants, and an inviting atrium lounge with a huge fireplace made of king-size boulders; European-style breakfast buffet. In winter you can cross-country ski and access the lifts from the lodge. If you decide to stay more than a day or two, condominiums and cabin rentals in the village are the way to go (800-794-3866).

CALAVERAS BIG TREES STATE PARK (all ages)

Four miles east of Arnold, on Highway 4; (209) 795–2334. Open all year.

In spring white-flecked branches of blooming mountain dogwood hover over your vehicle as you drive into the park on South Grove Road. Like red Christmas candles, snow plants burst up in flaming spikes through the last remnants of snow.

The really big trees, the sequoias, are here. One giant stands 320 feet high, and another measures 27 feet around. The biggest trees—1,300 of them—are found in the South Grove, 1 mile from the parking lot up the Big Trees Creek Trail. Short nature trails are accessible near the visitor center, and a network of trails leads to high ridgetops above the valley.

Winding through the park, the Stanislaus River has sandy, pebbly beaches for swimming and wading. Developed campsites are set up for RVs to 27 feet, and environmental campsites are available for backpackers.

The park is a popular cross-country ski area. A 1-mile loop near the main parking area and an outer 3-mile loop are groomed; snowmobiles are not allowed. At 4,800 elevation, snow is not always present, so it's best to call ahead for snow conditions.

BEAR VALLEY MOUNTAIN RESORT (all ages)

P.O. Box 5038, Highway 4 at Highway 207, Bear Valley 95223; (209) 753–2301; www.bearvalley.com.

A real family-oriented ski mountain, one of the last family-built and -operated ski resorts in the West. The emphasis is on beginner and intermediate skiing. Special programs are set up for little kids ages 4 to 8 (Skiing Bears), for 9- to 12-year-olds (Bear Scouts), and for teens and adults. There is all-day "Bear Care" too. The Grizzly Snowboard Den is a "boarder only" rental and lesson center; snowboarders have a snazzy new terrain park.

First-timers are VIPs, with **Free** guided ski tours of the mountain on weekends. Lift ticket and rental prices are considerably cheaper here than at Lake Tahoe ski resorts. You can ski to Bear Valley Village on Lunch Run or Home Run or get to and from the village on the **Free** shuttle.

The cross-country ski area has the largest track system in the central Sierras, 65 miles of groomed trails with warming huts and endless acres of unmarked meadows. There is also a sledding hill (www.bearvalleyxc.com).

BEAR VALLEY ADVENTURE COMPANY

1 Bear Valley Road, Bear Valley 95223; (209) 753–2834. Open all year.

In the summer, families can rent kayaks, canoes, and mountain bikes here, and get fishing equipment and bait. You can rent a fishing pole for $5.00. This is a good place to get maps and advice about recreation in the area. Ask about the new family bike trail to Lake Alpine. You can also arrange here for half-day kayaking lessons on Lake Alpine and for "Moonlight Paddles."

In the winter Bear Valley offers cross-country skiing, sledding, ice skating, and snowshoeing.

TAMARACK PINES INN AND CROSS-COUNTRY SKI CENTER

18326 Highway 4, 2.5 miles west of Bear Valley, Tamarack-Bear Valley 95223; (209) 753–2080; www.tamarackpinesinn.com.

Families return every year with their young children for the easily accessible Nordic skiing on 90 kilometers of groomed trails here, and they make this a summer headquarters for the myriad of outdoor-recreation activities nearby. The place is very child-oriented. The lodge rooms are simple and fresh, with small kitchens, and there is a complimentary continental breakfast. The common room for all guests has a fireplace, refrigerator and microwave oven, satellite TV, a VCR and video library, books, and a children's play area. Some rooms have extra-long twins, sofa beds, and child's beds; no pets allowed. There is a little sledding hill, and sleds are available to use. Ask about ski packages. $–$$

LAKE ALPINE

 Two miles northeast of Bear Valley, off Highway 4; (209) 795–1381.

The closest lake to the village, Lake Alpine is popular for kayaking, canoeing, and sailing and is regularly stocked with rainbow trout. Hiking and equestrian trails lead to the Carson-Iceberg Wilderness and into the Mokelumne Wilderness. Situated around the lake are four campgrounds and a backpackers' camping area.

A snow-play area lies just south of the parking lot. Snowmobilers and cross-country skiers head from here into the backcountry on the road to Mosquito Lake.

UTICA, UNION, AND SPICER MEADOW RESERVOIRS

 Four miles west of Bear Valley, off Highway 4; (209) 795–1381.

Quieter and less developed than the popular Lake Alpine and great for launching your own small boat and fishing for trout, bass, and catfish. No waterskiing, no Jet Skis—ah, heaven. A lyrical day-trip can be had by renting lightweight kayaks and a car rack and spending the day paddling and picnicking and messing around on one of the reservoir lakes. Surrounded by dark forest and sun-warmed boulders, with plenty of shallow spots for wading, these glittering gems are easily accessible.

A new campground is available at Spicer; day-use facilities include picnic tables, barbecue grills, and restrooms. Boating here is restricted to a speed limit of 10 miles per hour.

Where to Eat

Red Dog Lodge. *Bear Valley Village; (209) 753–2344.* Casual family dining, featuring burgers, ribs, steak, and pasta. $

Headwaters Coffee House. *In the Village Center, Bear Valley; (209) 753–2454.* Yummy baked goods, ice cream, and bistro lunches. $

Where to Stay

Bear Valley Condominium and Cabin Rentals. *Alpine Condo Management; (209) 753–2503. Bear Valley Condo Management; (209) 753–6201. Bear Valley Real Estate; (209) 753–2334.* $$–$$$

U.S. Forest Service Campground Reservations. *(209) 795–1381.* $

Lake Alpine Lodge. *Two miles from Bear Valley, off Highway 4; (209) 753–6358.* A family-oriented resort on the lake, offering housekeeping and tent cabins, a general store, a restaurant, boat and bike rentals, laundry facilities, and showers. $–$$

For More Information

CalTrans Highway 4 Road Conditions. *(209) 948–7858.*

Yosemite National Park

Spring in Yosemite means wildflowers and waterfalls. The shining water curtains of Bridalveil, Nevada, Vernal, and Yosemite Falls are all visible from the valley floor. Within the spectacular view corridor of Yosemite Valley are Half Dome, El Capitan, Cathedral Spires, Royal Arches, and myriad more granite columns, domes, and pinnacles created by millions of years of glacial activity. Like the Grand Canyon, Yosemite Valley is one of those places that you and your children must see, at least once in your lifetime.

Campgrounds, lodges, and most of the public facilities—including grocery stores, theaters, and restaurants—are located in the eastern end of the valley. Sightseeing in the valley is best done on foot, on 9 miles of bike trails, and on **Free** shuttle buses.

When the snow flies in Yosemite, the number of visitors drops dramatically and activities center on Crane Flat, Badger Pass Ski Area, and Yosemite Valley. Rangers lead snowshoe walks and ski tours from several locations. With icicle-clad Half Dome looking on, skating is fun to try or to watch at the outdoor rink in Curry Village. Winter brings a new perspective to Yosemite, when rain curtains and mists clothe the peaks. Like an Ansel Adams photo, bare cottonwood branches shiver in their crystal coats beside streams almost covered with ice.

If you are nervous about driving on snowy roads, take a two-hour, narrated winter sightseeing tour of Yosemite Valley in a comfortable motor coach with large windows.

VISITOR'S CENTER

Park at the Yosemite Lodge lot or the Curry Village lot and take the shuttle to the center; (209) 372–0299.

Get information here for a lively program of guided walks, hikes, classes, live theater, music, and exhibits that reaches a crescendo of daily choices at midyear. Informational slide shows and a bookstore with guidebooks are also here.

ANSEL ADAMS GALLERY

Near the visitor center, on the shuttle route; (209) 372–4413.

 Paintings and photos depict the history of humans and nature in Yosemite. Attend the **Free** documentary film about Adams's career and his lifelong love affair with Yosemite, screened on Sunday.

Free two-hour photography workshops with professional teachers are held at the gallery, with walks nearby. Parents and little snappers have enjoyed the photo workshops since 1902, and some were lucky enough to meet Ansel Adams himself, who taught these classes for over fifty years.

There are also Sunrise Camera Walks from Yosemite Lodge (209-372-0299).

HAPPY ISLES NATURE CENTER (ages 5–12)

On the shuttle route; (209) 372–0287.

Films, puppet shows, exhibits, and wildlife programs designed for kids. Here and at Tuolumne Meadows, a Junior Ranger Program is conducted for 8- to 12-year-olds. To earn a Junior Ranger patch, the children listen to interpretive talks on ecology, Native Americans, and wildlife and go on ranger-guided treks. Junior Snow Rangers get their patches in the winter.

At the Happy Isles bookstore, consider purchasing an Explorer Pack, a daypack filled with a guidebook and activity suggestions. Each pack has a theme, such as "Featuring Feathers," a bird identification kit, and "Rocking in Yosemite," for rock and mineral discoveries.

You can leave children at Happy Isles for **Free** one-hour walks and talks on nature, birds, and forest lore. Happy Isles is the start of several trails, including the Mist Trail.

MIST TRAIL TO VERNAL FALL (ages 8 and up)

About 1.5 miles (one-way).

The most popular hike in the valley and a spectacular one, although the complete route is strenuous and slippery for the average child under 7 or 8. Rewards are close-up views of the fall dropping over a 317-foot cliff and knockout vistas of many peaks, domes, and water cascades. The last 0.5 mile to the top is steep and switchbacky, but many 9- or 10-year-olds make it with their older siblings and parents.

The upper step of the "Giant's Stairway," 594-foot Nevada Fall feeds Vernal Fall, which plunges 317 feet toward the valley in a wide white curtain encircled by rainbows at its base.

*E*veryone Comes to Yosemite

One million people visit Yosemite in July and August, 80 percent of them remaining in the valley, which is just 1 percent of the park, where most of the public facilities and the best-known postcard views are found.

To avoid crowded campgrounds, high-season traffic, and people glut, opt to come in spring or fall. If summer is your only choice, come on weekdays and stick to the two quieter but no less attractive areas of the park, Wawona and Tuolumne. The southern section of the park, Wawona, is loaded with historic architecture, shady camping spots along a tributary of the Merced, and some of the tallest and oldest trees in the world.

You can get away from people and midsummer heat by heading for the Tuolumne High Country, to campgrounds, lakes, and cool, wildflower-bedecked Tuolumne Meadows at 8,600 feet.

MIRROR LAKE

On the shuttle route.

An easy, 0.5-mile walk to a small lake named for its glassy reflection of surrounding mountains, best in spring and early summer when the water level is highest. To avoid the more popular part of the trail, bypass the paved path and take the bridle trail along Tenaya Creek, keeping your eyes and ears alert for horses. Among the live oaks and Douglas firs, dogwood blooms in creamy white clouds in spring, while maples flame in fall.

 YOSEMITE FALLS

On the shuttle route.

Walk a short path to the base of the third highest waterfall in the world, dropping 2,425 feet in two mighty cataracts.

 AHWAHNEE HOTEL

Yosemite Village in midvalley; (559) 252–4848 or (209) 372–1488; www. yosemitepark.com. Room rates begin at about $250 for a double; packages are available.

An Art Deco, circa 1927 masterpiece built of granite blocks and concrete beams convincingly stained to look like redwood. In a forest glade of aspens and conifers, below the sweeping stone arcs and spires of Royal Arches, the hotel is a museum of priceless Native American baskets, Persian rugs, and charming early photos and artworks.

Hung with baronial chandeliers, the 130-foot-long dining room is world-famous for its beauty and views through sky-high windows. A pianist plays for dinner, and the food is better than it has ever been in the history of the hotel—top-notch California cuisine and a good wine list, plus choices that kids like. The dining room is elaborately decorated and glowing with candles and merriment every Christmas season, when the Medieval-style Bracebridge Dinners are held.

The gift shop is the best place in the valley to shop for souvenirs and books. There is a pool with a dining terrace for light meals, afternoon tea in the Great Lounge, and you can walk or bike from here, or take the shuttle, to all valley sights.

Rooms have been redone, and they are fabulous, with king-size beds, cushy fabrics, upscale mountain- and Native American decor, sitting areas, and huge windows with spectacular views. Now that the food and the accommodations are tops, the Ahwahnee lives up to its spectacular outdoor setting and atmospheric interiors. High season is booked well in advance; I like late fall, winter, and early spring, when we often have the public rooms to ourselves.

For $12.50, you can arrange for "Kid's Night Out," which includes supervised dinner, stories, and games on Monday nights, while parents take a break. And if you are interested in the gala off-season Vintners' Holidays and Chefs' Holidays special banquets and events, babysitting can be arranged.

A Very Beary Place

Bears live in Yosemite and they love campers' food. A few precautions are essential or you may be awakened in the middle of the night by a furry creature eating your hamburger and marshmallows.

- Put every bit of food into the bear lockers provided, never in your car.

- Or, hoist your food by rope 10 feet or more up into a tree, and hang pots and pans from your food bag as an alarm.

- If bears arrive, make as much noise as possible and throw rocks.

- Before you set up in a campground or High Country hike-in site, ask a ranger about bears in the area.

- Take your children to the talk entitled "Thinking Like a Bear," held once a week at Happy Isles Nature Center.

VALLEY CAMPGROUNDS

Call the National Park Reservation Service, (800) 436–PARK, for information.

Lower River, Upper River, and North, Upper, and Lower Pines are large and crowded in the high season. Although they can be noisy with road traffic and RV generators, they're conveniently located for walking and biking to most public places and trailheads. If your family is interested in the classes, interpretive hikes, and performances scheduled throughout the high season, a valley campground may be your best choice. Children like the nightly campfires at Lower Pines Campground.

CURRY VILLAGE

On the eastern end of the valley; (209) 253–5639.

Sprinkled about under cedars, Kellogg oaks, and Jeffrey pines are a variety of accommodations, including tent cabins, housekeeping cabins, hotel rooms, and loft rooms sleeping six or more. All are clean and quite basic; some can be noisy. There is a cafeteria and an outdoor cafe with good, basic American food.

The outdoor skating rink here is a cozy place to be, with a warming hut, skate rentals, and hot drinks. You can rent one-speed bikes, a great way to get around the valley on 8 miles of bike paths in addition to the roads.

GLACIER POINT

Required sightseeing. Early morning or late afternoon is the best time for the 32-mile road trip to Glacier Point, to avoid gridlock and to see the dazzling array of granite monoliths when the light is most dramatic (early morning is when hang gliders sail off Half Dome).

From Glacier Point, a rock outcropping hanging out over the edge of the valley, you get a breathtaking bird's-eye view from 3,200 feet. Looking down into the chasm of the valley, your children will spot the river snaking far below and antlike cars crawling on the main roads. With the help of the plaques provided, it's fun to search for the landmarks. The Ahwahnee is easy to locate, at the foot of Royal Arches; Happy Isles is right below your feet; and Half Dome, with half its roundness chopped off as if by a tomahawk, seems to fill up half the sky to the east. Look for climbers making their ascent to the 7,000-foot summit of El Capitan, a startling vertical mass four times as large as the Rock of Gibraltar. The faint booming sound you hear in springtime is Nevada Fall, 2 miles away.

A relaxing way to get to Glacier Point is on a narrated bus tour that runs 3 times a day from the valley (about $20 round-trip for adults, and $10 for kids). You can also take the bus one-way up and walk all the way down to the valley, a 4.8-mile, three-and-a-half-hour hike for the superfit family.

TUOLUMNE MEADOWS

Overnight backpacking requires a Wilderness permit, which is **Free** *and not necessary for day hikes. Trailheads have quotas that are occasionally "sold out" in the high season, so request permits by mail in advance: Wilderness Office P.O. Box 577, Yosemite 95389; (209–372–0310). A hiker's bus from the valley will drop you off near Tioga Road trailheads.*

An enormous open space at 8,600 feet, bordered by the snow-fed Tuolumne River and surrounded by peaks and glacier-polished domes. The boiling waters of two forks of the river come together here, then drop into the Grand Canyon of the Tuolumne and finally into Hetch Hetchy Reservoir miles below, the drinking fountain for San Francisco.

A hub for backpacking trails, the 2.5-mile-long meadow is the largest in the Sierras at the subalpine level. It may sparkle with frost or be awash in purple nightshade, golden monkey flowers, and riots of magenta lady's slipper orchids. A variety of ranger-guided walks begin here. The "Night Prowl," an after-dark caravan around the meadow, turns up great gray owls, spotted bats, and other nocturnal denizens of the High Sierras.

For good fishing and swimming, take the 1.5-mile one-way trek to Dog Lake, a little steep at first, but easy enough for kids age 6 and up.

WAWONA

Southern section of the national park, 36 miles south of Yosemite Valley on High-way 41.

Families with small children love Wawona for the quiet, riverside campground; for the fun of the Mariposa Grove tram ride; and for the Pioneer Yosemite History Center, where costumed docents reenact nine-teenth-century life. Beaches and swimming spots are easily accessible on the South Fork of the Merced River as it runs through Wawona.

Even toddlers can manage part of the 3-mile, flat loop trail around Wawona Meadow, and they like watching the herds of grazing deer (do not feed or touch them).

WAWONA HOTEL

Near the south gate of the park on Highway 41; (209) 252–4848. Rates start at about $100 for a double, ski packages available.

Riding the edge of Wawona Meadow like a glistening white ocean liner, the oldest resort hotel in the state was built in 1870s, and she is in fabulous shape. Rooms in several beautiful, vintage buildings and cot-tages vary in size, and many have been redone in sumptuous fabrics, with armoires, new furnishings, and nice bathrooms with amenities. Some families return every summer to stay in their favorite rooms; some of the best choices are number 137 (three beds); Little White cottage (three adjoining rooms and private porch); and upstairs in the main building, connected rooms with shared baths. There is a beautiful pool, sweeping lawns, a 9-hole golf course, wonderful walking trails, tennis, horseback riding, and the Merced River nearby for swimming and fishing. Or you can just sink into a rocker on the covered porch. You don't need a car: just jump on one of the **Free** shuttles to the valley and the Mariposa Grove, operating year round.

The beautiful Victorian dining room, open for all meals, now has a fabulous chef. The menu is a cross between California cuisine and com-fort food, with seasonal specials; don't miss the pine nut pie and the summer barbecues.

Only One Day

Only One Day It's unbelievable, really, but some families have just a day to spend in Yosemite. Here are my top sights to see in a day, including the easiest and most accessible trails in the valley. Hop on the Free valley shuttle for the first four stops.

- **Lower Yosemite Fall.** Walk ten minutes to the base of the fall, where a wispy, watery wonderland awaits you (an additional 0.5-mile loop goes over the bridge and back to the parking lot).

- **Mist Trail.** From Happy Isles, it's 0.7 mile on a paved trail to Vernal Fall bridge for zowie views of the waterfall (if you have more time, continue on a 0.5-mile steep trail to the top of the fall).

- **Mirror Lake.** Popular, scenic 0.5-mile walk to see Half Dome in all its glory.

- **Ahwahnee Hotel.** My favorite place in Yosemite—I always feel like whispering as I wander around the lobby of this living Art Deco museum, still a thriving, popular lodge. Sit right down in a big arm-chair in the Great Room, put your feet up in front of the big stone fireplace, and contemplate the fabulous stained-glass windows faded into soft Indian colors. Take a look at the old photos and paintings of the 1920s and 1930s. Walk into the main dining room, a two-story, trestle-beamed hall with floor-to-ceiling windows looking onto Royal Arches, a monumental granite cliff that is breathtaking when glazed with snow and ice, and when the aspens at its base are molten gold in the fall.

- **Bridalveil Fall.** At the junction of Highways 140 and 41 in the park is a parking lot where a short, paved trail leads to the base of the water-fall. Look up to a sheet of water floating 620 feet to the valley floor. This fall never disappoints, as it flows year-round and is often deco-rated by rainbows. In springtime turn around to get a view of Ribbon Fall, the highest single fall in the park, at 1,612 feet.

- **Tunnel View.** Just below the entrance to the Wawona Tunnel, park at the turnout to see a classic, panoramic view of the valley with the famous and mighty monoliths El Capitan and Half Dome.

- **Glacier Point Road.** Enjoy 32 miles of dazzling alpine scenery topped by the stupendous view from Glacier Point, 3,200 feet above the val-ley, with peaks, domes, and massive cliffs in a dizzying array before you. Save a roll of film for this one.

PIONEER YOSEMITE HISTORY CENTER (all ages)

A compound of circa 1880 buildings, offering antique horse-drawn vehicles, a covered bridge, a real live blacksmith, and stagecoach rides. About 200 yards upstream from the covered bridge are small swimming and wading pools in a river tributary, the warmest waters in the park. You can leave your vehicle on the side of the road and wade across to big, flat boulders warmed by the sun—one of my favorite places to picnic. A small grocery store and deli are located here.

MARIPOSA GROVE

A five-minute drive east of the Pioneer Yosemite History Center.

The largest of three sequoia groves in Yosemite. It's the home of the 209-foot, 300-ton **Grizzly Giant,** the **Columbia** (290 feet) and dozens more 2,000- to 3,000-year-old sequoias, the world's largest living things. One branch of the Grizzly Giant is more than 6 feet in diameter, and the cinnamon-brown bark is 24 inches thick.

The narrated, open-air tram tour stops frequently for passengers to hop on and off to wander nature trails on the way to a vista point at 6,810 feet, overlooking the vast Wawona forest basin. Instead of taking the tram back to the parking lot, wander the 2.5-mile, easy downhill route on footpaths beneath the fragrant branches. In the cool stillness you'll hear only bustling chipmunks and the prattle of Stellar's jays; trillium and wild iris spring from carpets of moss and fern.

BADGER PASS SKI AREA

Off Glacier Point Road; (209) 372–1244. Lift tickets for adults $22 to 28, ages 12 and under $13; inexpensive equipment rental, lessons, and tours. Ask about family ski packages at Yosemite Lodge and Wawona Hotel.

Six lifts take skiers to the 8,000-foot summit; Nordic skiing is fine on 350 miles of trails and roads and on 23 miles of machine-groomed tracks and skating lanes. The emphasis is on beginners and intermediates at both the downhill and the cross-country ski schools. This is the oldest ski school in the state, and still one of the best and most reasonably priced.

Gas Up There are no gas stations in Yosemite; the closest station is in El Portal, 16 miles from the park, and at Crane Flat, 18 miles away on Highway 120.

Except on holiday weekends, you won't wait in lift lines; the dining decks and all facilities are just steps away from the lifts. Take it easy, and take the comfortable shuttle buses from your accommodations up the (sometimes icy) hill to Badger.

Kids ages 4 to 6 like the Badger Pups program, which has short group lessons and supervised play.

A two-hour, ranger-guided, narrated snowshoe hike is only $3.00, including equipment.

SNOW PLAY

Two locations: Crane Flat on Highway 120, and another just outside the southern entrance of the park, on Highway 41 at Fish Camp.

Developed snow play and rentals; no charge to play!

Where to Eat

Marriott's Tenaya Lodge. *1122 Highway 41, Fish Camp 93623; (800) 635–5807.* The Sierra Restaurant offers an upscale casual atmosphere, fresh fish, local produce, Italian cuisine, a fireplace, and mountain views. The Parkside Restaurant is a casual coffee shop, serving sandwiches, salads, and deli take-out. Breakfast, lunch, and dinner are offered at both restaurants. $$

Degnan's Deli/the Loft. *In Yosemite Village, near the visitor center.* Sandwiches, salads, and barbecue burgers to take out; sit-down meals too, including steak, burgers, and chicken dishes. Don't expect gourmet cuisine. $

Pets *Kennel facilities, (209) 372–1248.* Pets are allowed in the national park if they are leashed at all times and never left unattended. No pets are allowed on trails, in the backcountry, or in lodgings.

Where to Stay

Yosemite National Park. *National Park Reservation Service (campgrounds); (800) 436–PARK. Yosemite Reservation and Information service (cabins; lodge/hotel rooms); (209) 252–4848.* For sites requiring reservations call three months to a year in advance to ensure your space. For campgrounds operating on a first-come, first-served basis, be sure to arrive early in the morning in order to avoid disappointment.

Yosemite Lodge. *Midvalley; (209) 252–4848.* Four hundred eighty-four simple rooms, from traditional rooms with balconies to rustic cabins, with or without baths. The compound that includes a cafeteria and restaurants with good, plain food; a post office; gift shops; a swimming pool; an outdoor theater; and a tour desk. Free nightly programs. $

Bridalveil Creek Campground.
Twenty-five miles from Yosemite Valley on Glacier Point Road; (800) 436–PARK. A compromise between accessibility to the valley and a quieter, prettier place to camp at an elevation of 7,200 feet. One hundred tent and RV sites with bear lockers.

High Country Campgrounds at Yosemite. *(800) 435–PARK.* Cabins are available at six High Sierra camps; only the rustic **Tuolumne Meadows Lodge** and the **Tuolumne Meadows Campground** can be reached by car. Tuoloumne Meadows is the largest campground in the park, with 325 sites; the most desirable are on the east side near the river. Campfire programs and special children's get-togethers with songs and stories are held most nights. Nearby are a grocery store, stables and a restaurant in a tent beside the river, serving substantial American fare. Tent cabins with wood stoves are in a picturesque setting near the river. **White Wolf Campground** is summertime-only headquarters for backcountry trails, with rustic tent cabins, a "first-come" campground, store, stables, and a lovely old clapboard dining hall that serves simple meals all day.

The Redwoods. *Chilnaulna Falls Road off Highway 41, Wawona, in the national park; (209) 375–6666; www. redwoodsguestcottages.com.* Choose from more than one hundred privately owned cabins and houses to rent in a wooded setting near the river. Homes are in varied sizes, all fully furnished and equipped. Make reservations for holidays starting February 15 of each year. $$–$$$

Wawona Campground. *Fourteen miles from Oakhurst, within the national park, five minutes from the southern gate; (800) 436–PARK.* Open year-round, the one-hundred-site first-come, first-served campground stretches for 1 mile along on the banks of the Merced, with river-view sites the most coveted. $

Yosemite View Lodge. *11159 Highway 140, El Portal, fifteen minutes from the national park entrance; (800) 321–5261.* Two swimming pools, three spas, kitchenettes, fireplaces, restaurant. A large motel with balconies overlooking the Merced River. $–$$

Yosemite's Four Seasons. *7519 Henness Circle, near the Wawona entrance to the national park; (800) 669–9300.* Rooms, studios, homes, and apartments to rent, from simple to luxurious. $$–$$$$

For More Information

Yosemite National Park. *P.O. Box 577, Yosemite 95389; general information, (209) 372–1000; reservations for cabins and lodge/hotel rooms, (209) 252–4848; reservations for campgrounds, (800) 436–PARK; road and weather information, (209) 372–0200 or (209) 372–2009. Admission to the national park: $20 per car.* Weather changes rapidly in the Sierras; snow can fall as early as September, and storms can occur any month of the year. Before you leave home, call to check on weather, road, and trail conditions, and ask about the availability of campsites if you plan to camp without reservations.

Sierra National Forest Ranger District. *(209) 841–3311, (209) 372–1000, (209) 372–0265, or (209) 372–0264.*

Yosemite Web Sites

www.yosemitepark.com. Yosemite Concession Services site with information on lodging, shopping, dining, activities, and links.

www.reservations.nps.gov. Camping reservations.

www.yosemite.org. Yosemite Association, visitor information, bookstore, classes and seminars, weather, and live-camera views.

www.nps.gov/yose. Official National Parks Association site.

www.yosemite.com. Travelers' information, lodging, road conditions, and weather.

Y.A.R.T.S. *(877) 98–YARTS; www.yosemite.com/yarts.* Fares are $10 to $15 round-trip, including park admission. A new motorcoach service from Merced, Coulterville, Mariposa, and Mammoth with bike racks, making personal vehicles unnecessary.

Oakhurst

Between Yosemite and Kings Canyon National Park, the Lake Country of the Central Sierras remains relatively undiscovered by vacationers. Some 700 miles of trout streams, along with numerous lakes, reservoirs, and campgrounds, make this an area your family will want to explore.

Fourteen miles from the southern Yosemite gate, Oakhurst is an antiques center and a busy stopover point for travelers on the way to the national park and the national forests. Just up the road at an elevation of 3,400 feet lies the popular recreation area of Bass Lake, with rustic resorts and campgrounds; marinas for sailing, fishing, and waterskiing boats; and endless hiking trails in the surrounding Sierra National Forest.

My favorite time of the year in the Central Sierras is after Labor Day. Traffic is light, and the weather has cooled from the high nineties of midsummer to the seventies. Nights are delightfully crisp, and color is beginning to show in the maples, dogwoods, and oaks.

YOSEMITE COFFEE ROASTING COMPANY
40879 Highway 41, in the Silver Creek Center, Oakhurst 93644; (559) 683–8815.
Fun from dawn to late at night, the place features an ice cream parlor and luscious bakery treats, sandwiches, bistro food, and live music on weekends. $

H it the Trail

- **Oakhurst River Parkway.** *Oakhurst Community Park, Civic Circle, Oakhurst; (209) 683–7766.* An oak-shaded 3-mile loop trail along the Fresno River and Oak Creek.

- **Lewis Creek National Recreation Trail.** *Five miles south of the southern Yosemite Gate, off Highway 41; (209) 683–4665.* From the highway parking area, walk 0.25 mile south on the trail to Corlieu Falls, then 1.8 miles north to Red Rock Falls, through dogwood, azalea, and pines along Lewis Fork Creek. The creek is stocked with trout and is popular with anglers.

- **Shadow of the Giants Trail.** *Ten miles north of Oakhurst on Highway 41, take Sky Ranch Road for 6 miles.* A National Recreation Trail, an easy, 1 mile with interpretive signs along the banks of Nelder Creek, leading to a miraculous grove of over 100 specimen sequoias and one of the largest trees in the world, the **Bull Buck**. Insiders know that this trail is less traveled and more beautiful than the Sequoia grove trails in Yosemite. The biggest and best trees are at the far end of the loop, so get there!

- **Way of the Mono Trail.** *Along Road 222 at Bass Lake, trailhead between the Forks Resort and the California Land Management Office.* A nice, easy 0.5-mile walk to learn some American Indian history and see some great views of the lake.

- **Goat Mountain Trail.** *Trailheads at Spring Cove Campground and Fork Campground at Bass Lake; (209) 683–4665.* Four strenuous miles one-way to the summit and the fire lookout, with nonstop views of the lake and the forested valleys along the way. Cut the distance and the degree of difficulty of this beautiful trail in half by starting at one campground, leaving a car at the other, and turning back where the two trails meet on the way up.

FRESNO FLATS HISTORICAL PARK (all ages)

One mile from Oakhurst, on Road 427; (559) 683–6570.

A re-created western town from the region's early timber and ranching era. Old buildings have been moved from all over the county—jails, schools, barns, wagons, buggies, and a furnished home.

YOSEMITE MOUNTAIN SUGAR PINE RAILROAD (all ages)

Between Oakhurst and Yosemite, on Highway 41; (559) 683–7273; www.ymsprr.com.

A major destination for families with younger children. You might want to plan a couple of hours here riding the train, picnicking, and enjoying the beautiful forest. An eighty-four-ton vintage locomotive—the largest ever built for a narrow-gauge track—pulls open cars 4 miles through forestlands into Lewis Creek Canyon. It's exciting to climb aboard at the tiny station while steam rolls out from under the huge engine and black smoke belches into the sky. A conductor spins tales of when the railroad hauled timber out of the Sierras.

From June through September a "Moonlight Special" evening train excursion ends with a steak barbecue and live music around a campfire. Cross-country skiing is excellent throughout the Sugar Pine area.

Next door at the **Narrow Gauge Inn,** the Victorian era and the Old West come together in the restaurant and Bull Moose saloon—cozy in cool weather when logs burn in the big stone fireplaces (209-683-7720).

BASS LAKE (all ages)

Fourteen miles from Oakhurst off Highway 41, on Road 222; (559) 683–4665.

The warm waters of this popular lake reach seventy-eight degrees in summer. Situated in the Sierra National Forest at 3,400 feet, the lake is good spring and fall fishing for trout, bass, catfish, and bluegill and in summer for partaking in water sports and camping. You can rent windsurfers and boats for canoeing, sailing, rowing, and waterskiing. At three main resort areas—Pines Village, Forks Resort, and Miller's Landing—are shops, groceries, gas, and rentals of all kinds.

SIERRA MONO MUSEUM (all ages)

Between North Fork and South Fork, at Malum Ridge Road (Road 274) and Mammoth Pool Road (Road 225), North Fork; (559) 877–2115.

A major exhibition of American Indian artifacts, baskets, and California wildlife displays. In August the **Sierra Mono Indian Fair Days and**

Pow Wow is held here, featuring Indian foods, traditional dances, crafts, games.

Where to Eat

Ducey's on the Lake. *Pines Village, Bass Lake 93644; (559) 642–3131.* Every Friday evening from late May through late August, live jazz outdoors and fireworks! On a sunny deck overlooking the lake, offering grilled chicken, salads, burgers, fresh fish, and pasta. $

The Pines Resort. *Pines Village, Bass Lake 93644; (559) 642–3121.* Good barbecue and American food; indoor/outdoor casual dining. $$

Yosemite Forks Mountain House Restaurant. *Highway 41 at the Bass Lake turnoff 93644; (559) 683–5191.* A real family-oriented place, serving burgers and steaks, chicken and fish, with take-out and box lunches. $

Castillo's. *49271 Golden Oak Loop, Oakhurst 93644; (559) 683–8000.* Terrific tacos and homemade Mexican food. It's a cantina, too—try the blackberry margaritas. $

Meadows Ranch Cafe. *5023 Highway 140, Mariposa 95338; (209) 966–2065.* On the way to Yosemite, a great place to stop for breakfast, lunch, or dinner. Very family oriented, with a huge menu of comfort food, from steak to chili, pasta, burgers, gourmet pizza, barbecue, and luscious desserts; plus a large kids' menu. $–$$

Where to Stay

Marriott's Tenaya Lodge. *1122 Highway 41, Fish Camp 93623; (800) 635–5807; www.tenayalodge.com.* A destination resort overlooking forested mountains and valleys, five minutes from the southern gate of Yosemite National Park. The two-story atrium lobby and the restaurants have a casual yet luxurious feel and are decorated with Indian artifacts and Western-style furnishings. The spacious, elegant rooms were delightfully renovated recently and include many amenities. ironing boards, coffeemakers, Nintendo; some have two double beds and a sitting area with sofa bed. Recreational facilities include a full-service spa and fitness center, saunas, indoor and outdoor pools, and a playground. Tours from the hotel get you into the park and to the Badger Pass ski area.

Kids check in at their own station at the front desk and pick up an activity pack. "Camp Tenaya" day camp is popular with 5- to 12-year-olds, who like volleyball, Ping-Pong, swimming, games, movies, music, crafts and nature hikes. Campers get personal attention and special meals, and there are evening programs, too. Baby sitting can be arranged for toddlers. There is a nice playground on the grounds, and a snow-play area.

You can hike right from the lodge, through pine forests and along streamsides. Bikes are available at the hotel, and you can walk to a stable for guided horseback rides. Cross-country ski out the door and rent equipment here too, to ski on your own or take a guided tour.

Barbecue evenings start with a horse-drawn wagon ride to the cook-out, with campfire singing and marshmallow roasting with cowpokes. $$$

Yosemite Gateway Inn. *40530 Highway 41, Oakhurst 93944; (800) 545–5462 or (559) 683–2378.* Motel and family units in a parklike setting, with oak trees, some kitchens, indoor and outdoor pools, restaurant, barbecue area, playground, laundry, and mountain views. Some two-bedroom family units. $$

The Pines Resort. *Right on Bass Lake, P.O. Box 109, Bass Lake 93604; (800) 350–7463; www.basslake.com.* Rustic condos and chalets at the lake and luxury suites; restaurant; tennis, swimming pool, sauna, hot tub; boat rentals. $

U.S. Forest Service (USFS) Campground Information and Reservations. *(800) 280–CAMP.* Summerdale USFS Campground at Fish Camp has a nice, streamside location. $

For More Information

Yosemite Sierra Visitors Bureau. *40637 Highway 41, Oakhurst 93644; (559)683–4636; www.yosemite.sierra.org.*

Bass Lake Chamber of Commerce. *P.O. Box 126, Bass Lake 93604; (559) 642–3676; www.basslake.com.*

South Bay and East Bay Towns

The cities and the countryside surrounding San Francisco are easily accessible and packed with opportunities for family adventures—from ridge-top hikes in the East Bay hills to science museums, ethnic festivals, and a wild water park.

Hop a fast underground train to Berkeley for a day on a university campus, or shop in the outlet stores, and later take a hike in a ridge-top forest. Ride the ferry to Oakland for a seafood dinner in Jack London Square and to an art museum that kids like. Spend the day in San Jose at high-tech play-and-learn centers; you will need another whole day to play at Paramount's Great America theme park, and yet another to explore a mystery house and a cool museum of mummies and Egyptian tombs.

Highway 280 is the fastest route south to San Jose. Take Highway 80 across the Bay Bridge to Oakland and Berkeley, or a ferry or BART across the bay.

Berkeley

Just a skip and a jump across the bay from San Francisco, Berkeley is the home of one of the largest and most beautiful university campuses in the western United States, the University of California at Berkeley. Attractions here for visiting families are the campus itself, ethnic and vegetarian restaurants, and recreation in Tilden Regional Park in the verdant hills above the city. You might also enjoy the reasonably priced accommodations and the factory outlet stores.

At the base of a range of forest-covered hills overlooking San Francisco Bay, the small city is laid out on either side of University Avenue, which stretches from a lively marina to the campus.

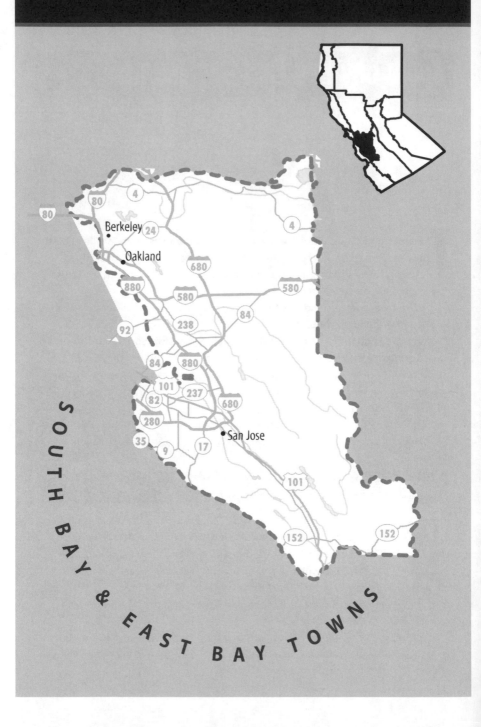

SOUTH BAY & EAST BAY TOWNS

UNIVERSITY OF CALIFORNIA (all ages)

101 University Hall, at Oxford Street and University Avenue, Berkeley; (510) 642–5215.

Budding scientists in your family will find a plethora of fascinating museums, as well as the world-famous Lawrence Hall of Science, on the campus. Student-led campus tours are offered several times a day, and you can get maps for a self-guided tour at the visitor center. Maps are also posted at the campus entrance, and you can get one by mail by sending a self-addressed stamped envelope to 2200 University Information Center, 2200 University Avenue, Berkeley, CA 94720. Call ahead for tour reservations.

I went to school here and now find the campus a little more crowded with buildings and students but still a great place to spend an afternoon, wandering the garden pathways and having a picnic beneath one of the century-old redwoods or oak trees. The oldest of the UC campuses, established in 1868, this one has a fascinating variety of architectural styles. Delicatessens and casual cafes are clustered on the streets near each campus entrance.

ADVENTURE PLAYGROUND AND SHOREBIRD NATURE CENTER (ages 7–12)

West end of University Avenue, west of Highway 80, Berkeley Marina; (510) 644–8623. Open daily in summer, weekends off-season; call first. Admission is **Free**.

For children 7 and older, a special playground for junior carpenters, a place to build, climb, and play around. Staff hand out paint, brushes, hammers, and nails and keep an eye on the kids. Great bay views and a one-hundred-gallon aquarium.

BERKELEY PIER/CESAR CHAVEZ PARK (all ages)

West end of University Avenue, west of Highway 80, Berkeley Marina.

Extending 3,000 feet out into the bay, the pier is a good place to stroll, take photos of the skyline, and watch freighter traffic. Many people fish for perch and flounder, and you may see sharks and stingrays caught too. The dependably breezy waterfront park is the site of the annual Berkeley Kite Festival in July, when amateur and professional kite flyers compete.

Highlights of the UC Campus

- **Sather Tower.** *Central campus, visible from Sather Gate on Bancroft; (510) 642–5215.* A campus landmark built in 1914 as a replica of St. Mark's campanile in Venice. Take a heart-stopping ride to the top for 360-degree views of the Bay Area. The last elevator of the day leaves at 3:00 P.M.; on Sundays, at 1:30 P.M. Tickets cost $1.00.

- **Lawrence Hall of Science.** *Centennial Drive near Grizzly Peak Boulevard; (510) 642–5132. Admission is $6.00 adults, $4.00 students, and $2.00 kids ages 3 to 6.* Get involved in interactive displays of lasers, computers, medicine, dinosaurs, and outer space; pretend to be a doctor, an archaeologist, and an astronaut. Planetarium shows and physics and biology labs are here too. The littlest kids like "OK-to-touch" frogs, tarantulas, rabbits, and other animals. Call for a schedule of special weekend events.

- **Valley Life Sciences Building/Museum of Paleontology.** A huge collection of fossils are laid out in the hallways, and a triceratops skull awaits in the library. A two-story-high *Tyrannosaurus rex* presides in the atrium, while a pterosaur flies overhead. Cool!

- **Essig Museum of Entomology.** *211 Wellman Hall.* Bees, beetles, butterflies and more—bugs galore—are on display in the hallways.

- **Phoebe Hearst Museum of Anthropology.** *Kroeber Hall on Bancroft at College Avenues; (510) 643–7648.* California Native Americans are featured, plus ancient artifacts from all over the world.

- **International House.** *2299 Piedmont Avenue; (510) 642–9456.* A chance to have a meal in the company of students from all over the world. Good, basic international cuisine is served from a buffet in a unique Spanish/Moorish–style restaurant, indoors or on the garden patio. $

HABITOT CHILDREN'S MUSEUM (ages 1–7)

2065 Kittredge Street, Berkeley 94704; (510) 528–6319.

A brand-new learning center for children, from babies to 7-year-olds: water play, costume shop, wind-tunnel climbing and exploration, and a small-scale town.

TILDEN REGIONAL PARK (all ages)

In the hills above Berkeley, accessed from Spruce Street, from Centennial Drive, and from Grizzly Peak; (510) 525–2233.

A vast, green open space that is a haven for hikers, bikers, and picnickers. A popular site for tykes is Little Farm, where children can pet and feed domestic animals and birds. There are pony rides here, together with a 1911 carousel with beautifully painted animals, a merry-go-round, and a small lake—a day is hardly enough time! Lifeguards are on duty for swimming from spring through fall in Lake Anza, which has a sandy beach and is particularly well set up for toddlers.

On the east end of Tilden, take a ride on a miniature steam train that winds through the redwoods and a tunnel.

An easy 1-mile walk through woods and meadows circles Jewel Lake, leading to a marshy pond where frogs and ducks hold court. Longer hikes start from Little Farm.

Where to Eat

Fatapple's Restaurant and Bakery. *1346 Martin Luther King, Jr. Way, Berkeley 94704; (510) 526–2260.* Wildly popular with families, for burgers, chili, and homemade pie and bakery goods, all at reasonable prices. $

Long Life Vegi House. *University Avenue at Shattuck Avenue, Berkeley 94704; (510) 845–6072.* Rub elbows with students, professors, and families who like good, inexpensive vegetarian and seafood specialties. Try the mu-shu veggies. $

Hana Sushi Buffet. *1722 University Avenue, Berkeley 94704; (510) 841–9500.* In a casual atmosphere, dozens of kinds of sushi and hot dishes, plus a salad bar. All you can eat for a minimum price. $$

Pizza Rustica Cafe and Tapas Bar. *5422 College Avenue, Berkeley 94704; (510) 654–1601.* Some say this is the best pizza in town. $

Where to Stay

Radisson Hotel Berkeley Marina. *200 Marina Boulevard on the waterfront, Berkeley 94704; (510) 548–7920.* Glistening from a multimillion-dollar renovation, a big hotel conveniently located to the entire Bay Area. Each room has a balcony or patio. Outdoor pool and indoor lap pool, fitness center, guest laundry, *Free* shuttle to BART, restaurant. $$–$$$

Claremont Resort Hotel. *Ashby and Domingo Avenues, Berkeley 94704; (510) 843–3000.* The only resort in the East Bay, a classic Victorian-style hotel within elaborate gardens and grounds, along with a major tennis complex and a complete spa. Olympic-size pool, lap pool, children's wading area, playground, par course, restaurants, and babysitting service. $$–$$$

For More Information

Berkeley Convention and Visitors Bureau. *2015 Center Street, ½ block west of the downtown Berkeley BART station, Berkeley 94704–1204;*

(510) 549–7040 or (800) 847–4823; recorded information on events and more: (510) 549–8710; www.berkeleycvb.com.

Fourth Street Shops and Cafes To reach the restaurant and factory outlet ghetto on Fourth and surrounding streets, take the University Avenue exit off Highway 80, then the first left turn; then turn left again onto Fourth Street.

- **Bette's Oceanview Diner.** *1807 Fourth Street, Berkeley; (510) 644–3230.* My family's favorite restaurant in the East Bay, and a favorite with the people who stand in line to get in. This all-American, circa-1940 cafe with booths and a counter opens at 6:30 A.M. and goes full blast all day long, through dinner; take away as well as eat in. The epitome of comfort food. $

- **Royal Robbins.** *841 Gilman Street off Fourth, Berkeley; (510) 527–1961.* Top-quality outdoor recreation equipment and clothing, at a discount. My husband has Royal Robbins shorts that's he's worn every summer for twenty years. Really!

- **HearthSong Toys.** *1810 Fourth Street, Berkeley; (510) 849–3956.* Toys that run on imagination instead of batteries. Games, audiotapes, books, and toys from all over the world.

- **Earthsake.** *1805 Fourth Street, Berkeley; (510) 559–8440.* Interesting eco stuff, including toys, games, and books.

- **REI.** *1338 San Pablo Avenue, near Fourth Street, Berkeley; (510) 527–4140.* Top-of-the-line camping and outdoor recreational equipment, clothing, bikes, a climbing wall, boots, running gear, guidebooks, and ski stuff.

- **Nature Company.** *740 Hearst Avenue off Fourth; (510) 649–5448.* All sorts of toys, books, clothing, music, games, and puzzles with environmental, nature, and world themes.

- **Sweet Potatoes.** *1716 Fourth Street; (510) 527–5852.* Fabulous bright cotton duds for babies and toddlers.

Oakland

The main family attractions in the port city of Oakland are Jack London Square and Lake Merritt. You can get here by ferry and on BART.

LAKE MERRITT AND CHILDREN'S FAIRYLAND (ages 1–8)

Grand Avenue and Bellevue Street, Oakland; (510) 425–2259.

For younger children, a three-dimensional nursery-rhyme playground, a merry-go-round, a puppet theater, train rides, and farm animals. A 3-mile paved path runs around the lake, and you can rent paddleboats, rowboats, and canoes.

JACK LONDON SQUARE

Broadway at Embarcadero, Oakland; (510) 814–6000.

On the Oakland estuary, the city was founded in the 1850s to ship lumber and supplies to the miners of the Gold Rush. Named for the notorious and prolific adventure story author Jack London, who was a roustabout in Oakland early in this century, the waterfront is a hodgepodge of old and new seafood restaurants and cafes, souvenir shops, a few historic sites, and the beginnings of the gentrification soon to come. The Sunday farmers market is great fun, and so is the monthly antiques fair. There is a movieplex here, and inexpensive hotels within easy reach of the Oakland airport, good choices for Bay Area visitors who are on a budget. Ferries ply the bay between here and downtown San Francisco, Pier 39, Fisherman's Wharf, and Angel Island. The gigantic new Barnes & Noble is open late and has a cafe with tables in a shady grove of trees.

U.S.S. *POTOMAC* (all ages)

At the foot of Clay Street, corner of Embarcadero at Jack London Square; (510) 839–8256 or (510) 839–7533; www.usspotomac.com. Admission for adults $3.00, ages 6 to 17 $1.00, ages 5 and under **Free***; family rate is $5.00 for all, with two parents.*

FDR's "Floating White House" is a sweet reminder of a beloved president who escaped humid Washington summers and the pressures of World War II and the Depression by cruising on this yacht, which has been beautifully restored. While browsing the artifacts of that tumultuous era, you can imagine FDR playing poker with his buddies and poring over his stamp collection.

COST PLUS

101 Clay Street, Jack London Square 94607; (510) 834–4440.

Cut the kids loose with ten bucks each and look for them an hour later, loaded up with imported wooden toys, candy bars, ethnic jewelry, posters, candles, and art supplies. The warehouse-style store offers the world for cheap, from rattan furniture to placemats, and baskets and china from China. This is the all-time best place in town for Christmas shopping on a budget.

EBONY MUSEUM OF ARTS AND STORE (all ages)

30 Jack London Square, Oakland 94607; (510) 763–0745.

From Africa, everything is handcrafted and everything is fabulous: baskets, sculpture, art, jewelry, masks, clothing, and crafts.

ROCKRIDGE (all ages)

From the beginning of College Avenue at Broadway, up College to the Oakland/Berkeley border.

Spend an afternoon strolling, noshing, and shopping in a charming, leafy neighborhood that seems lost in the early twentieth century. Shop the fresh produce, fruit, cheese and bakery vendors at the pleasant, open-air Market Hall; peruse the spectacular tile murals at the BART station, buy outdoor- and nature-oriented books and gifts at Sierra Club Books; discover the antiques shops and children's stores along College; grab a pizza at Zachary's, and a treat at Buttercup Bakery.

OAKLAND MUSEUM (all ages)

1000 Oak Street at Tenth Street, Oakland 94607; (510) 834–2412.

Not just another boring museum, this one is a playful construction of three tiers topped by a four-acre roof garden of outdoor sculpture and a koi pond. The open layout makes this a child-friendly, comfortable place to see contemporary and vintage California art. Stop at the video stations to watch Native American demos and interviews with artists. A cafe serves sandwiches, salads, and yummy desserts.

Where to Eat

Ratto's. *Corner of Ninth and Washington Streets, Oakland 94607; (510) 832–6503.* A fancy food shop, gourmet deli, and cafe, serving fantastic soups, pastas, salads, and sandwiches. $

Zachary's Chicago Pizza. *5801 College Avenue, Oakland 94607, (510) 655–6385; and 1853 Solano Avenue, Berkeley 94704; (510) 525–5950.* The best. $

Red Tractor Cafe. *5634 College Avenue across from Market Hall in the Rockridge district; (510) 595–3500.* Down-home comfort food, from macaroni and cheese to sumptuous meat loaf and gar-lic-mashed potatoes, barbecued chicken and chicken-fried steak and gravy. Kids meals are served on Big Bird plates. Lunch, dinner, weekend brunch. $

Vi's. *724 Webster Street, Oakland 94607; (510) 835– 8374.* A long-established, popular, fresh and clean, simple cafe serves dynamite Vietnamese noodle soup and stirfried dishes; the less adventurous will like the rice and veggies. $

Where to Stay

Executive Inn. *1755 Embarcadero, near Jack London Square, Oakland 94607; (800) 346–6331.* On the Oakland Estuary. Complimentary breakfast, airport shuttle, pool, guest laundry, refrigerators. $$

Best Western Inn at the Square. *233 Broadway at Jack London Square, Oakland 94607; (800) 633–5973.* Garden courtyard setting. Pool, coffee shop, refrigerators. $$

For More Information

Oakland Convention and Visitors Bureau. *1000 Broadway, Oakland 94607; (800) 262–5526.*

San Jose

Families visiting in the Bay Area may have heard of Paramount's Great America theme park, but many are unaware that several other fantastic family-oriented attractions are located in the South Bay. Your big and little cyber-nerds will spend their time in three dazzling technology museums: the Tech, the Intel, and the Children's Museum.

In San Jose's trendy arts and dining hub, SoFA (South First Street), it's fun to explore sidewalk cafes, galleries, and bookstores. At the Fairmont Hotel's Fountain Restaurant, monumental ice cream concoctions are served at tables under a grove of palm trees; on hot days in the public plaza across the street, kids splash and play in an assemblage of 4-foot-tall water spouts.

A newly refurbished "Old Town" district downtown, San Pedro Square is a dining mecca with delightful new shade trees, landscaping and sidewalk cafes.

"Tuckered out" tourists rest on the lawns and benches of Plaza de Cesar Chavez, and kids run up and down on 3 miles of landscaped paths and parks in Guadalupe River Park. Look for the new carousel and a visitor center in the south end of the park at Arena Green.

Adding to San Jose's value as a family destination are a water park, the urban oasis of Kelley Park, an eerie mystery mansion, and one of the premier Egyptian museums in the world. Sports fans line up for pro-hockey Sharks tickets, and for minor league Giants baseball and Earthquakes soccer games.

Annual events that families like best are the Japanese Obon Festival in July, the Cinco de Mayo parade and festival in May, and Hoi Tet—the Vietnamese New Year celebration in February. The wildly colorful International Folklórico Festival is held in May at the new Mexican Heritage Plaza, a lively headquarters for Hispanic music, art, and performing arts events all year (www.mhcviva.org).

With the fastest-growing economy in the country, Silicon Valley caters to businesspeople during the week, so accommodations can be hard to find; reserve well in advance, and ask about special weekend discounts.

KELLEY PARK

1300 Senter Road, San Jose 95110; (408) 277–3000.

Happy Hollow Zoo, a miniature train ride, the Historical Museum, an outdoor complex of Victorian buildings, a trolley barn, and a firehouse with old engines—tons of fun things to do are in this wonderful city park laid out on beautiful Coyote Creek.

CHILDREN'S DISCOVERY MUSEUM OF SAN JOSE (ages 3–12)

180 Woz Way, San Jose 95110; (408) 298–5437; www.cdm.org. Tickets are $6.00 for adults, $4.00 for kids ages 2 to 18.

In a bright purple building designed by a world-famous Mexican architect, the largest hands-on science facility in the West is loaded with educational and fun activities for children through grade school age: Drive a fire truck, make tortillas, climb on a movable jungle gym, invent thingamajigs, crawl through tunnels, play on computers, conduct an orchestra, walk through an ambulance, get your face painted.

Light spills in through two-story glass walls onto indoor city streetscapes complete with traffic lights. The museum shop sells great toys, games, and puzzles, and there is a cafe. Get here early (the facility opens at 10:00 A.M.) to avoid crowds and noise, pick up a map to the 150 exhibits, and let the kids go.

THE TECH MUSEUM OF INNOVATION (ages 5 and up)

201 South Market Street, San Jose 95113; (408) 294–TECH; www.thetech.org. Admission is $6.00 for adults and $4.00 for students/seniors; kids 5 and under are admitted Free.

Silicon Valley is the birthplace of the personal computer and world headquarters for technology-oriented businesses. It's no wonder that their dazzling $91 million mango-colored edifice of learning and tech fun for high schoolers is state-of-the art. One hundred exhibits are mostly interactive, including experimenting with the virtual bobsled simulator, piloting a real robot on the ocean floor, floating in a jet pack like the astronauts, designing a roller coaster, making your own movie, and much more— an IMAX theater, a Robot Zoo, computer games, demos of high-tech inventions, and a cafe. For the techie in your family, this could be an all-day affair.

Cool Things to Do in San Jose

- **Tech Museum of Innovation**: Shake hands with a robot.

- **San Jose Arena**: Watch a shark attack.

- **Winchester Mystery House**: Walk with ghosts and spirits in 160 crazy rooms.

- **Rosicrucian Egyptian Museum**: Discover marvelous mummies; explore creepy underground tombs.

- **Paramount's Great America**: Scream your brains out on the Demon; turn your world upside down in the Vortex.

- **Raging Waters**: Slip and slide.

- **San Jose Flea Market**: Spend your allowance on junk.

INTEL MUSEUM (ages 7 and up)

Take the Montague Expressway exit off Highway 101 to 2200 Mission College Boulevard, Santa Clara 95052; (408) 765–0503; www.intel.com/intel/intelis/museum. Admission is Free.

Learn about the life and times of the microprocessor chip through exhibits and demos that make tech science comprehensible to all of us. You can also find out about clean rooms, transistors, and memory technology, and try out the new hands-on computer-based learning lab. A new gift shop is great fun, with techie souvenirs, clothing, and semi-conductor jewelry.

WINCHESTER MYSTERY HOUSE (ages 6 and up)

525 South Winchester Boulevard, San Jose 95128; (408) 247–2000, www. winchestermysteryhouse.com. Admission for adults and ages 13 and up $15.00, ages 6 to 12 $9.00; under 6 are **Free**.

In a Victorian mansion with 160 rooms, doors open into blank walls, stairways lead nowhere, and ghosts and spirits are afoot in a strange and spooky atmosphere. Also here is a large collection of antique Tiffany glass windows. The house tour is guided, but you can wander the vast, glorious gardens on your own.

ROSICRUCIAN EGYPTIAN MUSEUM (all ages)

1342 Naglee Avenue, San Jose 95191; (408) 947–3636.

Do you love your mummy? Sphinxes, temples, chariots, statues from ancient Thebes, gods of the Nile, a pharaoh's tomb, and delightfully scary, shrouded mummies are a few of the artifacts and reproductions here. A large collection of fascinating stuff, the largest Egyptian museum in the West. Kids love it. Little ones can run around in the gardens.

RAGING WATERS (ages 5 and up)

233 South White Road, San Jose, 95148; (408) 654–5450; www.rwsplash.com.

A fourteen-acre water park with more than thirty exciting slides. The little ones have their own wading pools and minislides; big kids take off in the Barracuda Bluster! Adjacent to the water park, Lake Cunningham Regional Park offers picnic areas, windsurfing, bike paths, fishing, and a marina with pedal boat, canoe, and sailboat rentals.

PARAMOUNT'S GREAT AMERICA (all ages)

Great America Parkway, Santa Clara 95052; (408) 988–1776; www.pgathrills. com. Admission for adults and ages 7 and up $37; ages 3 to 6 $20, children under 3 or under 48 inches tall go **Free**.

Plan one long day here for fifty coasters and rides and spectacular, Broadway-style shows; movies and TV are on the menu. The big thrills are the world-famous roller coasters—the Top Gun suspended jet coaster; the Grizzly, a traditional Coney Island–style coaster; the Demon, the Tidal Wave, and the Edge; and a rare stand-up coaster, the Vortex. The world's first flying coaster, Stealth, twists and turns at an alarming 50 miles an hour while riders "fly" face down, zooming sometimes within 10 feet of the ground. One admission price gets you on all the rides and into live and filmed extravaganzas. At the Days of Thunder motion simulator, strap yourselves in and get ready to scream around a stock car racetrack. Take the littlest kids to the audience participation Flintstones show and to Rugrats. See IMAX movies, live ice shows, and rock bands. Fort Fun and the Smurf Woods are filled with rides and entertainment for toddlers.

LOS GATOS CREEK TRAIL (all ages)

Above Los Gatos, at Lexington Reservoir; (415) 691–1200.

For biking, walking, and skating, 9 miles of trail along a riparian corridor.

CASTLE ROCK STATE PARK (all ages)

15000 Skyline Boulevard, Los Gatos; (408) 867–2952.

Some 3,600 acres of semiwilderness, with big views, waterfalls, forests, meadows, hiking and horse trails, and picnic areas.

STANFORD LINEAR ACCELERATOR CENTER (ages 11 and up)

2575 Sand Hill Road, Menlo Park 94025; (650) 926–2204; www.slac.stanford. edu. Call ahead to book the Free, two-hour tour of the accelerator, the Gallery (offering an incredible photo-op of the 2-mile tunnel), the Collider, and more.

On the Stanford University campus, the Klystron Gallery is the longest building in the world, housing 2 miles of cutting-edge scientific machines and devices. If you have children who are mad scientists and interested in subatomic collisions, synchroton radiation, antimatter, quarks, and leptons, they will love this place (you may not know what these words mean, but your children probably do).

BARBIE DOLL HALL OF FAME (ages 3–12)

433 Waverly Street, north of University Avenue, Palo Alto 94306; (408) 326–5841.

The world's largest collection—14,000!—of Barbies, from hippie Barbie to astronaut Barbie: a fascinating display of fashion trends of the last several decades.

Where to Eat

Sam's Bar-B-Que. *1110 South Bascom Avenue, San Jose 95110; (408) 297–9151.* Beloved by the locals and serving barbecued brisket, ribs, chicken, and burgers. A model train entertains the youngsters. $

Las Brasas. *763 East Julian Street, San Jose 95110; (408) 971–9639.* One of the best *taquerias* in a town that knows tacos. Go for outside service on balmy summer weekend nights, and don't miss the melt-in-your-mouth spicy beef, *suadero.* $

Old Spaghetti Factory House. *51 North San Pedro Avenue, San Jose 95110; (408) 288–7488.* Good, traditional Italian food, fun, casual surroundings. $

Chevy's. *5305 Alamaden Expressway, San Jose 95110; (408) 266–1815.* A chain restaurant with good, mainstream Mexican food and a fun children's menu. Kids get crayons and a coloring book, plus balloons, and they can watch tortillas being made in a glass-sided machine. $

Where to Stay

Hyatt San Jose. *1740 North First Street, San Jose 95110; (800) 233–1234.* A big hotel, with an airport shuttle, a pool and garden courtyard, a fitness center, a par course, an on-site jogging path, some refrigerators, and a coffee shop and pool cafe. Tennis nearby; hotel is near main San Jose attractions. $$

For More Information

San Jose Convention and Visitors Bureau. *333 West San Carlos Street, Suite 1000, San Jose 95110–2720; (408) 295–9600 or (888) SAN–JOSE (recorded events: 408–295–2265); www.sanjose.org.* Ask about travel packages that include lodgings and admission to local attractions and events, and about 50-percent-off weekend hotel discounts.

Valley Transportation Authority (VTA). *(408) 321–2300 or www.vta.org.* Light-rail service in San Jose, Santa Clara, and throughout Silicon Valley, and historic trolleys downtown.

Bay Area Rapid Transit (BART). *(510) 441–2278.* High-speed trains between major cities in the Bay Area, including Santa Clara.

San Francisco

It's a new era for children and families in one of America's favorite vacation cities. A major new complex in Yerba Buena Gardens, in the South of Market district, is one of the most impressive commitments to youngsters ever made by a city. The $56 million childrens' Rooftop includes the Zeum, a high-tech visual, performing, and media arts center for ages 8 to 18; an ice skating rink; a bowling center; an historic carousel in a glass house; and a space-age play and learning garden. Looming above all this, Sony's Metreon is a three-story, blockbuster family entertainment center.

The Embarcadero from Fisherman's Wharf to China Basin has been transformed into a dazzling waterfront esplanade, with a wide sidewalk for jogging, biking, walking, and baby "strollering." Tall palms, historical plaques, Victorian-style benches and lamp stands, cobblestones, antique trolley cars, restaurants, and a Major League baseball park are all part of the shiny and new bayside sweep.

Old favorite attractions are the cable cars, Alcatraz, Golden Gate Park, and Chinatown. More than 200 parks and playgrounds are places to let off steam and picnic. Kids love the outdoor recreation and amusements on Marina Green and Fisherman's Wharf, while parents like the romantic Victorian neighborhoods, the museums, and the choice of over 3,500 restaurants—more per capita than any other American city. A visit to San Francisco is not complete without a ferry ride around the bay and a walk across the Golden Gate Bridge!

Only locals know of the more than 300 hidden stairways that wind up and down the hills, through forest glades and lush gardens. With a little investigation your family will discover the stairways and other hidden treasures, such as mysterious Chinese temples smoky with incense, a museum of antique nickelodeon games, and a students' cafe with knockout views and yummy, inexpensive food.

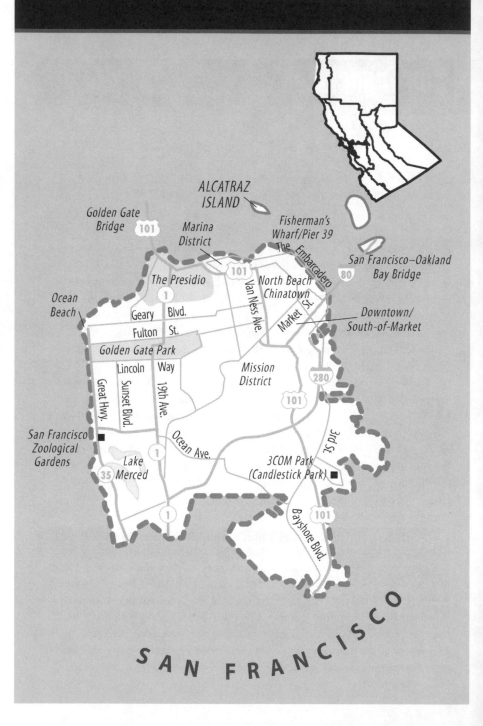

ALCATRAZ
ISLAND

Golden Gate
Bridge 101

Marina
District

Fisherman's
Wharf/Pier 39

The Embarcadero

San Francisco–Oakland
Bay Bridge 80

The Presidio 1

North Beach

Chinatown

Van Ness Ave.

Market St.

Downtown/
South-of-Market

Ocean
Beach

Geary Blvd.

Fulton St.

Golden Gate Park

Lincoln Way

Mission
District

280

Great Hwy.

Sunset Blvd.

19th Ave.

101

San Francisco
Zoological
Gardens

Ocean Ave.

Lake
Merced 35

3COM Park
(Candlestick Park)

3rd St.

1

Bayshore Blvd.

101

SAN FRANCISCO

This is a photogenic city, from the hairpin turns of the world's crookedest street to the pagodas of Chinatown. When I spend a day in the city with my granddaughters, I buy each of them one of those little disposable cameras so they can shoot their own record of Baghdad-by-the-Bay.

Walking is the best way to explore the ethnic districts of North Beach, the Hispanic Mission District, and Chinatown, as well as the neighborhoods inhabited by the "Painted Ladies," as the city's thousands of turn-of-the-century mansions are called.

Running, walking, and in-line skating; sailing on the bay; and indoor sports are some of the most popular activities for San Franciscans, when they aren't watching the Forty-niners or the Giants on TV. Local mariners share the bay with visitors on sightseeing sails, whale-watching cruises, and deep-sea fishing expeditions. Whale-boaters row, kayakers paddle, and flotillas of windsurfers flit like butterflies.

Parking is scarce and expensive, and streets are congested throughout the city, so preplanning and lots of walking is advised, with the occasional use of a taxi to get from one district to another. Bay Area Rapid Transit (BART), the clean, safe and on-time subway and commuter rail system, connects the city with the East and South Bays and the San Francisco International Airport, commonly referred to as SFO. "Muni", the streetcar and bus system, is neither clean, safe, nor on time; the newly refurbished vintage streetcars running along the Embarcadero and Market Street are the exceptions. Bicycles are more popular than ever, with all garages and ferries required to have bike parking.

Bring light jackets for the city's mild but changeable marine climate. Summer mornings and evenings can be chilly, due to foggy fingers blowing in through the Golden Gate, the city's natural air-conditioner. Fall and spring are the best seasons to visit, when days are sparkling-clear and warm and the summer crowds are gone. Year-round temperatures seldom drop below forty-five degrees or rise above seventy-five.

Marina District

  ### MARINA GREEN (all ages)
Along Marina Boulevard between Scott and Webster.

A vast greensward on the edge of the bay and a yacht harbor, the most popular place in town for jogging, walking, and kite flying. You can get picnic goodies at the Safeway across the street.

THE EXPLORATORIUM (ages 3–16)

3601 Lyon Street in the Palace of Fine Arts, San Francisco 94123; (415) 561–0360; www.exploratorium.edu/. Admission is $2.50 to $9.00 (kids under 3 admitted Free) and all are Free the first Wednesday of some months.

Called the best science museum in the world, the Exploratorium is housed in the Palace of Fine Arts, a fanciful Greco-Romanesque remnant from the Panama-Pacific Exposition of 1915. Here kids and adults are encouraged to play with and explore more than 600 exhibits. It's fun to bend lights, step into a giant kaleidoscope, fly without leaving the ground, watch a tornado, make bubbles 3 feet across, and create on computers. The Playsquare has climbing structures and role-playing venues for toddlers, as well as a place for infants to play with mirrors and experimental toys. Reservations are necessary for the Tactile Dome, a labyrinthine, pitch-black, crawl-through experience of a lifetime! (Call 415-561-0362). Special exhibitions have featured animation, digital technology, TV editing; the biology and stimuli of memory with live nerve cells; and body imaging and the physics of sight.

When you're all reeling from cerebral stimulation, grab a snack in the indoor cafe or a hot dog at the outside food cart, take a walk around the lake, and relax on the lawns. On weekends you'll see wedding parties in full regalia, having their photos taken in the elegant pink rotunda of the Palace of Fine Arts.

 FORT MASON (all ages)

On the east end of the Marina yacht harbor at Bay and Franklin Streets; (415) 556–0560.

A sea-breezy complex of former military buildings on the waterfront, where cultural events are held on weekends. There are small museums and frequent weekend festivals; parking is Free for up to four to twelve hours, depending on the parking spot location. **The Children's Art Center** in Building C offers drop-in and extended art workshops such as clay, printing, and painting for children 27 months to 10 years (415-771-0292, www.childrensartscenter.org).

Every year the **San Francisco Blues Festival** (415-826-6837) is held on the lawns above Fort Mason. There are easy-to-find public restrooms in each of the Fort Mason buildings.

GULF OF THE FARALLONES MARINE SANCTUARY (all ages)

The Presidio, Fort Mason Building 201 at Crissy Field, San Francisco 94129; (415) 561–6622; www.nos.noaa.gov/nmsp/gfnms. Admission and parking are **Free**.

Near a small beach and walking paths, with views of the Golden Gate Bridge and the bay, this is a small visitor's center for a vast, federally protected area of the ocean than runs from Bodega Bay south almost to the Golden Gate, and twenty-seven miles out to sea. Photos and exhibits show an extraordinary variety of sea creatures, including the greatly feared white sharks that breed around the Farallone Islands. Kids can touch sea animals in a living tidepool, look through a telescope, and find out about educational trips, such as guided kayaking and tidepooling. On a computer, you can browse information on beaches, trails, fishing, and outdoor recreation throughout the Bay Area.

It's a nice, short walk from here to the marina along the recently restored wetlands of Crissy Field. About sixty species of birds now inhabit the lagoon (www.crissyfield.org).

COOKS AND COMPANY (all ages)

Building B at Fort Mason; (415) 673–4137.

A terrific take-out sandwich, soup, and scrumptious dessert counter. Picnic tables are just outside, or you can take a five-minute walk to the lawns on the marina. $

GOLDEN GATE PROMENADE/EMBARCADERO (all ages)

Along the North and East Waterfronts, from Fort Point under the Golden Gate Bridge to Pac Bell Park at China Basin, about 5 miles.

A wide sidewalk perfect for in-line skates, baby strollers, and your feet. Cruise along through Crissy Field, past the small craft harbor and the Marina to Aquatic Park, Ghiraradelli Square and the Cannery, past Fisherman's Wharf to Pier 39. Continue along the commercial piers to the Ferry Building and Justin Herman Plaza, beyond the Oakland Bay Bridge and the outdoor cafes of South Beach, to Pac Bell Park, enjoying the fishing piers, benches, historic markers, restaurants, and rest stops along the way. Take the F Line trolley back from Market Street to Fisherman's Wharf.

Where to Go in San Francisco The most popular family attractions are located in these districts of the city.

MARINA DISTRICT *In the shadow of the Golden Gate Bridge, bordered by San Francisco Bay, Van Ness Avenue, Pacific Avenue, and the Presidio.*

- Marina Green
- The Exploratorium
- Fort Mason
- The Presidio
- Fort Point
- Golden Gate Promenade

NORTH WATERFRONT *From the Marina east to the Embarcadero.*

- Hyde Street Pier and Maritime National Historical Park
- Fisherman's Wharf
- Maritime Museum
- The Cannery
- Pier 39
- Alcatraz
- Blue and Gold Fleet Ferries

NORTH BEACH *The old Italian district, bordered roughly by Broadway, Mason, Kearny, Lombard, and Telegraph Hill.*

- Washington Square
- Coit Tower
- Italian restaurants
- North Beach Museum

GOLD GATE PARK/OCEAN BEACH

- Japanese Tea Garden
- Steinhart Aquarium
- California Academy of Sciences
- Natural History Museum
- Outdoor Recreation
- Beach Chalet
- San Francisco Zoo

DOWNTOWN/SOUTH-OF-MARKET

- Yerba Buena Gardens
- MOMA, the San Francisco Museum of Modern Art
- Zeum/Rooftop
- Cable cars
- Sony's Metreon

CHINATOWN

- Chinese Historical Society Museum
- Chinese restaurants and shops

MORE SAN FRANCISCO *Other attractions well worth a stop if time permits.*

- Mission Dolores
- 49-Mile Scenic Drive
- SkyDeck
- China Beach
- Mission Cliffs

THE PRESIDIO OF SAN FRANCISCO (all ages)

Near the Golden Gate, bordered by Baker Beach, the bay, Lyon Street, and West Pacific Avenue; (415) 561–4115. Maps and information at the Presidio Museum, corner of Lincoln Boulevard and Funstan Avenue; (415) 561–4331.

These 1,480 acres of wooded highlands, beaches, and vintage buildings that were used by the military for more than 200 years, from the Spanish and Mexican Armies to the U.S. Army, from Civil War times to the 1990s. Now part of the National Park System, this magnificent park is threaded by quiet roads and paths for walking and bike riding. You can easily spend a day here, starting with a ranger-led tour or a self-guided expedition of the museums and architectural relics, from seventeenth-century bronze Spanish cannons to Civil War barracks, pre-earthquake Victorians, adobe walls built by the Spanish conquistadors, and picturesque rows of Queen Anne–style officers' homes. Call for tour reservations: (415) 556–0865. Easy two-hour walks focus on history, architecture, nature, or historical personalities.

Secluded trails wind through cypress, pine, and eucalyptus forests. Picnic tables are found in sunny meadows, hidden in lush rhododendron groves, or perched on breezy headlands with sea views. A meandering creek and a spring-fed pond are habitats for hundreds of birds.

On the west side of the Presidio, Baker Beach is unsafe for swimming but great for sunning and shore fishing, and there are World War II bunkers to explore. Smaller, more sheltered beaches and a waterfront promenade are found at Crissy Field beside the bay—also part of the Presidio.

Off-limits to the public since 1895, the 18-hole **Presidio Golf Course** is now open to golfers who reserve tee times in advance (415-751-4063). It's a beautiful, challenging course with an upscale restaurant and clubhouse.

FORT POINT NATIONAL HISTORIC SITE (all ages)

Under the Golden Gate Bridge adjacent to the Presidio, take Long Avenue to Marine Drive; (415) 556–1693. **Free** *admission.*

A Civil War–era fort where costumed docents show you around a gunpowder storehouse, barracks, jail cells, and a museum of military artifacts. Little boys really go for the swords, guns, and cannons.

Take photos here of the bridge with waves crashing and sailboarders in the bay. You can fish along the seawall. A beach at the foot of the cliffs on the west side of Fort Point is sometimes enjoyed by nude sun worshippers.

BEPPLE'S PIES (all ages)

2142 Chestnut Street, San Francisco 94123 ; (415) 391–6226.

Just like at Grandma's house, luscious pies sit in the open window, driving you crazy with their savory aromas. You can watch the pastry chefs put together deep-dish fresh fruit pies, old fashioned cream pies, and chicken and veggie pot pies, chock-full and covered in flaky, home-made pastry. Take pies away to reheat, or sit at a little table and have soup, salad, and pie right here. The 1934 Union Street branch is take-away only. $

WAX MUSEUM (all ages)

145 Jefferson Street, San Francisco 94133; (800) 439–4305 or (415) 202–0400; www.waxmuseum.com. Admission for adults and children ages 12 and up $12.95, ages 4 to 11 $6.95, children under 4 Free.

It's downright spooky to see Princess Diana, George Burns, and King Tut in the (waxed) flesh. From their posts in 100,000 square feet of elaborate, movielike settings, more than 300 celebrities and historical figures look you right in the eye: Caruso, Castro, Chaplin, Cinderella, even Bruce Willis. This is a fun but pricey experience, a genuine Fisher-man's Wharf tourist trap. The Rainforest Cafe has a beautiful, huge aquarium, live birds and a three-story indoor waterfall. If you decide to go for it, come at opening time, 9:00 A.M., to avoid the crowds.

North Waterfront

HYDE STREET PIER AND MARITIME NATIONAL HISTORICAL PARK (all ages)

Hyde and Jefferson Streets at Fisherman's Wharf; (415) 556–3002. Admission is adults $4.00, kids ages 12 to 17 $2.00, kids under 12 Free. *A family ticket costs $10.00 up to six people.*

The only floating national park, anchorage for the world's largest collection of historic ships. Dozens of antique vessels are open to explore and clamber on, from tiny fishing boats to steam tugs, a house-boat, an 1895 lumber schooner—with 100-foot beams in its hold—and an ornate 1886 square-rigger. Vintage autos line the decks of the *Eureka,* a circa 1890 ferry. Knot tying, sail raising, and sea-chantey singing take place on weekends. Annual events include the Haunted Halloween Ship, storytelling, engine room tours, birding tours on the pier, navigation, and more. Every Saturday from 2:00 to 2:45 P.M. rangers give Free presentations, especially for kids: scrimshaw, signal flags, stories, ship models, and knot tying.

FISHERMAN'S WHARF

On the waterfront, from Aquatic Park to about Powell Street, www.
fishermanswharf.org.

The bawdy, brawny Barbary Coast of a century ago is a warren of seafood restaurants, shopping complexes, commercial fishing wharves, museums, tourist traps, and one of the great waterfront promenades in the world.

NATIONAL MARITIME MUSEUM (all ages)

Foot of Polk Street, Fisherman's Wharf; (415) 556–3002. **Free**.

A glorious and historic Art Deco building resembling a cruise ship, awash with ship models, figureheads, maritime paintings, photos, and artifacts. Watch ships in the bay through the telescope on the "bridge," and translate Morse code in the WWII-era radio room.

THE CANNERY

2801 Leavenworth, at the foot of Columbus overlooking the bay; (415)
771–3112; www.thecannery.com.

The largest peach cannery in the world at the turn of the century, this three-story brick complex now holds dozens of smart shops and restaurants, with an olive-tree-shaded patio for **Free** entertainment and dining. The cable car turnaround is ½ block away.

BAY BICYCLE TOURS (ages 3 and up)

In the Cannery; (415) 436–0633.

Take an independent or guided bike tour of the city, or go on the 9-mile, easy guided ride across the Golden Gate Bridge to Sausalito, with a ferry ride back, including helmet, sightseeing stops, ferry ticket and snacks, for about $35.

PIER 39 (all ages)

The Embarcadero at Jefferson Street; (415) 981–7437.

One of the most popular tourist attractions in the country, Pier 39 is a carnival of entertainment, shopping, restaurants, and places to enjoy the outdoors. The long pier juts out into the bay on the northernmost point of the city, making for glorious sea views from many of the more

Top Shops for Kids

- **F.A.O. Schwarz.** *48 Stockton Street, San Francisco 94102; (415) 394–8700.* Guarded by a soldier in a red coat at the front door, three stories of the newest and classic toys and games, dolls, vehicles, and books—a child's dream.

- **Esprit Outlet.** *499 Illinois Street, San Francisco 94102; (415) 957–2500.* Huge, trendy clothing outlet beloved by young teens.

- **NIKEtown.** *Corner of Stockton and Post Streets, San Francisco 94102; (415) 392–6453.* Go into the lobby to see the athletic shoes atop tall platinum tubes, and the neato sports star videos. Conveniently nearby is a Disney Store.

- **Sanrio's Hello Kitty.** *39 Stockton, in Union Square 94102; (415) 981–5568.* Little girls know and love Sanrio's Japanese-designed accessories and toys.

- **Quantity Postcards.** *1441 Grant Avenue, in North Beach 94133; (415) 986– 8866.* Some 10,000 new and vintage postcards. Honestly, you'll have a hard time getting your kids out of here.

- **Basic Brown Bear Factory.** *444 DeHaro Street, South-of-Market; (800) 554–1910.* Take a teddy tour from 1:00 P.M. daily and from 11:00 A.M. on Saturdays. Stuff your own bear: Staff helps kids stuff their bear on a machine, then sew it up, give it a bath, and choose clothing and accessories! How about a Beary Godmother?

- **Virgin Megastore.** *2 Stockton Street, San Francisco 94105; (415) 397–4525.* A tower of musical power, the largest music store in the western states is overwhelming. Three glitzy floors are packed with over 150,000 CDs and cassettes. Dozens of teens and their parents stand silently with headphones on, listening before they buy. The latest of videos and best-selling books are all here, too, and the cafe serves pretty good, basic sandwiches and salads. Open until 10:00 P.M. on weekdays and midnight on weekends.

- **Lark in the Morning.** *2801 Leavenworth Street, the Cannery, 94133; (415) 922–4277. www.larkinam.com.* Kids can try playing fruit and veggie "shakers" and frog rasps, steel drums, panpipes, zithers, drums and flutes, accordions, xylophones, and strange instruments they never imagined existed. This fabulous world music and instrument store has a traditional music and dance festival in May and other events during the year, such as free children's drum workshops.

■ **Nature Company.** *900 Northpoint, San Francisco 94133; (415) 776–0724.* Surrounded by a musical background of nature sounds or a world beat, displays are pleasantly earth-friendly, with rainforest palms and tiger T-shirts, world globes, weather monitors, and posters, plus wildlife, science, and travel books. You can choose from a nice variety of telescopes and binoculars, and kids really like the squeeze-and-squirt frogs, glow-in-the-dark stars, plastic dinosaurs, puzzles, sea shells, and animal- and nature-oriented games and books.

■ **Wound About. Pier 39,** *San Francisco 94111; (415) 986–8697.* Thousands of wind-up toys that rock and roll, gallop, crawl, waltz, and waddle—a noisy place guaranteed to make you laugh.

than 100 shops. Prices are high, but there are plenty of gadgets and souvenirs in the $5.00-and-under range. Each shop focuses narrowly on some catchy type of merchandise, such as gifts for your feline at Kitty City, zillions of magnets at Magnetron, the Marine Mammal Store, Russka Babushka Dolls, and Santa's Workshop. The atmosphere is clean and commercial in a Disneyesque way. It is the best shopping center in town for kids because there is plenty of **Free** entertainment—musicians and performers outdoors, sea lions, a carousel, plus a big games arcade. Seaview cafes and snack carts serve fresh seafood and ethnic specialties, and they are expensive. Every twenty minutes, a motorized cable car departs from here for a $3.00, twenty-minute trip downtown.

 ### UNDERWATER WORLD (all ages)
At Pier 39; (415) 623–5300.

    A diver's-eye-view aquarium, where you walk beneath the waves via a 300-foot clear tunnel. The fish are looking in at you! Hundreds of schooling fish and deep-sea predators, including bat rays and sharks.

 ### K-DOCK (all ages)
At Pier 39.

    Herds of sea lions put on a daily show, barking, cavorting, and showing off on the docks at the end of the pier. The males can be 7 feet long and weigh 1,000 pounds.

NAMCO CYBER STATION and NAMCOLAND (ages 3 and up)

Pier 39, San Francisco, 94133; (415) 399–1909.

Bring money for this high-tech amusement arcade, one of the largest on the West Coast. Namcoland is for ages 3 to 12, while Cyber Station is geared to ages 12 and up, with action games, some of them with rather violent images. While older kids enjoy the arcade, little ones might be better off riding the nearby Venetian-style carousel, a stunning work of art made in Italy.

TURBO-RIDE (ages 6 and up)

At Pier 39.

A wild big-screen trip in hydraulic seats to see the *San Francisco Experience,* a half-hour, multimedia extravaganza depicting the history and sights of the city, including a jolting reenactment of the 1906 earthquake. The Turbo-Ride gives new meaning to the term *moving pictures.*

ALCATRAZ (all ages)

Pier 41; (415) 546–2896. Fee for self-guided or guided tours adults $9.00– $11.00, ages 12 to 18 $7.75–$11.00, ages 5 to 11 $4.50–$5.75, ages 4 and under Free.

Site of the notorious federal penitentiary that once housed Al Capone and Machine Gun Kelly, the island in the middle of the bay is a top tourist attraction. The Alcatraz experience takes about three hours and includes a ferry ride, a walk in the sea breezy outdoors, narrated or self-guided tours of the echoing, empty cell blocks and other historic buildings, and stunning views of the Bay Area. A new electric tram trundles people and wheelchairs up the steep hill. An abbreviated version of the daytime trip, an "Alcatraz After Hours" tour, offers dazzling sunset and night skyline views, fog permitting.

ISLAND HOP (all ages)

Pier 41 at Fisherman's Wharf, San Francisco 94133; (415) 705–5555. Tickets for adults $31, students $30, ages 5 to 11, $18.25, ages 4 and under Free.

A popular new five-hour tour combines visits to Alcatraz and Angel Island State Park, both islands in the bay. Included are ferries, admission fees, an audio tour of Alcatraz, and a motorized, narrated, open-air tram tour of Angel Island—great fun for all ages. Sandwich lunches are available for purchase on Angel Island, or you can bring a picnic. On clear days—almost every day in the spring and fall—the islands and the ferries offer unequaled views of the city skyline and much of the Bay Area, and five of the region's eight bay bridges.

RED AND WHITE FLEET GOLDEN GATE BAY CRUISE (all ages)

Pier 43½, Fisherman's Wharf; (415) 447–0597. Tickets are adults $15.00, kids ages 12 to 18 $12.00, and kids ages 5 to 11 $8.00.

If you have time for just one quick boat trip, this is the one: a one-hour sail under the bridge and around the bay past Angel Island and Alcatraz, including personal audiotape with historical overview, in your choice of six languages. From Pier 43½ or from the ferry building, Red and White also offers ferry tours to the aircraft carrier, *USS Hornet*, in Alameda.

North Beach

Adjoining the North Waterfront, sunny, sheltered North Beach is a microcosm of Italy in a square mile of peaks and valleys between Telegraph Hill and Russian Hill. Beneath the towers of the Romanesque masterpiece Church of Saints Peter and Paul, Washington Square is the residents' outdoor meeting hall and social center, where Chinese practice tai chi, Italian grandpas sit on park benches, and artists set up their easels. Surrounding streets are crowded with family-style Italian restaurants, pizza joints, bakeries, and more than a dozen espresso cafes. Picturesque against the frescoes and murals of Cafe Roma and Cafe Viva, people from all over the world sip cappuccinos. At Caffé Verdi and Cafe Puccini, you'll hear opera; at Cafe Italia, the click of pinball and pool.

COIT TOWER (all ages)

On top of Telegraph Hill; from Washington Square take Muni bus #39 up the steep hill; parking is limited; (415) 362–0808.

Overlooking the entire north Bay Area, this 210-foot-tall Art Deco tower is decorated with 1930s murals of early California. Return to North Beach by way of the woody Filbert Street steps past mansions, pre-earthquake cottages, and gardens. Sit quietly on a bench and you may see raccoons or a small red fox.

MARIO'S BOHEMIAN CIGAR STORE CAFE

566 Columbus Avenue, San Francisco 94133; (415) 362–0536.

A tiny corner cafe with windows looking onto Washington Square, Mario's is famous for focaccia sandwiches and rich ricotta cheesecake. Meatball sandwiches are the traditional choice. This is an authentic, century-old North Beach hole-in-the-wall, where Italian grandpas, tourists, and businesspeople crowd in together for cappuccinos, Italian biscotti, pastries, and snacks. You can also take out food for a picnic in the square. Breakfast, lunch, and supper; open late. $

 ### MOLINARI'S DELICATESSEN

373 Columbus, San Francisco 94133; (415) 421–2337.

The smell of dozens of kinds of Italian cheeses and salamis is as intoxicating as a glass of Chianti.

 ### NEW WORLD SPORTS (ages 6 and up)

1365 Columbus Avenue, San Francisco 94133; (415) 776–7801; www. newworldsports.com.

Awesome is the word for the Friday Night Skate, when several hundred in-line skaters head out together from here for a fun glide through the city. Everyone is welcome, from beginners to pros. Get free lessons and rent the newest blades, safety gear, helmets, and accessories. The owners have been blading since the sport was invented, not so many years ago, and their enthusiasm is catching. They also sell snowboards, tennis rackets, and sports clothing.

 ### NORTH BEACH MUSEUM (all ages)

1435 Stockton Street, San Francisco 94133; (415) 989–2220. Free *admission.*

Tucked away on the mezzanine of a bank, a cache of fascinating old photos and a few artifacts make old Italian North Beach, Chinatown, and Fisherman's Wharf come alive. Black and white images appear dreamlike, with Chinese women in silk robes and tiny bound feet, men in long pigtails carrying live chickens and ducks tied by the neck, masted sailing vessels in the bay, and Victorian ladies in long, cinch-waist dresses and feathered hats.

Golden Gate Park/Ocean Beach

In the 1,017-acre garden that is one of the world's greatest metropolitan parks, you can row on a lake, ride a horse, play tennis, take long walks, browse in museums, or just laze on the lawns. A Golden Gate Park Explorer's Pass saves 30 percent on admission to six cultural attractions: the **Japanese Tea Garden,** the **Steinhart Aquarium,** the **California Academy of Sciences,** the **Natural History Museum,** the **deYoung Fine Arts Museum** and the **Asian Art Museum.** Admission is 𝐅𝐫𝐞𝐞 on the first Wednesday of every month.

My kids, grown-up now, still love having tea and cookies in the Japanese teahouse when the cherry trees bloom in early spring. The Japanese Tea Garden is a fairy tale of a place, with a moon bridge, a brightly painted pagoda, a brooding bronze statue of Buddha, and lily ponds swimming with koi fish. Glorious maples blaze in autumn, and clouds of rhododendrons and azaleas burst into flower in spring. Flower and plant lovers, my girls and I always make a stop at the **Conservatory of Flowers,** a monumental glass greenhouse shipped around Cape Horn from England in the 1870s. Inside is a steamy, dreamy, five-story jungle of trees, exotic plants, and flowers, a sort of Victorian biosphere. On a huge network of walking and biking trails, you will pass people playing bocci and tennis, tossing horseshoes, fly casting, and even playing checkers and chess in the checkers pavilion.

 ## *B*est Playgrounds

- **Golden Gate Park Children's Playground.** *Bowling Green Drive between John F. Kennedy and Martin Luther King Drives, Golden Gate Park;* *(415) 753–5210.* Climbing equipment, slide, swings, sandboxes, circa 1912 carousel with sixty-two vintage animals. Restrooms.

- **Chinese Recreation Center.** *Washington and Mason Streets, Chinatown;* *(415) 292–2017.* The usual playground equipment, an ethnic mix of kids. Restrooms.

- **North Beach Playground.** *Lombard and Mason Streets; (415) 274–0201.* Olympic-size pool with special hours for kids, a big playground, and an excellent children's library. Restrooms.

- **Huntington Park Playground.** *At California and Taylor Streets on Nob Hill.* A grassy spot with play equipment and a fountain that is a replica of a famous fountain in Italy.

Golden Gate Park Stables offers pony rides for children ages 1 and up for $4.00; turn the pony ride into a riding lesson for $12.00. For a relaxing tour of the park on horseback, take a one-hour park trail ride for $25.00 (415–668–7360).

Snacks and light meals are available in the museum cafes, but for pot stickers to pizza, make a quick side trip to a clutch of restaurants at Ninth Avenue and Irving Street.

On Sunday afternoons the main park road is closed to vehicles, and impromptu Rollerblading and skateboarding happen; I mean, they really *happen*—fantastic **Free** entertainment. As in any large urban park, it's advisable to stay together, leave before dark, and avoid isolated areas. Guided walking tours are offered **Free** on weekends; call ahead for times and location (415–263–0991). Maps of the park are available at McLaren Lodge, at Stanyan and Fell, weekdays.

SKATES ON/OFF HAIGHT (ages 6 and up)

1818 Haight Street, near Golden Gate Park; (415) 752–8375; www.skates.com.

Within a short distance of the eastern entrance of Golden Gate Park, a popular and friendly shop for skateboard, Rollerblade and pad rentals, groovy skater duds, and **Free** lessons. A second store is at 1219 Polk Street.

CLIFF HOUSE (all ages)

1090 Point Lobos, on the west end of Golden Gate Park at Ocean Beach, San Francisco 94121; (415) 386–3330; www.cliffhouse.com.

Built in 1863 as a resort, then rebuilt in 1895 after it burned to the ground, the Cliff House reigns loftily over the beach and Seal Rocks, where hundreds of sea lions and swirling seabirds perform daily. Sea views and seafood are the specialties; the food is okay, the prices are high, and the place is often filled with tour bus passengers. On the terrace is an odd replica of Leonardo da Vinci's invention, the camera obscura, a sort of giant magnifier through which you can watch the wildlife. Breakfast, lunch, dinner, Sunday brunch. $$

BEACH CHALET

1000 Great Highway, San Francisco 94122; (415) 386–8439;
 www.beachchalet.com.

A terra-cotta-tiled 1925 masterpiece of Willis Polk architecture overlooking Ocean Beach, this a museum and park visitor center on the ground floor, with Depression-era murals, mosaics and wood carvings, a model of Golden Gate Park, and historic exhibits. There is also a shop selling San Francisco logo souvenirs, guidebooks and old street signs, and city memorabilia. Upstairs is a great place for a sunny Sunday brunch or lunch; it's rather noisy, so squirmy kids attract little notice. The bistro and brewery menu is robust, featuring sausage sandwiches, beer-battered prawns, macho onion rings, grilled fish, and Cajun/Creole specialties, with some plain choices that kids like. Try the "sand castle" chocolate truffle cake. The museum is **Free**, and makes a convenient restroom stop at the beach. Daily lunch and dinner. $$

MUSÉE MECHANIQUE (ages 4 and up)

At the Cliff House Restaurant; (415) 386–1170.

Play with a large and fabulous collection of coin-operated antique arcade games. This is a good place to park older kids with a handful of change while you watch the sun set and the whales blow from the nearby terrace.

LAND'S END TRAIL (all ages)

Take Geary Boulevard west to the Cliff House Restaurant, where the trail begins; (415) 556–0560.

An easy, 2.5-mile walk, with views of the Golden Gate, the Marin Headlands, and the shore, plus seabirds and marine mammals for company. There are benches along the way.

SAN FRANCISCO ZOO (all ages)

Three miles south of the Cliff House Restaurant, Sloat Boulevard at Forty-fifth Avenue, San Francisco 94116; (415) 753–7083. Admission is $6.50 for adults, $3.00 for kids 12 to 15, $1.00 for kids 6 to 11, and **Free** *for kids 5 and under.*

The zoo shelters many rare and endangered animals, such as black rhinos, snow leopards, condors, elephants, and Prince Charles—a rare white Bengal tiger. In the world's largest naturalistic gorilla exhibit resides a family of lowland gorillas, including an adult male silverback and adorable youngsters. The feeding of the African lions and the highly endangered Sumatran and Siberian tigers takes place at 2:00 P.M., a big hit with all ages. A walk through the magical aviary of Rainbow Landing is an intimate encounter with some of the most colorful birds in the world—rainbow lorikeets. Kids can feed them nectar from their hands, then take home a photograph of themselves with these beautiful Australian birds. A sweet new home for the North American river otters has climbing logs, pools, and waterfalls. Little ones like the circa 1920 carousel and the Children's Zoo, where they can feed, pet, and play with barnyard animals. This is an old-style zoo with many animals in small concrete and iron cages; a gradual process of replacing these old venues is underway.

KATE'S KITCHEN (all ages)
471 Haight Street, San Francisco 94117; (415) 626–3984.

Locals know this is one of the best breakfast spots in town. Let out your belts, belly up to the blue-and-white-checked tablecloths, and tuck into big chunks of French toast, biscuits and sausage gravy, piles of bacon and cheddar cornmeal pancakes, and gigantic scrambled egg concoctions. Tops on the lunch menu are meat loaf sandwiches, homemade chicken soup, and incredible pie. Now, walk the 15 blocks to Golden Gate Park. Breakfast and lunch daily. $

Downtown/South-of-Market

YERBA BUENA GARDENS (all ages)
Bordered by Third, Folsom, Fourth, and Howard Streets, South-of-Market district.

A new art and culture ghetto and urban park South-of-Market, Yerba Buena Gardens was built atop the underground Moscone Convention Center. A greensward surrounded by astonishing contemporary architecture, museums, and theaters, Esplanade Park is a place to sit at an outdoor cafe, lounge on the lawns, and enjoy the larger-than-life sculpture flanked by a 60-foot-wide, torrential sheet of water that creates a misty grotto for trees and a butterfly garden.

MOMA, THE SAN FRANCISCO MUSEUM OF MODERN ART (ages 4 and up)
At Yerba Buena Gardens, 151 Third Street, San Francisco 94103; (415) 357–4000. Admission is $9.00 for adults, $5.00 for students with ID, and **Free** *for children 12 and under who are accompanied by an adult. Tickets are half price on Thursdays, 6:00 to 9:00 P.M.* **Free** *admission on the first Thursday of each month.*

Like a striped spacecraft about to lift off, a dazzling brick and glass temple to the arts designed by world-famous Swiss architect Mario Botta. Step inside to see the gigantic, upslanting skylight pouring light into the atrium. A whirl of gallery floors flow one into another, showing the works of Matisse, Kline, Warhol, and countless more contemporary masters. A glitzy cafe, an upscale shop, and a truly fabulous children's department with educational and artistic toys and games complete the MOMA experience. When popular exhibitions are in residence, avoid standing in line by coming a few minutes before the museum opens at 11:00 A.M. (10:00 A.M. during the summer).

Museum Activities

Golden Gate Park/Lincoln Park/Yerba Buena Gardens

Tops with younger kids are the Saturday drop-in art and activity workshops and gallery tours at the deYoung Museum in Golden Gate Park and the California Palace of the Legion of Honor in Lincoln Park (Free with museum admission; (415–790–3658). Meanwhile, parents take the opportunity to cruise the museums.

At the Asian Art Museum, myths and legends are told every Sunday at 1:00 P.M. (415–379–8801). At Family Sundays at the Museum of Modern Art, introduce your child to modern art at hands-on workshops in a light-filled workroom, with docent-led gallery activities, live music, and performers, often related to the current special exhibition (415–357–4000).

ZEUM (ages 8–18)

Corner Fourth and Howard Streets, San Francisco 94103; (415) 777–2800; www.zeum.org. Tickets are $7.00 for adults, $5.00 for kids 5 to 18, $4.00 for kids 5 to 12, Free for kids under 5.

Leonardo da Vinci meets R2-D2 at this 34,000-square-foot, pumpkin-and-mauve-colored visual, performing, and media arts center, where young people ages 8 to 18 get involved in multimedia production, and tech-based art and drama. Families can just enjoy the exhibitions and performances, or your kids can jump into interactive play and learning. Teenage "masters" lead youngsters through the process of using state-of-the-art equipment to mix sound, create special effects, and integrate live performance and an archive of clips to produce videos Changing exhibits may feature sound and light, fine art produced by computer, animation, sculpting, backstage theater production, or puppetry. In the spiraling Media Gallery, visitors stand in a round room or perch on balconies to see videos projected on two-story walls. An average visit is about three hours.

THE ROOFTOP (ages 2–8)

Fourth and Howard Streets, Yerba Buena Gardens, San Francisco 94103; (415) 522–9860.

Like a flying saucer floating among the skyscrapers, this is a children's play center for the new millennium. The Rooftop incorporates an outdoor amphitheater, where frequent performances are held for young audiences, a kid-sized hedge labyrinth, a lawn bowl, robot sculptures, and free-play areas with rubberized surfaces designed for safe tumbling.

YERBA BUENA BOWLING CENTER (ages 6 and up)

Third and Mission Streets; Yerba Buena Gardens, San Francisco 94103; (415) 777–3727.

Twelve lanes of high-tech bowling with new-fangled "bumpers" that pop up on either side of your lane, the better to corral the ball. For beginners and kids, this makes bowling a lot more fun. Upstairs, Mo's makes their famous smoky grilled burgers, thick shakes, sandwiches, and salads, to be consumed in front of incredible views of the Gardens and the surrounding cityscape.

YERBA BUENA ICE SKATING CENTER (ages 2 and up)

740 Folsom Street, Yerba Buena Gardens, San Francisco 94103; (415) 777–3727. Admission is $6.00 for adults, $4.50 for ages 12 and under; skate rental $2.50.

Brian Boitano is the resident "celeb" at this sparkling new indoor ice palace. Surrounded by windows with stunning views of the city, it is a photogenic place with plenty of action to watch, even if you don't skate. Synchronized ice dancers, hockey players, and Brian and his friends practice and perform frequently on the 100-foot-long, NHL-regulation-sized rink. The public is invited to skate and take lessons every day.

METREON (all ages)

101 Fourth Street at Yerba Buena Gardens, San Francisco 94103; (415) 369–6000; www.metreon.com.

A four-story silvery dazzler of a family entertainment complex, Metreon houses fifteen cinemas, several restaurants, shops, and a children's world of interactive play. The only IMAX theater in town features an 80 x 100-foot screen with 2- and 3-D. Stadium-style seats are high-backed, comfy rockers, the better to be blasted by the action and nature flicks. A destination in itself, the glass lobby offers a panoramic view of the high-rise skyline. Maurice Sendak–designed "Where the Wild Things Are" is larger than life, with a maze, a bubbling cauldron, and a 17-foot-high puppet. Teens like the futuristic video games in the "Airtight Garage." In the Sony store, play with the high-tech gadgets, and listen to the latest CDs, and explore computers at Microsoft SF. Lots of places to spend money, lots to see that is **Free**.

 ### CARTOON ART MUSEUM (all ages)

Near Yerba Buena Gardens, Third and Townsend Streets 94103; (415) 227–8666.

11,000 pieces of film and print cartoon art from the late 1700s to today, with a children's museum, an interactive CD room, and exhibits of Hanna-Barbera characters, Peanuts, Calvin and Hobbes, and more.

 ### CABLE CARS (all ages)

Call (415) 673–6864 for information. Tickets are $2.00.

National Historic Landmarks, the famous cable cars of San Francisco are fun, rain or shine. You get fresh air, great photo ops, and roller-coaster rides up and down the steep hills. To avoid standing in line, very early in the day during the week is the best time to hop on and off the Powell–Hyde, Powell–Mason, and California Street lines, each ending at a "turnaround." From the Powell–Hyde turnaround on Market Street, walk 2 blocks up to Union Square for an exciting ride on one of the St. Francis Hotel's thirty-two-story glass elevators, an eye- and ear-popping, 1,000-feet-per-minute flight with dizzying views at the top.

 ### JUNGLE FUN AND ADVENTURE (ages 1 to 12)

*555 Ninth Street between Bryant and Brannan, on the upper level of the Toys "R" Us center 94103; (415) 552–4386. Admission is **Free** for adults, $5.95 to $6.95 for children, with discounts some evenings.*

A special treat for very, very good children ages 1 to 12: a three-level, indoor play facility with cargo nets, slides, tubes, ball pools, track slides, and games, plus a special venue for toddlers. Crafts and videos teach about endangered species. As in all of these commercial play venues, the noise is deafening, and very young children may be overwhelmed and even frightened. Adults who can't stand the din are welcome to relax in "Quiet Rooms." The Gorilla Cafe serves pizza and healthy snacks.

SAN FRANCISCO PUBLIC LIBRARY (all ages)

100 Larkin Street, San Francisco 94102; (415) 557–4400; http://sfpl.lib.ca.us. Free *admission.*

When they can't keep it to a whisper, kids at the brand new, state-of-the-art main library take a break on the outdoor terrace of the Children's Center, or head to the cafe for a healthy snack or a drink. Students love the hundreds of new computers with free Web access. Here and at twenty-six branches throughout the city are preschool story times and crafts workshops, a chess and checkers club, book clubs, film screenings, seasonal music, history programs, and even homework help for grades K to eight.

Chinatown

Beginning at the ornate Chinese Gate at Bush and Grant, most of Grant Avenue and the streets and alleys off Grant, 24 square blocks.

Stand on Grant Avenue and look in both directions at the blizzard of neon signs, pagoda roofs, and dragon-bedecked lampposts, all in the colors of China—blood red, gold, and bright green. Flying from the rooftops of the more elaborate buildings are banners and flags heralding the family and benevolent associations that unite Chinese people with a common heritage. At one of these, the Chinese Six Companies building at 843 Stockton, the steps between the green dogs are a good place for a family photo.

The best time to explore Chinatown is in the early morning, when chattering housewives flock around produce stands and little kids walk to school with their grannies. As handcarts clatter along, heaped with winter melons and crates of live

Do You Know About the Golden Gate Bridge?

- Length: 1.7 miles
- Height of roadway above water: 220 feet
- Height of towers above water: 746 feet
- Color: International orange
- Toll in 1937: 50 cents
- Toll in 1998: $3.00 southbound
- Cables: The two great cables on which the bridge is suspended contain 80,000 miles of steel wire, enough to encircle the equator three times
- Best photo: North side of the bridge from the Marin Headlands (take the Alexander Street exit)

chickens, you'll hear nary a word of English. In Portsmouth Square rows of people move in silent unison, practicing their daily tai chi exercise.

The larger souvenir stores and Asian antiques emporiums are on Grant, while the small shops are found in the forty-one narrow alleys crisscrossing the main street. As you prowl the alleys, watch out for laundry dripping from balconies overhead.

On Washington Street look through the open doorways of the fragrant shops and watch herbalists concoct potions and medicines by scooping fungus, powdered horn, roots, spices, and herbs into paper packets.

A meal in a Chinatown restaurant is a must, from an elegant dining room to a hole-in-the-wall noodle shop or a dim sum emporium. Most of us are familiar with Cantonese-style food—chow mein, sweet-and-sour dishes, fried rice—and you can get that all over Chinatown, but it's fun to try "hot pots" and noodle dishes from northern China or hot-and-spicy Szechwan-style cuisine. In dim sum teahouses, steamed dumplings and stuffed buns and turnovers are rolled by on carts. You choose by pointing to what looks good. It may be delicate shrimp in a translucent pastry cover, spiced rice wrapped in fragrant leaves, or sweet, spicy pork in a puffy white dumpling coat. Take your chances and pay by the plate.

ROYAL JADE SEAFOOD RESTAURANT

675 Jackson Street, Chinatown 94108; (415) 392–2929.

Dim sum in a three-level teahouse, noisy and bustling, with a multicultural clientele. $$

R AND G LOUNGE

631 Kearny Street, San Francisco 94108; (415) 982–7877.

Don't bother to open the huge menu, just ask what fresh seafood specialties are being prepared today. From the province of Canton, the dishes are primarily seafood—wonderful whole steamed fish, crispy fried catfish, salt-and-pepper-roasted Dungeness crab, and savory clay pot casseroles that may be anise-scented oxtails or spicy chicken. As in most Chinese restaurants, the dining room is plain and brightly lit; group tables are upstairs, which is nicer. Lunch and dinner. $–$$

CHINATOWN KITE SHOP (all ages)

717 Grant Street, San Francisco 94108; (415) 391–8217.

At one of the world's great kite shops, there are Asian fighting kites; multilevel, dual-control stunt kites; dragon kites; windsocks; and even plain diamond-shaped paper kites you put together yourself. The nicest ones are made of fabric, and they make dramatic decorative pieces for the home, especially in a child's room. The best place in town to fly kites is on the Marina Green, where you have plenty of room to roam and the chance to see some fabulous, big kites in the air on weekends.

GREAT WALL GINSENG AND HERBS
821 Pacific Avenue, San Francisco 94108; (415) 397–2040.

This is the archetype of the colorful, fragrant, crowded Chinatown shops where herbalists concoct potions and medicines by scooping fungus, powdered horn, roots, spices, and herbs into paper packets—quite an exotic environment. They don't mind if you watch and ask questions.

GOLDEN GATE FORTUNE COOKIES COMPANY
56 Ross Alley, Chinatown 94108; (415) 781–3956.

Workers sit at machines from the 1920s, twisting fortunes into hot cookies as they come off the press. You are welcome to step in and sample the goodies.

TEN REN TEA COMPANY
949 Grant Avenue, Chinatown 94108; (415) 362–0656.

Wide open to the street, welcoming you for **Free** samples of steaming green, jasmine, or black teas. More than fifty varieties of special teas, priced up to $60 a pound, are scooped from big canisters. When tea samples are poured for you, tap your fingers or knuckles on the table to show thanks.

CHINESE CULTURE CENTER (all ages)
Holiday Inn, 750 Kearny Street, San Francisco 94108; (415) 986–1822; www.c-c-c.org. Admission is **Free**.

In the lobby of the hotel is a small, impressive museum of antique Chinese pottery and musical instruments, beautiful ancient statuary, and the gold-adorned costume of an empress. An annual holiday bazaar is held in December, when reasonably priced Chinese ceramics, toys, gifts, and home accessories are on sale.

CHINESE HISTORICAL SOCIETY OF AMERICA (all ages)

644 Broadway, Fourth Floor, San Francisco 94123; (415) 391–1188. Admission is Free.

Displays of clothing and slippers of nineteenth-century Chinese pioneers, a colorful 1888 Buddhist altar, antique swords, photos, parade dragons, opium pipes, a fishing sampan, and other artifacts tracing the history of Chinese immigration in America from the early 1880s to today. The gift shop here is a good place for inexpensive souvenir shopping.

CHINESE NEW YEAR (all ages)

January and February; (415) 391–2000.

The most spectacular of annual festivals in the city, starting with the New Year Flower Fair in late January, on Grant and Pacific Streets: plants, flowers, produce, traditional dance, music, art, and cultural displays. A mid-February weekend is the big deal, with a Chinatown Community Fair—kite and lantern making, arts demos, folk dance, puppet shows—and the big nighttime New Year Parade. With kids and grandkids in tow, my family prowls the parade route for a prime spot where the smaller children can see, and we wait breathlessly to hear the first blast of the firecrackers. Up the street come the glowing lanterns, crashing cymbals, marching bands, booming drum troupes, and famous dragons—roaring, fire-breathing, twisting, leaping, and sparkling red, gold, and green, accompanied by costumed attendants holding long strings of popping firecrackers. When the parade is over, having cleverly made dinner reservations in advance, we then have a big Chinese dinner, usually at Brandy Ho's (217 Columbus; 415-362-6268).

More San Francisco

MISSION DOLORES (all ages)

Dolores Street at Sixteenth, in the Mission District; (415) 621–8203.

The beating heart of the city's Hispanic community, the mission is the oldest and one of the most beautiful structures in the city; it was founded in 1776, five days before the signing of the Declaration of Independence. Within the thick adobe walls a miraculous painted ceiling glows in early Native American designs. Next door the larger church was built in 1918. In a tiny cemetery lie literally thousands of the Mexican, Spanish, Indian, and Irish builders of America's favorite city by the bay.

MAKE A CIRCUS (ages 3–15)

Various locations around the city; (415) 242–1414; www.makeacircus.org.

If your child yearns to run away with the circus, perhaps Make A Circus will keep him or her close to home. In three-hour events at **Free** Circus Days, held at several parks in the city during the summer, kids learn juggling, stilt walking, acrobatics, human-pyramid building, and clowning, then participate in zany shows. Call for dates, hours and locations.

MISSION CLIFFS ROCK CLIMBING CENTER (ages 4 and up)

2295 Harrison Street, San Francisco 94110; (415) 550–0515; www. mission-cliffs.com.

No, Virginia, there are no mountains in San Francisco, but you can learn to climb on 16,000 square feet of cavernous indoor terrain. Rock climbing is a happening sport in California, and this state-of-the-art climbing gym in the Mission District is a fascinating place to visit, even if your family doesn't have the desire to hang upside down from great heights. There is a large "bouldering" area, short top-roping routes for beginners, longer routes for experts, and lead-climbing routes as long as 55 feet for those who are Half Dome– and Everest-bound. The gym is membership based, with day passes available to the public for $14. There are free weights, exercise machines, locker rooms, showers, and saunas. A lively schedule of classes, clinics and world-class competitions goes on, with programs for kids, too.

ESPN X GAMES (all ages)

Piers 30 and 32 and other locations; (415) 392–9830; www.xgames.com.

A spectacular series of sports events can be watched **Free** in June and July, from skateboarding to bicycle stunts, in-line skating, sport climbing, snowboarding, sky surfing and street luge. For aspiring sports stars, the chance to see 400 of the world's best alternative sports athletes is tons of fun, in spite of huge crowds.

CHINA BEACH (all ages)

Just west of the Golden Gate Bridge, Seacliff and Twenty-eighth Avenue; (415) 221–5756.

One of the few beaches safe for swimming, with lifeguards in summer, changing rooms, barbecues, and a sundeck. The water is *cold!*

Where to Eat

Mel's Drive-In. *2165 Lombard Street 94123; (415) 921–3039.* No longer a real drive-in, Mel's is *American Graffiti* revisited. Jukeboxes are stationed at every booth, burgers come in a car box, shakes are thick, and crayons, balloons, homemade apple pie and banana splits are abundant. $

David's Deli. *474 Geary, near Union Square 94102; (415) 771–0431.* Kids like to sit at the counter for gigantic deli sandwiches, hot pastrami to die for, New York–style cheesecake, and huge slices of pie. $

Sears Fine Foods. *439 Powell Street, at Union Square 94102; (415) 986–1160.* For years and years, breakfasts of sourdough French toast and tiny Swedish pancakes for tiny tots, plus all-American favorites for breakfast and lunch. $

San Francisco Art Institute Cafe. *800 Chestnut, in North Beach 94133; (415) 749–4567.* The view is tremendous, and the prices are downright cheap for homemade soup, sandwiches, and super desserts. While here, take a look at the Diego Rivera murals. $

Swan Oyster Depot. *1517 Polk Street 94109 ; (415) 673–1101.* Since 1912 just a counter with twenty stools and just the best clam chowder, cracked crab, and other fresh seafood in town. Breakfast and lunch. $

Hard Rock Cafe. *1699 Van Ness Avenue 94109; (415) 885–1699.* Noisy and fun, a 1950s dream of hot cars and hot music and *the* place to meet young people and families from all over the world. $$

St. Francis Fountain. *2801 Twenty-fourth Street, San Francisco 94114; (415) 826–4200.* Since 1918, the city's best sodas and root beer floats, homemade ice cream, grilled cheese sandwiches, BLTs, and burgers. $

La Taqueria. *2889 Mission Street, San Francisco 94110; (415) 285–7117.* Among the many *taquerias* (little cafes specializing in tacos) in the Mission District, this one has remained for twenty-five years and continues to be wall-to-wall busy. Whimsical murals create a festive backdrop for fresh-fruit sodas, smoky *carne asada, carnitas* (slow-cooked pork), grilled chicken, and steak tacos and burritos. The neon sign says, THE BEST TACOS IN THE WHOLE WORLD. It could be true. You can sit on a bench inside or outside to eat, or take away. $

Where to Stay

Suites at Fisherman's Wharf. *2655 Hyde Street, at the North Waterfront, San Francisco 94133; (800) 227– 3608.* In a garden courtyard, one- and two-bedroom suites with sofa beds, laundry, and rooftop terrace for bay watching. Free continental breakfast, parking, and shuttle to downtown. $$

Hotel del Sol. *3100 Webster Street, San Francisco 94123; (415) 773–1066 or (800) 738–7477.* Looking just like a California beach town motor lodge from the 1950s, the two-story Del Sol is Day-Glo yellow, bright orange, royal blue, and flaming red inside and out, with fabulous striped canvas drapes to pull across the carports. With low rates, a small swimming pool, free parking, a sauna, even hammocks, and an unbeatably convenient location near the Marina and Union Street shopping, this is a rare find in this city. Smallish rooms and spacious suites. $$

Hotel Metropolis. *25 Mason Street, San Francisco 94102; (415) 775–4600; www.personalityhotels.com.* In a glitzy new boutique hotel, a specially designed children's suite has bunk beds, a separate parlor with a sofa bed, and a connecting room for parents. Furniture is scaled for kids, and there is a vibrant artwork created by children. **Free** are arts and crafts materials, books, games and toys, and even kids' toothpaste and bubble bath. Peanut butter and jelly sandwiches and cookies are served on a silver tray! **Free** morning transportation to key destinations. $$$

Seal Rock Inn. *545 Point Lobos Avenue, San Francisco 94121; (415) 752–8090.* At the beach near the Cliff House Restaurant, simple units with an ocean view, some with fireplaces, kitchenettes. $

Motel Row. *On Lombard Street, between Baker Street and Van Ness.* Several inexpensive and medium-priced motels are located on Lombard Street within walking distance of the waterfront, restaurants and public transportation. Reasonable choices are the Buena Vista Motor Inn (800–835–4980), the Lombard Motor Inn (800–835–3639), and the Cow Hollow Motor Inn (415–921–5800). All have **Free** parking and connecting rooms. $$

Radisson Hotel. *250 Beach Street, San Francisco 94133; (800) 333–3333 or (415) 392–6700.* A block square of over 400 rooms with parking and an attractive, Tuscan-style indoor/outdoor restaurant. Upper rooms have balconies overlooking the bay. Year-round heated pool, several restaurants. $$$

San Francisco Hotel Reservations. *(888) 782–9673 or (415) 974–4499; www.sfvisitor.org.* 220 hotels and inns are described by location, type, price range, services, neighborhood, comfort level, and quality ratings, with availability up to twelve months in advance and photos.

San Francisco International Hostel. *Bay and Franklin, above Fort Mason, 94123; (415) 771–7277; www.norcal hostels.org.* For families on a strict budget and/or for those looking for a unique experience, two- and three-bunk private rooms (bring sleeping bags) and a communal kitchen; brief chores are required. The location above Fort Mason is unbeatable. $12–$15 per person; also family rates. For a brochure describing all Northern California hostels, call (415) 863-1444 (fax 415-863-3865).

For More Information

San Francisco Convention and Visitors Bureau. *900 Market Street, corner of Powell, P.O. Box 429097, San Francisco, 94142-9097; (415) 391–2000; www. sfvisitor.org.*

Bay Area Rapid Transit (BART). *(650) 992–2278 or (510) 465–BART; www.bart.gov.* Subway and rail connecting San Francisco with Colma, Daly City, and the East and South Bay, including Oakland Airport. Ticket prices start at $1.10; ages 4 and under ride Free. Call for schedules, discounts, stations.

Passport. *(415) 673–MUNI.* Purchase at Visitor Centers and the cable car terminals at Fisherman's Wharf and Ghirardelli Square. Prices are one-day $6.00, three-day $10.00 and seven-day $15.00 for unlimited travel on citywide Muni buses, cable cars, trolleys, and streetcars. Regular Muni adult fares are $1.00 and 35 cents for seniors and youth to age 17, ages 5 and under Free. Exact change is necessary.

Streetcars. One of the nicest ways to ride about the city is on the colorful, historic streetcars. Beginning at Embarcadero Station, five streetcar lines (J-Church, K-Ingleside, L-Taraval, M-Ocean View, and N-Judah) take you along Market Street to various stops west and southwest in the city, including Ocean Beach. The F-line extension runs from Pac Bell Park to the Ferry Building and around the Embarcadero to Fisherman's Wharf every ten minutes, stopping frequently. The city recently purchased beautiful refurbished antique streetcars from Milan, Italy.

Visitor Information Twenty-four-Hour Hotline. *(415) 391–2001.* Updates on events in five languages.

CityPass. *Purchase at visitor center and at the major attractions on the pass. Prices are $29.95 for adults and $17.95 for youth ages 12 to 17; passes are good for seven days.* Save 50 percent admission price on the San Francisco Zoo, MOMA, the deYoung Fine Arts Museum and the California Academy of Sciences in Golden Gate Park, bay cruises, the Exploratorium, and the Palace of the Legion of Honor.

Airport Transportation. There is a free shuttle from SFO to the Millbrae Caltrain station, then a $2.00 train to the Caltrain station at Fourth and Townsend in San Francisco, a half-hour trip. Also popular is Super Shuttle (415–558–8500), a door-to-door van service from SFO to any address in San Francisco. For information on other ground transportation to SFO from Bay Area cities, go to www.quickaid.com/airports/sfo/l/city.html.

Golden Gate North: Marin County

Streaming out of the city like the tide under the Golden Gate Bridge, day-trippers escape into Marin County. Within a hour's drive are Pacific beaches, shady roads for bike rides, and footpaths beneath ancient redwood giants.

The profile of 2,600-foot Mount Tamalpais, the "Sleeping Maiden," lures mountain bikers and hikers into the canyons, forests, and meadows of Mount Tamalpais State Park. Scenic two-lane Panoramic Highway runs steeply over the mountain and down to Stinson Beach.

For freeway-free getaways take a ferry from San Francisco's Embarcadero to Tiburon or Sausalito for a day in the sun when the city is socked in with fog. With shops, restaurants, and waterfront promenades, the two Mediterranean-style villages overlook San Francisco Bay and the quiet inlet of Richardson Bay.

Miraculous double peninsulas that point jaggedly into the Pacific, Point Reyes National Seashore is one of the greatest coastal wilderness preserves in the world. The tiny towns of Inverness and Point Reyes Station are headquarters for provisions, meals, and lodgings near the national seashore. If your family craves oysters, head for Tomales Bay.

Inverness

A vacation village since the late 1880s, Inverness, population 1,000, is a day-tripper's rest stop and a community of country cottages in the dark forest of Inverness Ridge, overlooking Tomales Bay. Keep your eyes open for cafes, a small marina, and eye-popping scenery.

From February through early summer, the meadows and marine terraces are blanketed with California poppies, dark blue lupine, pale baby blue-eyes, Indian paintbrush, and some wildflowers existing only here. The summit of Mount Wittenberg, at 1,407 feet, is reachable in an afternoon's climb.

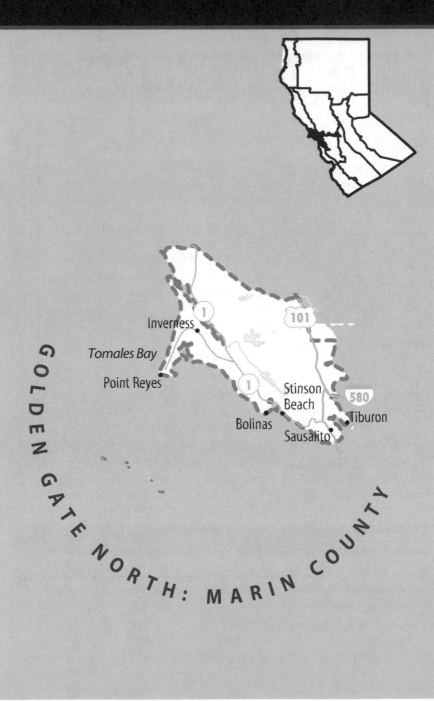

Inverness

Tomales Bay

Point Reyes

Stinson
Beach

Bolinas

Sausalito

Tiburon

GOLDEN GATE NORTH: MARIN COUNTY

A string of beaches and protected bays, hilltop and meadow trails, and an astonishing variety and abundance of birds and wildlife make the area a magnificent resource for families who love the outdoors. Often cool and foggy in summer, the weather is dependably clear and warm in spring and fall, and midwinter days can be surprisingly mild.

Tomales Bay

Thirteen miles long, a mile wide, and shallow, Tomales Bay is a quiet finger of water surrounded by acres of mudflats and salt and freshwater marshes. Commercial oyster farms line the eastern shore. More then 100 species of resident and migrating water birds are the reason you'll see anorak-clad, binocular-braced birdwatchers at pullouts on Highway 1 along the shore. At the head of the bay, the minitown of Tomales is a 2-block-long headquarters for crabbers, clammers, and surf fishermen. At low tide in the winter, catch a clammer's barge from Tomales out to the flatlands around Hog Island in the bay. If you don't care to dig for your dinner, stop at one of the rustic oyster joints.

Kayaking Marin
If you haven't been in a kayak since years ago when they were heavy and awkward, you have no idea how easy and safe they are these days. When they say, "for all ages," it's really true. I started kayaking when I became a granny in my forties, and I have a friend who started designing, selling, and paddling kayaks in her seventies.

Kayaking companies will teach you the basics, outfit you, and suggest short or long-paddling routes. Besides single "open deck" and sea kayaks, these proprietors rent junior-size kayaks, doubles, and triples. Even first-timers can learn in a few minutes with the Free instruction offered by the kayak companies; kids will feel secure riding with a parent or older sibling. Call ahead to reserve the boats.

- **Blue Waters Kayaking.** *Next to Barnabys by the Bay, 12938 Sir Francis Drake Boulevard, Inverness; (415) 669–2600, www.bwkayak.com.*

- **Tamal Saka Tomales Bay Kayaking.** *Marshall Boat Works, 8 miles north of Point Reyes Station; (115) 663–1743, www.tamalsaka.com.*

- **Open Water Rowing.** *85 Liberty Ship Way, Sausalito; (415) 332–1091, www.owrc.com.*

- **Sea Trek Ocean Kayaking Center.** *Schoonmaker Point, Liberty Ship Way, Sausalito; (415) 488–1000, www.seatrekkayak.com.*

HOG ISLAND OYSTER COMPANY (all ages)

20215 Highway 1, between Point Reyes Station and Tomales; (415) 663–9218.
Shucking knives, tables, and barbecue kettles are provided—and the best oysters in the world!

NICK'S COVE

23240 Highway 1, just south of Tomales, on Highway 1; (415) 663–1033.
On an outdoor deck right in the aromatic wetlands where the oysters grow. Barbecued oysters and seafood are on the menu, along with a list of beers as long as your arm.

TOMALES POINT HIKE

About 2.5 miles past Inverness, turn right onto Pierce Point Road, following signs to McClure's Beach, and continue 9 miles to white ranch buildings and the parking lot; (415) 663–1092.

A breathtaking route on the bluffs above the Pacific, windswept moors that remind some visitors of Scotland. Wildflowers float in the meadows, whales spout December through February, and a herd of Tule elk live in the grassy fields of Pierce Ranch. The entire loop is 6 miles round-trip.

POINT REYES NATIONAL SEASHORE (all ages)

Bear Valley Road, Highway 1 and Sir Francis Drake Boulevard, Point Reyes; (415) 663–1092; www.nps.gov./pore.
When the English explorer Sir Francis Drake sailed his *Golden Hind* into the great curve of Drake's Bay in 1579, he knew this was a bit of earth like no other. Part of the National Seashore, the bay remains largely as it was 400 years ago—fringed with sandy beaches and tidepools alive with anemones and crabs, sometimes even rays and leopard sharks. North from the point—Point Reyes, where the lighthouse stands—are miles of beaches accessible from Sir Francis Drake Boulevard. Exposed to the full force of storms and pounding surf, these beaches are unsafe for swimming or surfing. The headlands, tidepools, sea stacks, lagoons, wave-carved caves, and rocky promontories are alive with birds—endangered brown pelicans, cormorants, surf scooters, sandpipers, grebes, terns—and sea life such as giant anemones, sea palms, urchins, fish, and even the occasional great white shark offshore of Tomales Point.

At the visitor center are exhibits, guidebooks, trail maps, and daily postings of whale sightings. Rangers are on hand to orient you to the diverse ecosystem and the many destinations within the huge park.

Short, easy walks near the visitor center include Kule Loklo Trail to Miwok Village, where an ancient Indian site has been re-created. On the Earthquake Trail are photos of the effects of the 1906 earthquake and signs explaining earth movement; the entire peninsula was once located some 250 miles to the south!

The **Coastal Native American Summer Big Time** takes place here in July, with demonstrations of crafts, skills, music, and dancing. October brings the Acorn Festival, a celebration of Miwok Indian history.

The weather can be foggy and windy on any day of the year, so warm jackets are advisable.

BEAR VALLEY TRAIL (all ages)

Point Reyes National Seashore; (415) 663–1092.

The 4.4-mile trail to the Arch Rock overlook at the beach is the most popular and the easiest trail. The route wanders through forest tunnels, along creeks, and through meadows, ending on a bluff 50 feet above the sea. The last 2 miles are downhill. Bikes are allowed on all except the last 0.75 mile, where a bike rack is provided. From Arch Rock, you have several choices of return routes. Restrooms are located midway.

LIMANTOUR BEACH AND LIMANTOUR ESTERO RESERVE

Within Point Reyes National Seashore, at the end of Limantour Road; (415) 663–1092.

Just a few steps from the parking lot, this long stretch of windswept sand is good for surf fishing and sunbathing. Look for the Muddy Hollow Trail for a short birdwatching walk. Birdwatching is popular in the 500-acre Drake's Estero, a large intertidal lagoon with a giant tidepool.

POINT REYES LIGHTHOUSE (all ages)

Within Point Reyes National Seashore, at the end of Sir Francis Drake Boulevard; (415) 669–1534.

Until the lighthouse was built, in 1875, many shipwrecks occurred off the Point Reyes Headlands. The lighthouse is reachable by 400 steps leading downhill from a high bluff, and it can be a windy, windy spot. During whale-watching season, December through March, a shuttle bus operates between the lighthouse and the beach. Some 20,000 California gray whales travel the Pacific coastline south to breed in Mexico, returning a few months later with their babies to the Arctic.

POINT REYES STATION (all ages)

Highway 1 and Sir Francis Drake Boulevard.

Many century-old buildings remain on the short main street of a picturesque railroad town founded in the 1800s. The train depot is now the post office, the Fire Engine House, a community center. Dairy ranches and commercial oyster companies fuel the rural economy.

TOBY'S FEED BARN

Point Reyes Station; (415) 663–1223.

Hay, feed, souvenirs, T-shirts, and cool stuff crafted by local artists.

INTO THE BLUE (all ages)

In the Livery Stable, corner of Third and B Streets, Point Reyes Station; (415) 663–1147.

On the way to the beach, with kites and wind toys galore.

TOMALES BAY FOODS

Fourth and B Streets, Point Reyes Station; (415) 663–9335.

Owned by a graduate of Chez Panisse, the birthplace of California cuisine. An airy emporium of luscious take-out foods, hot and cold, plus organic produce, homemade ice cream, flowers, and more from local farms, ranches, and wineries. $$

Where to Eat

Knave of Hearts Bakery. *12301 Sir Francis Drake Boulevard, Inverness 94937; (415) 663–1236.* Luscious pastries, light lunches, and ice cream. $

Barnaby's By the Bay. *At the Golden Hinde Inn, 1 mile north of Inverness 94937; (415) 669–1114.* A glassed-in dining room and decks overlooking a marina on Tomales Bay; the only waterside restaurant in the area. Clam chowder, deep-fried calamari with cornmeal crust, fresh fish, and barbecued oysters, chicken, and ribs from the applewood smoker. $–$$

Station House Cafe. *Main Street, Point Reyes Station 94956; (415) 663–1515.* Eclectic American cuisine in a lively bistro atmosphere, specializing in oysters, mussels, and more local seafood. Live music on weekends. When accompanied by our toddler grandkids, we ask for a table in or near the garden patio. Reservations, definitely. Breakfast, lunch, and dinner. $$

Where to Stay

Point Reyes Seashore Lodge. *10021 Highway 1, Olema 94950; (415) 663–9000.* One of the few B&Bs appropriate for families, a luxurious country estate in an idyllic garden setting with sweeping lawns, large trees, and a creek. The best rooms for families have tiny, private patios; some have fireplaces and double Jacuzzis. Breakfast is generous, with ample bowls of fresh fruit, yogurt, granola, pastries, and breads. A large library of guidebooks and restaurant menus is a big help. The staff will arrange bike, kayak, and horse rentals for you. $$$

Golden Hinde Inn. *12938 Sir Francis Drake Boulevard, Inverness 94937; (415) 669–1389.* A fresh-looking, white-painted, unassuming motel on Tomales Bay, with a pool, fishing pier, fireplaces, and kitchens. $$

Point Reyes Hostel. *From Bear Valley Road, go about 6 miles on Limantour Road, P.O. Box 247, Point Reyes Station 94956;*

(415) 663–8811. A ranch house and bunkhouse, with spacious kitchen, outdoor barbecue, and common rooms with woodburning stoves. A family room is available by reservation. $

Olema Ranch Campground. *10155 Highway 1, Olema 94950; (800) 655–2267 or (415) 663–8001; www. campgrounds.com/olemaranch.* Thirty-two acres of shade trees and grassy meadows with 150 tent and 80 RV sites and cabins, showers, and laundry facilities. They've thought of everything: mountain bike rentals, kayak tours, volleyball, a U.S. post office, ice-cream socials, storytelling around a bonfire, and buffet breakfast Sunday morning. Dogs okay. $

West Marin Vacation Rentals. *P.O. Box 160, Point Reyes 94956; (800) 540–1776.* One- to three-bedroom vacation home rentals. $–$$$

For More Information

West Marin Chamber of Commerce. *P.O. Box 1045, Point Reyes Station 94956; (415) 663–9232; www.pointreyes.org.*

Weather Information for Point Reyes National Seashore. *(415) 663–1092.*

Sausalito/Tiburon

Tumbling down steep, forested hillsides to the edge of San Francisco Bay as if it were on the Mediterranean, the small tourist town of **Sausalito** makes a great day-trip destination. Running along the edge of Richardson Bay, the main street, Bridgeway, is chockablock with galleries and upscale shops, seafood restaurants, and yacht harbors, all sharing postcard views of San Francisco.

At midtown is the ferry dock from San Francisco and Tiburon.

A community of 400-plus houseboats, permanently located at the north end of Bridgeway, is a phenomenon in itself and fun to see. In this part of town you can take kayaking and windsurfing lessons on Richardson Bay.

On the opposite side of Richardson Bay from Sausalito, **Tiburon** is another hamlet of vintage mansions, with outdoor restaurants overlooking the San Francisco skyline and Raccoon Strait. You can get here via one of the Angel Island ferries, as well as by car. On opening day of yachting season in April, decorated pleasure craft sail and motor back and forth while families engage in springlike behavior on the grassy shoreline, such as flying kites and playing boom boxes.

BAY MODEL (all ages)

2100 Bridgeway, Sausalito; (415) 332–3870. **Free** *admission.*

From the ferry dock a pleasant, twenty-minute walk north brings you to the one-and-a-half acre, hydraulic working scale model of San Francisco Bay and the adjacent Sacramento River Delta. The natural and cultural histories of the bay are traced in exhibits of wetlands, wildlife, shipwrecks, antique equipment, videos, and video games—kids love it.

MARIN HEADLANDS (all ages)

Take the Alexander Avenue exit off Highway 1, the first exit north of the Golden Gate Bridge; (415) 331–1540; www.nps.gov./goga.

Part of the **Golden Gate National Recreation Area,** wild open spaces with miraculous views. Hiking trails above the Golden Gate are breezy and bracing, and kids like to climb around in the remnants of World War II fortifications. Stop at the visitor center at Field and Bunker Streets for maps to myriad hiking, biking, and equestrian trails and beaches. Besides the Marin Mammal Center (listed below), the main attractions are **Rodeo Beach, Rodeo Lagoon, Muir Beach,** and the **Point Bonita Lighthouse.** The lighthouse is perched on a bit of rock at the entrance to the Golden Gate, with incredible views and a (slightly) swaying footbridge over crashing waves; walk down and back on your own and get the history from the ranger in the tiny visitor center, or take the guided walk, which takes (it seems) forever. Precipitous clifftop trails near here are not for little kids.

MARINE MAMMAL CENTER (all ages)

Marin Headlands, Sausalito; (415) 289–SEAL.

A must-see for families fascinated by the largest denizens of the sea, the center serves as a hospital for orphaned, sick, and injured seals, sea lions, dolphins, otters, and whales. Many of the patients are endangered or threatened species, and you can watch them being fed, treated, and comforted. The twin goals of the center are (1) to ready the animals to return to their watery habitat, and (2) to create public understanding of and appreciation for our fellow creatures. During some months, there are few animals on view; call ahead. The gift shop has a nice array of kids' books and guidebooks, and some exhibits.

BAY AREA DISCOVERY MUSEUM (ages 1–10)

Fort Baker, 557 McReynolds Road, Sausalito 94965, at the south end of Sausalito near the Golden Gate Bridge; (415) 487–4398. Tickets are $7.00 for adults, $6.00 for children, Free for kids under 1; children must be accompanied by an adult.

A premier attraction for youngsters ages 1 to 10, in a complex of historic buildings at East Fort Baker, built by the U.S. Army at the turn of the century. Among the play-and-learn venues are a multimedia center with CD-ROMs for kids to play, a science lab, a maze of illusions with optical tricks, and a fishing boat that kids can climb aboard. Kid can also crawl through an underwater tunnel, make arts-and-crafts projects, touch sea animals, develop photos, drop in on a workshop, or ride a carousel. The Tot Spot is huge, with all kinds of hands-on fun for toddlers. The museum store sells interactive science projects and imaginative toys and books, and the cafe serves reasonably priced sandwiches, soups, and salads. The idyllic setting, with a fabulous view of the bridge, makes this a great spot for a short walk and a picnic; don't forget your jackets, as it can be windy and cool.

RICHARDSON BAY AUDUBON CENTER AND WILDLIFE SANCTUARY (all ages)

At the north end of the Tiburon Bike Path, 376 Greenwood Beach Road, Tiburon 94920; (415) 388–2524; www.egret.org. Admission is Free.

In this lovely wetlands preserve, thousands of waterfowl and birds and harbor seals show up in the wintertime. There is a self-guided nature trail and a bookstore adjacent to Lyford House, a lemon-yellow landmark Victorian open to the public.

NATURE CONSERVANCY RING MOUNTAIN PRESERVE

3152 Paradise Drive, Tiburon 94920; (415) 435–6465.

In the hills on the north end of Tiburon, a 377-acre ridge top offers walking trails and wonderful views of the Bay Area. It's less than 1 mile to the summit on an easy trail edged with knee-high native grasses dotted with wildflowers in the spring.

ANGEL ISLAND STATE PARK (all ages)

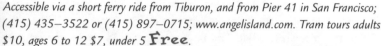

Accessible via a short ferry ride from Tiburon, and from Pier 41 in San Francisco; (415) 435–3522 or (415) 897–0715; www.angelisland.com. Tram tours adults $10, ages 6 to 12 $7, under 5 **Free**.

There are miles of hiking trails and mountain biking roads on this breezy island, plus gull's-eye views of three bridges and the skylines of the Bay Area. Among the historical sites are an ancient Miwok hunting ground, a cattle ranch, and a U.S. prisoner of war camp. The easy way to learn some history and get some fresh air is to take the narrated tour in an open-air tram.

Twenty-one-speed mountain bikes are available to rent, and you can take sea kayaking tours conducted around the island with historical and ecological interpretation. Less energetic family members can sit on the deck of the cafe with an espresso and a light lunch, watching sailboats and freighters gliding by. Environmental campsites (800–444–7275). No dogs, skateboards, or in-line skates are allowed.

CHINA CAMP STATE PARK (all ages)

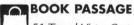

North San Pedro Road on the east side of Tiburon; (415) 456–0766.

Along San Pablo Bay, here is a hidden jewel of Bay Area parks, where the protected beach is often warm when fog chills the rest of Marin. Windsurfing is a big deal from May through October. Walk-in campsites are in lovely meadows about 1 mile from parking. Trails along the ridge have views of the north Bay Area, and there is a small museum and remnants of a late 1800s Chinese immigrants' shrimp fishing village. Leashed dogs are allowed.

BOOK PASSAGE

51 Tamal Vista, Corte Madera 94925; (800) 999–7909; www.bookpassage.com.

One of the largest and best independent bookstores in the country, with a big kids' and teens section, huge travel and mystery sections, and an indoor/outdoor cafe.

Where to Eat

Seven Seas. *682 Bridgeway, Sausalito 94966; (415) 332–1304.* The best in town for breakfast, indoors or on the patio. Lunch and dinner too. $

Harbor Grill. *305 Harbor Drive at Clipper Yacht Harbor, Sausalito 94966; (415) 331– 5355.* In a light-filled boathouse sort of place, checked tablecloths and a casual atmosphere, burgers, pasta, calamitously good clam chowder, crab cakes, and American comfort food, all at reasonable prices, indoors or out. $

Houlihan's. *660 Bridgeway Avenue, Sausalito 94966; (415) 332–8512.* Casual atmosphere with water view; seafood, pasta; lunch and dinner. $$

Sam's Anchor Cafe. *27 Main Street, Tiburon 94920; (415)435–4527.* One of the all-time best places in the Bay Area to sit on a sunny deck, contemplate the San Francisco skyline, and watch sailboats float by. Tuck into clam chowder, cracked crab, and fresh fish while the kids check out the seagulls and the boats. Bored older children can window-shop on Main Street, while you figure out how you can move to Tiburon. $–$$

Kitti's Place. *3001 Bridgeway, Sausalito 94966; (415) 331–0390.* In a homey atmosphere, comfort food extraordinaire, from homemade soup to Asian-inspired salads and entrees, and great sandwiches (try the portobello). Breakfast, lunch, and early dinner. $

Where to Stay

Corte Madera Inn. *1815 Redwood Highway, Corte Madera, five minutes north of Tiburon on Highway 101 94925; (800) 777– 9670; www.bestwestern.com.* One of the best choices in the North Bay for families, an attractive, comfortable motel arranged around gardens and lawns, with swimming and wading

pools, a laundry, playground, putting green, and an excellent coffee shop. Continental breakfast is Free, and so is the shuttle to the San Francisco ferry. Walk across the street to a large shopping center and around the corner to a world-class bookstore. Can't beat it! $$$

For More Information

Sausalito Chamber of Commerce Visitors Center. *29 Caledonia Street, Sausalito 94966; (415) 331–7262; www.sausalito.org.*

Tiburon Peninsula Chamber of Commerce. *96 Main Street, Tiburon*

94920; (415) 435–5633; www.citysearch.com/sfo/tiburon.

Marin County Convention and Visitors Bureau. *1013 Larkspur Landing Circle, Larkspur 94939; (415) 499–5000; www.visitormarin.org.*

Stinson Beach/Bolinas

A unique tropical undercurrent keeps the waters off Stinson Beach surprisingly warm year-round. Below the western slopes of Mount Tamalpais in a protected "banana belt," the white sand beach and the village enjoy a mild climate and are favorite destinations for San Franciscans escaping the fog.

A clutch of small cafes and shops, the village of **Stinson Beach** is ringed with eucalyptus and Monterey pines, where thousands of monarch butterflies spend the winter. Bolinas is even smaller and scruffier and is surrounded by spectacular wildlife preserves, beaches, and hiking trails.

Two ranches in the area are nature and wildlife preserves open to the public, with scheduled activities specially designed for children.

A rustic village inhabited by rogue artists and craftspeople, **Bolinas** has some charming nineteenth-century buildings, particularly near the old downtown along Wharf Road. Part of Smiley's Bar dates from 1852, and St. Mary Magdalen Catholic Church from 1878. The Bolinas Lagoon is 1,200 acres of saltmarsh, mudflats, and calm sea waters harboring great blue herons and egrets, migrating geese, and ducks—as many as 35,000 birds have been spotted in a single day.

A mile of shallow tidepools are exposed at low tide on the Bolinas Bay shoreline. In the vast intertidal area live gooseneck barnacles, ochre and pink sea stars, purple and giant red anemones, chitons, and more exotic sea life. This is a marine reserve, and not a thing may be removed. At the north end of the reef, Agate Beach is a small county park. Keep an eye peeled for the swift incoming tide.

STINSON BEACH PARK (all ages)

Highway 1 and Panoramic Highway, Stinson Beach 94970; (415) 868–0942.
A 3-mile-long sandy beach beloved by surfers and swimmers (many Marin beaches are not safe for swimming, due to undertows and currents; this one is an exception); great white sharks are occasionally sighted. Picnic tables, barbecues, restrooms, a snack bar, and, during summer, lifeguards. No pets.

AUDUBON CANYON RANCH (all ages)

Between Bolinas and Stinson Beach, 4900 Highway 1, Stinson Beach; (415) 868–9244. Open to the public from March through July on weekends and holidays. **Free** *admission.*

This research center is located in a beautiful valley. In the tops of redwoods and pines standing in deep, wooded canyons, herons and egrets make their nests. A short trail leads to fixed telescopes for nest-watching, and you can walk on two 3-mile-long loop trails and a short nature trail. Watch for newts, frogs, foxes, deer, and quail. Adjacent to a circa 1870 house are exhibits, a bookshop, and picnic tables.

SLIDE RANCH (ages 4–12)
2025 Shoreline Highway, Muir Beach 94965; (415) 381–6155.

A few miles south of Stinson Beach, on a hillside overlooking the sea, lies a ranch built in the early 1900s that is now an environmental education center where your children can milk a goat, harvest veggies, bake bread, and learn how to care for animals and nature. Special days are scheduled for ocean exploration and for children under 5. Call ahead for a reservation.

POINT REYES BIRD OBSERVATORY (all ages)
Four miles northwest from Bolinas, on Mesa Road; (415) 868–1221.

A lovely, short, self-guided nature trail and a small museum. You are welcome to observe the activities here, which include banding rufous-sided towhees, song sparrows, and other birds. This is the Palomarin Trailhead, leading to four freshwater lakes that are waterfowl habitats and to Double Point Bay, where harbor seals breed and tidepools are inviting to look into (don't touch). Three miles from the trailhead, watch for Bass Lake, a secret swimming spot. There are portable potties near the trailhead.

Where to Eat

Stinson Beach Grill. *3465 Shoreline Highway, Stinson Beach 94970; (415) 868–2002.* Breakfast, lunch, or dinner, indoors or on the heated deck; fresh seafood, barbecued oysters, pasta, and Southwest cuisine. $

Parkside Cafe. *43 Arenal, Stinson Beach 94970; (415) 868–1272.* Italian food, burgers, and pizza; breakfast, lunch, and dinner. $

Bolinas Bay Bakery and Cafe. *20 Wharf Road, Bolinas 94924; (415) 868–0211.* Organic-ingredient pastries, breads, pies, pizza, soups—some of the best picnic goodies in the Western Hemisphere. Lunch, dinner, and a great place for breakfast on the back porch. $

Where to Stay

Ocean Court. *18 Arenal, Stinson Beach 94970; (415) 868–0212.* Large, simple motel units with kitchens, near the beach. $

Steep Ravine Cabins. *801 Panoramic Highway, 1 mile south of Stinson Beach 94970; (800) 444–7275.* Simple, rustic cabins from the 1930s, each sleeping up to five people, with woodburning stoves, bunks, water, no electricity. These are rented through the state park. $

Golden Gate Hostel. *Building 941, Fort Barry, in the Marin Headlands; (415) 331–2777.* On the National Register of Historic Places, a spacious, homey place, with three kitchens, common rooms, a recreation room, a fireplace, and a piano. Family rooms with bunks. Walk right out the door onto a hiking trail. $

Seadrift Company. *2 Dipsea Road, P.O. Box 177, Stinson Beach 94970; (415) 868–1791; www.seadriftrealty.com.* Vacation home rentals. $–$$$

155 Pine. *155 Pine on Duxbury Reef, Bolinas 94924; (415) 868–0263.* A tiny B&B that welcomes families to stay in a cottage overlooking the ocean, within a short walk to the beach; fireplace, kitchen, decks. Sleeps up to six. $$

For More Information

Marin County Convention and Visitors Bureau. *1013 Larkspur Landing Circle, Larkspur 94939; (415) 499–5000; www.visitormarin.org.*

North Coast

To a child California's northern coastline means flying kites on the beach, camping in the redwoods, and watching a whale spouting offshore. Parents love the fishing villages and Victorian loggers' towns, the art galleries and cozy seaside cafes.

The main coastal route, Highway 1, twists and turns atop marine terraces and clifftops, some as high as 900 feet above the shore. Views of mountains and sea are legendary, but young backseat passengers will demand frequent stops. Several forays to the North Coast will create sweeter vacation memories than trying to see all the sights in just a few days.

Set up your headquarters in Mendocino, Fort Bragg, or Bodega Bay, and make day-trip expeditions to nearby beaches and forest parks. Take time to investigate the historic towns. In Mendocino, for instance, the entire town is a Historical Preservation District of early Cape Cod and Victorian homes and steepled clapboard churches. Point Arena is prime whale-watching country. A chain of beaches stretches north from Bodega Bay, a small fishing village where seals, sailboats, and windsurfers share a harbor.

Fort Bragg

A lumbering and commercial fishing town since 1857, Fort Bragg today carefully preserves a cache of vintage wood-frame houses. Families find that restaurants and accommodations are more reasonably priced here than in Mendocino. There are several coastal and forest state parks nearby, a picturesque fishing port at the mouth of the Noyo River, and the departure depot for the famous Skunk Train.

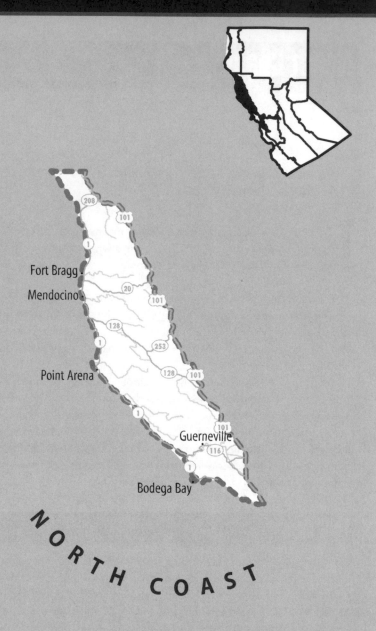

Fort Bragg

Mendocino

Point Arena

Guerneville

Bodega Bay

N O R T H   C O A S T

The annual Whale Festival in March is a two-weekend event with chowder, beer, and wine tasting; a doll show and classic car show; a run; banquet dinners; and a big arts and crafts fair with musical entertainment.

SKUNK TRAIN (all ages)

Laurel Street Depot at Main Street, Fort Bragg 95437; (707) 964–6371 or (800) 77–SKUNK; www.skunktrain.com. Tickets for adults about $26, ages 5 to 11 about $12, **Free** *for children under 5.*

Hauling logs to sawmills in the 1880s, the Skunk Train—actually several historic diesel and steam trains—now takes tourists on half- or full-day trips to Willits and back. The route runs along Pudding Creek through redwood forests, crossing thirty bridges and trestles; it's a beautiful train ride—perfect for the grandparents and younger grandchildren. In the Fort Bragg train depot are two dozen retail shops and places to eat, scattered among railroad and logging artifacts. Snacks and lunch are available to buy along the way, or you can bring a picnic. Special events, such as barbecue-dinner rides and "Tour de Skunk," a skunk ride one way and bike ride the other, are held annually.

MACKERRICHER STATE PARK (all ages)

Three miles north of Fort Bragg off Highway 1; (707) 927–5804.

A 1,598-acre park, 8 miles of beach and dunes, with a popular beach play area and tidepools at Pudding Creek, at the southern end of the park. Two freshwater lakes are stocked with trout. Horseback-riding, mountain-biking, and hiking trails are found throughout bluffs, headlands, dunes, forests, and wetlands. The headlands at Laguna Point are a prime spot for whale watching, and a permanent population of harbor seals reside here. The boardwalk affords wheelchair and stroller access, from the southwest corner of the parking lot. There are 140 developed campsites and RV sites for up to 35-foot vehicles, plus fire rings, and toilets. Stretching the entire 8-mile length of the park, the paved Haul Road, a former logging road, is a fabulous jogging, biking, and walking route with ocean views, crossing beautiful sand dunes.

MENDOCINO COAST BOTANICAL GARDENS (all ages)

18220 Highway 1, 1.5 miles south of Fort Bragg; (707) 964–4352; www. gardenbythesea.com. Admission is $6.00 adults, $3.00 kids ages 13 to 17, $1.00 ages 6 to 12, **Free** *for toddlers. Year-round birding tours at 8:00 A.M. on the third Tuesday each month are* **Free***.*

Acres of plantings, forest, and fern canyons on a bluff overlooking the ocean, from which you can see gray whales during their migrating season, with 2 miles of paths in lush gardens. Rhododendrons and roses, heathers, succulents, camellias, and literally thousands of other plants crowd the gardens. A picnic site perches on a scenic overlook. More than one hundred bird species visit the gardens. Smack in the middle of the Gardens, the **Country Garden Restaurant and Grill** serves lunch, dinner, and brunch at umbrella tables overlooking glorious blooming flowers and trees. Try the grilled fresh fish, grilled eggplant salad, mushroom crêpe torte, or the apple wood–rotisseried game hen.

Karen's Favorite Beaches Near Fort Bragg

Glass Beach. *At the foot of Elm Street.* The sand is sprinkled with pebbles of glass and china that have been tumbled and smoothed in the sea.

Pudding Creek. *North of town, past the first bridge.* Beach play area and tidepools.

Ten Mile River Beach. *Eight miles north of Fort Bragg.* Acres and acres of salt marsh and wetlands at the mouth of the Noyo River, inhabited by nesting birds and ducks; a 4.5-mile, duney stretch of sand extends south from the river.

NOYO HARBOR (all ages)

Located 1.8 miles south of Fort Bragg, at the mouth of the Noyo River.

Headquarters for a large fleet of fishing trollers and canneries. Barking and posing, sea lions lounge on the wooden piers, waiting for the return of the boats at day's end. You can rent a fishing rod here and fish off the piers or the rocks. One of a handful of seafood restaurants on the harbor, **The Wharf** is a casual, family-friendly place to enjoy some fresh fish and watch the sun sink slowly behind gangs of wheeling gulls *(707–964–4283)*.

FOR THE SHELL OF IT

344 North Main Street, Fort Bragg 95437; (707) 961–0461.

Shell jewelry, seashells, posters, rocks, minerals, folk art—and everything about shells.

LOST COAST ADVENTURES

19275 South Harbor Drive, Fort Bragg 95437; (707) 961–1143.

Kayak tours; mountain-bike, skin-diving, and scuba-diving rentals; boat charters for fishing, diving, and whale watching.

GUEST HOUSE (all ages)

343 North Main Street., Fort Bragg 95437;(707) 961–2823.

A beautiful home from before the turn of the twentieth century, this three-story house was built entirely of redwood and is filled with photos and artifacts of local history and antique logging equipment. There is also a lovely garden.

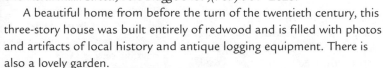

MENDOCINO CHOCOLATE COMPANY (all ages)

542 North Main, Fort Bragg 95437; (707) 964–8800, www.mendocino-chocolate.com.

Here you'll find handmade truffles and chocolates and edible sea shells. Or try these specialties: a dark, Rambo of a truffle, Mendocino Macho; Mendocino Breakers, dark-dipped caramels rolled in almonds; and old-fashioned Convent Fudge. **Free** samples; shipping worldwide.

Where to Eat

North Coast Brewing Company. *444 North Main Street, Fort Bragg 95437; (707) 964–BREW.* A hearty menu of local fresh fish, Cajun black beans and rice, ribs, Mendocino Mud Cake, burgers, nachos, and more. Voted Mendocino County Restaurant of the Year. Tons of fun. $$

Old Coast Bar and Grill. *101 North Franklin Street, Fort Bragg 95437; (707) 964– 6446.* Red-checked tablecloths give no hint of the sophisticated menu and big wine list: oysters, jambalaya, twenty varieties of pasta, fresh fish in imaginative sauces, house smoked ribs,

and kids menu. Warm and cozy on a cold night, delightful on the sun deck, live jazz on weekends. Lunch and dinner. $$

Redwood Cookhouse. *Redwood and Main Streets, Fort Bragg 95437; (707) 964–1517.* All-you-can-eat buffets; good food at reasonable prices. $

Purple Rose. *24300 North Highway 1, Fort Bragg 95437; (707) 964–6507.* Join the locals in this casual cafe for homemade tortillas filled with wonderful taco fillings, and other great Mexican dishes. $

Where to Stay

Grey Whale Inn. *615 North Main Street, Fort Bragg 95437; (707) 964–0640 or (800) 382–7244; www.greywhaleinn. com.* Built as a hospital in 1915, this three-story landmark has spacious rooms and public areas, with high windows looking out to the sea or inward through the trees to town. The inn welcomes children and offers plenty of room for them to roam. You can walk right out the back door of the inn to take a long walk along the waterfront on the Old Coast Road. Rooms have sitting areas with armchairs, deep tubs, some fireplaces, and lots of books; some have extra beds. Breakfast is a big buffet in the tiny dining room or in your room. Owner Colette Bailey wins prizes at the county fair for her coffee cakes and fruit breads. $$

Pomo RV Park and Campground. *17999 Tregoning Lane, 1 mile south of Highway 20, Fort Bragg 95437; (707) 964–3373.* Secluded, spacious sites in a parklike setting. $

Hi Seas Beach Motel. *1201 North Main Street, Fort Bragg 95437; (707) 964–5929.* Simple rooms, all with ocean view, adjacent to Haul Road walking/biking route. $

For More Information

Fort Bragg/Mendocino Coast Chamber of Commerce. *332 North Main Street, Fort Bragg 95437;* *(707) 961–6300 or (800) 726–2780; www.mendocinocoast.com.*

Mendocino

So closely does the town of Mendocino and this stretch of coastline resemble New England that much of the television show *Murder She Wrote* was filmed here.

Settled by Maine loggers in the middle nineteenth century, the town remained rough-and-tumble until the 1930s. The town languished for decades, only to be reborn as first an art colony and eventually a tourist destination. Couples come here for the galleries, the restaurants, and the romantic B&Bs. Families come to explore the beaches, to fish and whale-watch, to canoe up the rivers, and to hike in the forest parks.

The streets of Mendocino are crowded with country gardens that overflow picket fences, plus small shops, art galleries in historic buildings, and a few restaurants and inns. (Most of these are B&Bs that are inappropriate for children; plenty of family-oriented lodgings are found within a few miles north and south of town.)

MENDOCINO HEADLANDS STATE PARK (all ages)

Heeser Drive and Main Street, Mendocino; (707) 937–5804.

Wrapped around three sides of town, magnificent grassy headlands float high above swaying kelp beds in the sea, which boils through rocky arches and dark grottoes. With small children firmly in hand—there are no fences or railings—walk along clifftops and through meadows that in spring are abloom with wildflowers. From December through March you are likely to see whales not far offshore. Looking back at white storefronts, Victorian homes, and the distinctive water towers of town, you can easily imagine the days when horse-drawn carriages parked in front of the Mendocino Hotel and ladies with parasols swept along the boardwalks in their long gowns. Restrooms and a picnic area are on the north end of the park, along Heeser Drive.

BIG RIVER BEACH (all ages)

Accessed by a steep stairway from the Headlands Trail or from a small parking area off Highway 1, just below Mendocino; (707) 937–5804.

Where the deep Big River Valley meets the sea, a sandy, driftwoody beach and tidepools below the town of Mendocino. Swimming is safest and warmest in the river. Harbor seals, river otters, and great blue herons may share your swimming hole.

FORD HOUSE (all ages)

735 Main Street, Mendocino 95460; (707) 937–5397. Open 11:00 A.M. to 4:00 P.M. year-round. **Free**.

A visitor center for Mendocino Headlands State Park, a museum and a good place to get a perspective on how the town is laid out. A scale model of Mendocino in the 1890s shows the dozens of tall wooden water towers that existed then. More than thirty of the towers, some double- and triple-deckers, remain in the skyline today. A Whale Celebration is held at Ford House in March, with special exhibits, whale walks, and whale-size hot dogs.

KELLEY HOUSE MUSEUM (all ages)

Across the street from Ford House on Main Street, Mendocino; (707) 927–5791.

Set back from the street next to a huge water tower and a duck pond surrounded by an old garden. Among the historical photos in the house are those of burly loggers hand-sawing ancient redwoods. Lumber for shipbuilding and for construction of the Gold Rush city of San Francisco brought easterners here in the mid-1800s. It took them six months by ship to reach this wilderness of mighty river valley and seacoast, inhabited only by Indians and fur trappers.

 OUT OF THIS WORLD

45100 Main Street, Mendocino 95460; (707) 937–3335.

A zillion science- and nature-oriented toys and kits, plus binoculars, telescopes, robots, and puzzles.

 GALLERY BOOKSHOP

Main and Kasten Streets, Mendocino 95460; (707) 937–BOOK; www. gallerybooks.com.

Kids get lost in **Bookwinkle's Children's Bookshop,** their big corner of the bookstore, while parents browse in a huge selection of books about the coast and choose bestsellers for a day at the beach. You will find wonderful cards, music, and magazines, too.

 VAN DAMME STATE PARK (all ages)

Three miles south of Mendocino, on Highway 1; (707) 937–5804.

Accessible right off the highway, a popular beach and campground, plus hiking trails. The weird and wonderful Pygmy Forest, a Registered National Landmark, is seen on a 0.3-mile easy trail through a lush fern canyon and spooky woods of dwarf cypress, rhododendron, and other bonsailike plants and trees. A fifty-year-old cypress may be only 8 inches tall and have a trunk less than 1 inch in diameter. There are developed campsites.

 CATCH A CANOE AND BICYCLES, TOO!

Stanford Inn by the Sea, P.O. Box 487, Mendocino 95460; (707) 937–0273; www.stanfordinn.com..

Paddle canoes or kayaks from the mouth of the Big River, 7 or 8 miles upstream on an estuary—the longest unchanged and undeveloped estuary in Northern California—stopping for a picnic at a tiny beach or a meadow. The river is lined with fir and redwood groves, wildflowers, and wild rhododendrons. You will undoubtedly see ospreys, wood ducks, and blue herons; probably deer; and maybe even a small black bear. Time your canoeing expedition to paddle up the river when the tide is coming in, and be on the return trip as the tide goes out. The rental company can advise you on this, and they also rent mountain bikes, outriggers and other types of boats, and auto racks.

Trail of the Whale

Hundreds of majestic California gray whales parade off the North Coast each winter on their 12,000-mile round-trip from the Arctic Circle to Baja, California. On the Mendocino coastline, they are spotted in late November through January; they head north again in March.

Here are some of the best whale-watching sites:

- Jug Handle State Reserve, 3 miles north of Mendocino

- MacKerricher State Park, just north of Fort Bragg

- Mendocino Headlands State Park, in Mendocino

- Point Cabrillo Light Station, 4 miles north of Mendocino

- Russian Gulch State Park, 2 miles north of Mendocino

- Todd's Point, just south of Noyo Bridge on Ocean View Drive

For small children and for people who get seasick easily, Noyo Harbor is the best place to take a whale-watching cruise because whales are usually sighted within fifteen or twenty minutes. The cost is about $20 per person for a two-hour trip. Among the whale-watching cruise boats in the region are Anchor Charters (707–964–5440), Noyo Belle (707–964–3104), Tally-Ho (707–964–2079), and Telstar Charters (707–964–8770). Check the Chamber of Commerce Web site at www. mendocinocoast. com for updated information on when the whales are coming and going.

 ## STANFORD INN BY THE SEA

Highway 1 and Comptche-Ukiah Road, P.O. Box 487, Mendocino 95460; (800) 331–8884; www.stanfordinn.com.

On a hillside above the river near Mendocino lies a luxurious twenty-six-room country inn surrounded by fabulous gardens. Llamas and horses graze in the meadows; in the late spring baby llamas are much in evidence. Each spacious room has a fireplace or woodburning stove, sitting area, down comforters, and a private deck from which to watch the sun set over the sea. Wine and a bountiful buffet breakfast are included. There is spa, a sauna, and an Olympic size swimming pool enclosed in a greenhouse crowded with tropical plants. **Big River Nurseries** are also located on the grounds of the inn, and it's fun to browse the rows of organic plants, veggies, and herbs; you can buy herbal wreaths, sprays and braids, and herbs and spices and have them shipped home. There is also a terrific vegetarian restaurant on-site. $$$–$$$$

RUSSIAN GULCH STATE PARK (all ages)

Two miles north of Mendocino, on Highway 1; (707) 937–5804.

Sea caves, a waterfall, and a beach popular for rock fishing, scuba diving, and swimming in the chilly waters. From the headlands in the park, you can see the Devil's Punch Bowl, a 200-foot-long tunnel with a blowhole. Inland the park includes 3 miles of Russian Gulch Creek Canyon, with paved and unpaved trails in dense forest and stream canyons. A small campground here is quite lovely, and a special equestrian campground offers riding trails into Jackson State Forest.

JUG HANDLE STATE RESERVE (all ages)

Three miles north of Mendocino, on Highway 1; (707) 937–5804.

A 700-acre oceanside park notable for an "ecological staircase" marine terrace rising from sea level to 500 feet. Each terrace is 100,000 years older than the one below, affording a unique opportunity to see geologic evolution. The plants and trees change from terrace to terrace too, from wildflowers and grasses to wind-strafed spruce, second-growth redwoods, and pygmy forests of cypress and pine.

POINT ARENA PIER (all ages)

Highway 1 between Gualala and Elk, go west on Port Road.

A nice stop on the way up the coast, the fishing pier juts 330 feet out into the sea from the edge of a cove, where fishing, crabbing and whale watching are the main activities. In the rocks at the base of the cliffs, you can explore tidepools. A cliff-top trail leads to Schooner Gulch State Beach.

The original wooden fishing pier at Point Arena was dramatically smashed to pieces in a storm in 1983, along with all of the buildings in the cove. In a cafe on the pier—the **Galley at Point Arena**—are photos of the rip roarin' storm. The cafe serves chowder, snapper sandwiches, homemade pies, and crab in season. Adjacent to the pier are a few shops and other cafes.

POINT ARENA LIGHTHOUSE (all ages)

Lighthouse Road off Highway 1, 2 miles north of Point Arena: (707) 882–2777.

Erected in 1870, then reerected after the 1906 San Francisco earthquake, the 115-foot lighthouse is one of the best locations for gray whale watching. Scramble around in the lighthouse and visit the museum of maritime artifacts below; tours are conducted from 10 A.M. to 3:30 P.M. daily. Black oystercatchers and cormorants wheel over the offshore rocks, and sea lions and harbor seals are often seen in the waters just south of the point. The three, small **Point Arena Coast Guard Houses** here are available to rent. Neat and clean, with kitchens and fireplaces, they're perfect for a family (707-882-2777).

Where to Eat

Cafe Beaujolais. *961 Ukiah Street, Mendocino 95460; (707) 937–5614.* Nationally known, country-chic in a comfortable Victorian house surrounded by sumptuous flower and vegetable gardens. California cuisine extraordinaire for gastronomically adventuresome kids and parents. Reserve days or even weeks ahead; dinner only. $$

Bay View Cafe. *45040 Main Street, Mendocino 95460; (707) 937–4197.* Breakfast, lunch, and dinner, indoors or on the deck with a zowie sea view, upstairs in a water tower. Good, simple fare, such as burgers, salads, pasta, and steak. $

Mendo Burgers. *Lansing Street, Mendocino 95460; (707) 937–1111.* Beef, turkey, chicken, fish, and veggie burgers; cool 1950s decor; indoors or out. $

Tote Fete. *10450 Lansing, Mendocino 95460; (707) 937–3383.* California cuisine to go: apricot chicken salad, homemade meatloaf, calzone, focaccia sandwiches, dynamite desserts. $$

Mousse Cafe. *Corner of Kasten and Ukiah Streets, Mendocino 95460; (707) 937–4323.* In a cottage garden, a sophisticated cafe menu with things that children like to eat. People sit here all afternoon, having tea and munching chunks of Blackout Cake and bread pudding. Lunch and dinner daily; Sunday brunch. $$

The Ravens. *At the Stanford Inn, Comptche–Ukiah Road at Highway 1, just south of Mendocino 95460; (707) 937–5615.* The only fine restaurant on the Mendocino coast serving totally vegetarian food: soups, pizza, pasta, grilled veggies. $$

Where to Stay

Little River Inn. *7751 Highway 1, Little River 95456; (707) 937–5942.* A white wedding cake of a circa 1850 house anchors a beautiful country resort overlooking the sea, with an excellent restaurant, a fun 9-hole golf course, and tennis. Some of the spacious and comfortable rooms, each with ocean view and a deck, have two queens or doubles. You can walk from here to the beach and the Pygmy Forest at Van Damme State Park; Mendocino is ten

minutes away. The golf course is short, relatively easy, and inexpensive—perfect for beginners. $$$

Seafoam Lodge. *6751 North Highway 1, Little River, ten minutes south of Mendocino 95456; (707) 937–1827 or (800) 606–1827; www.seafoam.com.* Families and pets are welcome at this inn, located on a private cove. Ocean-view units, continental breakfast in your room, some kitchens, decks, refrigerators. $$

Sea Rock Bed and Breakfast Inn.
*11101 Lansing Street, 0.5 mile south of
Mendocino 95460; (707) 937–0926;
www.searock.com.* One- and two-bedroom garden cottages with ocean
views, Franklin stoves, feather beds,
hearty continental breakfast served in
an ocean-view dining room, some
kitchens. Children are welcome with
supervision. No pets. $$

Mendocino Coast Reservations.
*P.O. Box 1143, Mendocino 95460; (800)
262–7801; www.mcmca.com.* Vacation

home rentals, most with fireplaces,
ocean views, spas. $–$$$

Pacific Resorts Realty. *7675 Coast
Highway, Mendocino 95460; (800)
358–9879; www.Pacific-Resorts.com.* Vacation home rentals, most with ocean
views, and fireplaces. $–$$$$

North Coast Trailer Rentals. *(619)
648–7509.* Self-contained trailer
rentals, sleeping four to six, parked in
ocean-view campsites in the state
parks. $–$$

For More Information

**Fort Bragg/Mendocino Coast
Chamber of Commerce.** *332 North
Main Street, Fort Bragg 95437; (707)
961–6300 or (800) 726–2780; www.
mendocinocoast.com.*

Mendocino Area State Parks. *(707)
937–5804; www.mcn.org/1/mendoparks/
mendo.* Information about camping,
day use, and interpretive programs.
For campsite reservations, call (800)
444–PARK.

Bodega Bay

The warmest and some of the most beautiful Northern California beaches are
found near the fishing village of Bodega Bay. The climate is mild, even in winter. Dense fog occurs only about twenty days annually.

Weathered clapboard houses, a handful of seafood restaurants, and a few
shops and motels are scattered around the edges of a large, protected harbor
where pleasure boats from all over the world come to anchor away from the
open sea. Although the town was founded in the 1870s, most of the buildings
of architectural interest are circa 1910 California Craftsman–style bungalows.

Clamming in the tidal mudflats and windsurfing in the harbor waters are
two popular activities. The combination of freshwater wetlands and salt
marshes attracts a great variety of shorebirds and waterfowl, plus pond turtles,
harbor seals, and sea lions.

Almost a dozen Sonoma Coast beaches run from Bodega Bay 16 miles
north to Jenner, and each has its own treasures to discover. This stretch of

coastline is dramatic with sea stacks, sheer cliffs, rugged, rocky coves, and vast, wildflowery meadows—a spectacular drive. In April at Westside Park on the edge of the bay, the **Bodega Bay Fishermen's Festival** attracts crowds for the blessing of the fishing fleet, a decorated boat parade, a big outdoor fair with food and entertainment, a lamb and oyster barbecue, and arts and crafts.

BODEGA HEAD (all ages)

On the west side of the harbor entrance; parking at the end of Westside Road; (707) 875–3422.

A vast promontory overlooking the open sea. Rangers and docent volunteers are on hand during whale watching months to lead walks on the 1.4-mile bluff trail and answer questions. This is a bracing and beautiful walk at any time of the year, a trek accompanied by pelicans, oystercatchers, and sometimes even deer.

CANDY AND KITES

1425 Highway 1, Bodega Bay 94923; (707) 875–3777. Kite festivals in Bodega Bay will take place in April and July.

A must stop before you hit the sand, featuring a huge and colorful variety of kites and games for the beach.

BODEGA BAY GIFTS

Ocean Corner, 2001 Highway 1, Bodega Bay 94923; (707) 875–2449.

A big store, stuffed with seashells, games, T-shirts, and stuff.

UC DAVIS MARINE LABORATORY (all ages)

2099 Westside Road, Bodega Bay 94923; (707) 875–2211. **Free** *drop-in tours on Friday afternoons. Call ahead to tour other days.*

Half a mile of coastline and surrounding marine habitat is protected and studied by the university. Exhibits and working research projects such as aqua-farming are fascinating, and the student guides are great with kids.

BODEGA BAY SURF SHACK

Pelican Plaza, Bodega Bay 94923; (707) 875–3944, www.bodegabaysurf.com.
Headquarters for rentals, maps, and advice on biking, beachcombing, kayaking, surfing, and windsurfing. Lessons and guided tours are available; beachwear is for sale. Visit the Web site for fascinating satellite reports, maps, and forecasts about waves and weather.

*B*odega Bay Beaches

- **Doran Beach Regional Park.** *South end of the bay off Highway 1 on Doran Park Road.* A popular day-use beach for swimming, surfing, kite flying, clamming, and kayaking, with breezy RV and tent camp sites. Get information and maps for county parks at the office here. The Bodega Bay Sandcastle Building Festival is held at Doran Beach in September.

- **Bodega Dunes.** *On the north end of town off Westside Road, accessed on Bay Flat Road.* More than 900 acres of huge sand dunes, some as high as 150 feet. There is a 5-mile riding and hiking loop through the dunes, and a hiking-only trail to Bodega Head. In a spectacular show of color, thousands of monarch butterflies flock to a grove of cypress and eucalyptus trees adjacent to the dunes every October through February. Restrooms, RV, and tent camp sites.

- **Salmon Creek Beach.** Off *Highway 1, 2 miles north of Bodega Bay.* Two miles of wide, sandy beach edged with grassy dunes. The creek and lagoon are inhabited by throngs of seabirds. Restrooms. Ranger headquarters is located here (707–875–3540).

- **Portuguese Beach.** *Between Salmon Creek and Wright's Beach on Highway 1.* Best beach for rock fishing and surf fishing.

- **Wright's Beach.** *Between Portuguese Beach and Shell Beach on Highway 1.* With a large parking area at beach level, the easiest access for all ages and abilities.

- **Shell Beach.** *Between Wright's Beach and Goat Rock, on Highway 1.* A small, pretty beach with great tidepools; the best of the Sonoma beaches for shelling. Restrooms.

- **Goat Rock.** *Two miles south of Jenner on Highway 1; (707) 875–3483.* Although a dangerous place to swim, this beach is popular for beachcombing, shore fishing, and freshwater fishing at the mouth of the Russian River. Seals like it, too; a large herd is often seen sunbathing and surfing where the river joins the sea. In spring, they give birth to their pups here. This is protected territory for the seals, and visitors are advised to stay at a safe distance. More than 200 species of seabirds and shorebirds can be seen—great blue herons, white and brown pelicans, gulls, ospreys, even peregrine falcons.

POMO/MIWOK TRAIL

Across Highway 1 from Shell Beach; (707) 875–3540.

Up and over the hills to a small redwood forest, a moderately strenuous walk that takes about an hour and passes through meadows, over creeks, and under shade trees, with coastal views all the way. At the top hikers are rewarded with a redwood grove and creek, a perfect picnic spot. The path goes on from here to the Russian River and the Pomo/Miwok Campground.

VISTA TRAIL

Located 4.8 miles north of Jenner, off Highway 1; (707) 875–3483.

A wheelchair-accessible, 1-mile loop in a meadow on a bluff, offering wide ocean views and picnic tables.

CHANSLOR GUEST RANCH

2660 Highway 1, on the north end of Bodega Bay; (707) 875–2721.

Guided horseback rides on the beaches, along the bluffs, and through wetlands, plus haywagon and barbecue rides. Special rides for kids ages 4 and up on gentle horses, ponies, or donkeys.

SALT POINT STATE PARK

Located 15 miles north of Jenner, on both sides of Highway 1; (707) 847–3221 or (707) 865–2391.

Six thousand acres and 7 miles of coastline, with long, sandy beaches, rich tidepools, rugged cliffs, sunny meadows, and hiking and biking trails. The dense forestlands of Salt Point are inhabited by gnarly pygmy pines and cypress, their ghostly gray, mossy trunks tickled by maidenhair ferns. For tidepooling take the Gerstle Cove Campground turnoff and follow the road to Gerstle Cove parking. No collecting is allowed.

FORT ROSS STATE HISTORICAL PARK

19005 Highway 1, 11 miles north of Jenner; (707) 847–3286.

The Russians arrived here in 1812 to harvest otter and seal pelts and to grow produce for their northern outposts. Their small settlement of hand hewn log barracks, blockhouses, and homes, together with a jewel of a Russian Orthodox church, was protected with high bastions and a bristling line of cannons, just in case the Spanish decided to pay a call. Several of the buildings and the church remain in a magical greensward above the sea. Inside the restored buildings are perfectly preserved rifles, pistols, tools, furniture, and old photos. At the excellent visitor center are exhibits, films, and guidebooks. A delightful protected beach hides below the fort. Twenty coastal canyon campsites are open March through November; picnic areas, hiking trails, restrooms.

SEA RANCH LODGE

60 Sea Walk Drive, off Highway 1, 20 miles north of Jenner in Sea Ranch; (707) 785–2371 or (800) 732–7662; www.searanchlodge.com.

Headquarters for a unique residential development characterized by untouched open space and architectural restraint. Widely scattered, naturally weathered wood houses on the headlands and hillsides are barely visible. Many of the homes are available for vacation rental (Rams Head Realty, 800-785-3455).

From the lodge you can access several beaches (Shell Beach, Pebble Beach, and Black Point Beach are the best) and walk easy paths on the bluffs, as well as on quiet, paved country roads on the highway side of Sea Ranch. Wild azaleas, rhododendrons, and iris bloom in the spring. Wild mushrooms are colorful most of the winter and spring (don't touch).

A smashingly beautiful 18-hole, links-style golf course, laid out on the coastal bluffs and in the meadows and forestlands above the highway, makes this a prime weekend getaway destination.

The Bell Memorial

The children's bell tower in Bodega Bay is a magical place, a memorial for a local young boy, Nicholas Green, who was killed by highway robbers while vacationing in Italy with his family. His parents donated his organs to seven Italians waiting for transplants; their names are shown along with Nicholas'. *The Nicholas Effect,* a book written by his father, recounts the impact Nicholas had on people's lives after his tragic death. People from all over Italy continue to express their love and gratitude to the boy's family for the lifesaving organ donations. And, there has been a sharp increase in organ donor rates in Italy, along with the establishment of a foundation to further the cause of organ donation around the world. On the Bell Memorial are 140 bells, almost all sent by Italians—school bells, church bells, ships' bells, mining bells, and cow bells all chime when the wind blows. This is a lovely setting near cypress trees and green hills, with a glimpse of the ocean. The bells are located behind the Bodega Bay Grill, through the RV park. For more information contact the Nicholas Green Foundation, P.O. Box 937, Bodega Bay 94923; (707) 875-2263; www.nicholaseffect.com.

From the bluffs and the Sea Ranch restaurant, you can see whales in winter. The food is good—sandwiches, salads, homemade soups, fresh fish—at lunch and dinner. The lounge bar has a big fireplace. All with ocean views, rustic guest rooms seem to float in wildflowery meadows. $$

Where to Eat

Breakers Cafe. *1400 Highway 1, across from the kite shop on the north end of Bodega Bay, in the Pelican Plaza 94923;* (707) 875–2513. Great sea views from a sunny deck, killer breakfasts, fresh seafood and pasta, homemade pies. Breakfast, lunch, and dinner. $-$$

Sandpiper Dockside Cafe. *1410 Bay Flat Road, Bodega Bay 94923;* (707) 875–2278. Best kept secret, a little place hidden below the main road, featuring homemade everything, including crab cioppino. $-$$

Dinucci's. *Downtown Valley Ford on Highway 1, near Bodega Bay 94923;* (707) 876–3260. For decades a destination in itself. Huge home-style Italian dinners, seafood and steaks, a friendly longbar. $-$$

Negri's Italian Dinners. *3700 Bohemian Highway, Occidental 95465;* (707) 823–5301. Famous for decades for supercolossal, multicourse, family-style Italian dinners; very popular on Sunday afternoons and holidays. Choices include homemade ravioli, fried chicken, veal, antipasti, mine-strone, salads, and more—much more. Occidental makes a nice stop on the way to or from Bodega. Take the Bohemian Highway through Freestone for about twenty minutes on a winding mountain road to this tiny village and enjoy its restaurants, galleries, and shops. $-$$

Bodega Bay Grill. *2001 Highway 1, Bodega Bay 94923;* (707) 875–9190. In a small, clean cafe on the north edge of the bay, good fresh fish and chowder, and Mexican food. $

The Tides Wharf and Restaurant. *835 Highway 1, Bodega Bay 94923;* (707) 875–3652. On the wharf, with views of the bay and the boat action; a sunny deck for snacks and drinks, a tiny cafe, a souvenir shop, a gourmet food emporium and oyster bar, and a large, attractive restaurant serving great seasonal fresh seafood, from cracked Dungeness crab to cioppino, moist and crisp Petrale sole, a huge variety of fish, and seafood salads. Every table has a view, and the seals have view of you. $-$$

Where to Stay

Bodega Bay Lodge. *103 Coast Highway 1, on the south side of Bodega Bay 94923;* (707) 875–3525 or (800) 368–2468; www.woodsidehotels.com. Perched above the bay and bird-filled marshes, all rooms and luxury suites with sea views, terraces or decks, cozy comforters, Jacuzzi tubs, robes; some fireplaces. In the lobby are a giant stone fireplace and two 500-gallon aquariums filled with tropical fish. Fresh, contemporary decor, swimming pool, spa, sauna, fitness center, complimentary bikes, golf packages. $$-$$$

Inn at the Tides. *800 Highway 1, Bodega Bay 94923; (800) 541–7788; www.innatthetides.com.* On a grassy, landscaped hillside overlooking the town, a large complex of spacious, two-story units with fireplaces, sitting areas, a protected indoor/outdoor pool, and a spa. A top-notch restaurant serves California cuisine. $$$

Bodega Coast Inn. *521 Highway 1, Bodega Bay 94923; (707) 875–2217.* Each motel room has an ocean view, balcony, and refrigerator; some have fireplaces and spas; one is a two-bedroom with kitchenette. $$

Vacation Homes. *(707) 875–4000.* From cabins to spacious vacation home rentals in the Bodega Bay area. $-$$$

Pomo/Miwok Campground. *Where the river meets the sea at Bridgehaven, ten minutes off Highway 1; (800) 444–7275.* Forty walk-in tent sites in a dense redwood forest at the end of a paved road (a beautiful road for biking and walking). A few sites are near the parking lot; it's a five- to fifteen-minute walk to the others. If you arrive with no reservation, check the bulletin board to find available sites. Fire rings, picnic tables, and portable potties. $

Fort Ross Lodge. *20705 Coast Highway 1, Jenner 95450; (707) 847–3333.* Comfortable ocean-view rooms and suites, some with fireplaces and spas. Barbecues on your private patio; a convenience store across the road. $-$$

For More Information

Bodega Bay Chamber of Commerce and Sonoma Coast Visitors Center. *850 Highway 1, Bodega Bay 94923; (707) 875–3422; www.bodegabay.com.*

Department of Parks and Recreation, Russian River District. *P.O. Box 123, Duncans Mills 95430; (707) 865–2391.* Information on private campgrounds.

Wine Country

Due north across the Golden Gate, rugged mountain ranges and rich agricultural valleys shelter lakes, rivers, and a scattering of small, historic towns. Country pleasures are what families seek in Sonoma, Lake, and Napa Counties—everything from boating and fishing to biking and hiking, camping, and vestiges of California's early days.

The 1700s come alive in the small mission town of Sonoma, which contains the largest remaining Spanish plaza in the state. A few minutes away, in the Valley of the Moon, is a state park with riding trails and a delightfully spooky ruin in a redwood forest.

Kids like watching hot air balloons and glider planes in the Napa Valley, and parents are surprised to find that there's a lot to do and see besides wineries. The waters of Lake Berryessa attract vactioners for summer waterskiing and swimming and for year-round trout and bass fishing.

Primary destinations are the oceanarium and wildlife theme park, Six Flags Marine World, and Safari West near Calistoga, a preserve for African plains animals.

Flowing from the valleys to the sea in western Sonoma County, the Russian River offers fishing holes and campgrounds, redwood groves and sandy beaches.

Families that love to fish and water-ski head north to Clear Lake. The smooth green flanks of 4,200-foot Mount Konocti, a dormant volcano, loom dramatically above the placid blue waters, which hold more fish per acre than any other lake in the country.

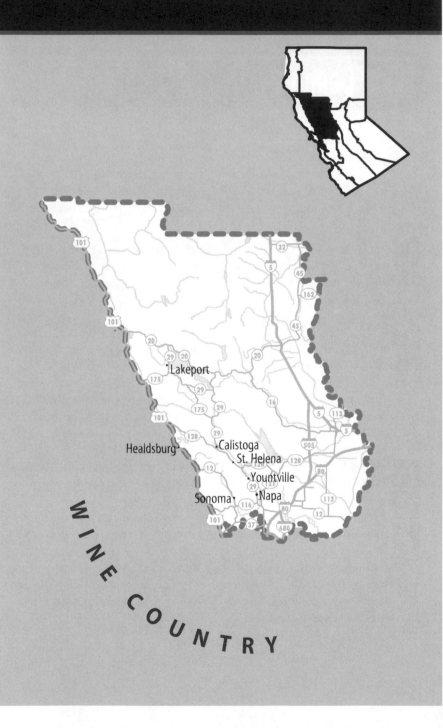

WINE COUNTRY

Lakeport

The largest town on the shores of Clear Lake, Lakeport features a few historic buildings and an old-fashioned band shell and playground in a grassy lakefront park. Several smaller towns and small resorts are scattered around the lake. When school's out, families begin arriving with their boats, camping gear, fishing rods, and water sports equipment. The largest natural lake in the state and rated the number one bass lake in the western United States, Clear Lake is ringed with family-oriented resorts, marinas, and campgrounds.

Pomo Indian tribal heritage is prominent throughout the county at the museum, at Anderson Marsh State Park, in the crafts and art found in retail shops, and at annual Native American events.

Winters are mild here, a good time for fishing expeditions, rock hounding, and birdwatching. You are likely to see bald eagles, and you can't miss the tremendous number of waterfowl and other migrating birds from Alaska and Canada that come to spend the season.

LAKE COUNTY MUSEUM (all ages)

255 North Main, Lakeport 95453; (707) 263–4555.

 In a beautiful 1877 building that served as a school for more than fifty years, a big collection of stone tools, arrowheads, pioneer costumes and exhibits, and antique firearms, as well as a shop selling jewelry made by local Native Americans. The highlights of the collection are the superb Pomo Indian baskets.

CLEAR LAKE STATE PARK (all ages)

5300 Soda Bay Road, Kelseyville 95451; (707) 279–4293; (campground reservations: 800–444–7275).

 Here you can camp beside the lake, fish, swim, and birdwatch. Interpretive displays on local history and the natural environment and wildlife are at the visitor center. Behind the center look for great blue herons on the banks of Kelsey Creek; the large nests in the treetops are heron rookeries. A 700-gallon aquarium shows Clear Lake fish and aquatic life. On Cole Creek are shady picnic sites, barbecues, and a swimming beach with lifeguards.

ANDERSON MARSH STATE HISTORIC PARK (all ages)

Highway 53, between the towns of Lower Lake and Clearlake; (707) 994–0688.

Herons, pelicans, ducks, grebes, coots, cormorants, bald eagles, and other species of water-fowl are seen regularly here. The sight of a bald eagle fishing for its din-ner is a moment to remember. Birdwatching is best in early spring and early in the morning when the birds are feed-ing. Numerous ancient Native American sites date from 8000 B.C., when the shores and swamps surrounding Clearlake were almost exactly as they are today. In the historic Anderson Ranch House are a small museum and visitor cen-ter. To get very close to the wetlands wildlife, hike through the Redbud Audubon Society's McVicar Preserve within the state park, or rent a boat or canoe at Garner's Resort (707-994-6267) or Shaw's Shady Acres (707-994-2236), nearby.

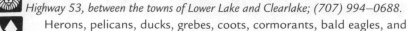

Rock Hounding Hunting for "Lake County diamonds" and other minerals is popular around Clearlake, particularly in winter, when rains expose the stones. Go first to one of several rock shops in the area to see the "diamonds" on display and set in jewelry. Experts at the shops will teach you how to recognize the stones (not true diamonds) in the field and give you maps to good hunting grounds. Top rock-hounding spots are on Perini Road near Lower Lake, in a streambed at Middle Creek Camp-ground north of Upper Lake, and at Highland Springs Reservoir.

- **Crystal Phoenix Rock Shops.** *14590 Lakeshore Drive, Clearlake; (707) 995–9219.*

- **Manzanita Hill Rock Shop.** *7325 Pyle Road, Nice; (707) 274–4489.*

KONOCTI HARBOR RESORT AND SPA (all ages)

8727 Soda Bay Road, Kelseyville 95451; (800) 862–4930; www.konoctiharbor.com.

In the shadow of Mount Konocti, this sprawling lakeside resort and marina has two large swimming pools with lifeguards, lighted tennis courts, minigolf, playgrounds, a video games arcade, volleyball, and a lot more. The staffed Kids' Club provides child care and activities all summer and during concert evenings. If your family wants to stay put and enjoy the lake, this is the place. Older children particularly enjoy it, as there are kids to meet, beach volleyball, pool tables, and video games, plus Jet Skis, pedal boats, kayaks, and fishing poles to rent. Also here is a complete health spa, with exercise classes, a lap pool, and body and beauty treatments. Live, top-name entertainment occurs year-round in 1,000- and 5,000-seat venues—mostly country western, with some rock stars. The facility offers a wide variety of accommodations, including motel rooms, beach cottages, condo units, and family rate packages. The atmosphere is family-oriented and casual. Restaurants serve hearty American fare. $$

ON THE WATERFRONT
60 Third Street, Lakeport 95453; (707) 263–6789.

Parasailing, plus rentals for Jet Skis, pedal boats, ski boats, and fishing and "patio boats"—an easy-to-handle sort of a barge, just the thing for families. Purchase beachwear and water-ski accessories here too.

OUTRAGEOUS WATERS (ages 4 and up)
Highway 53 at Highway/Dam Road, Clearlake; (707) 995–1402; www. outrageouswaters.com.

Four scary water slides are thrilling and cooling on a summer's day. Little kids will like the "Lazy River" and a huge kid's pool with waterfalls. A mini–Grand Prix race track, batting cages, and, of course, video games are available.

PATHWAYS HIKING AND BIKING TOURS
Maps and information at Visitor Center, 875 Lakeport Boulevard, Clearlake; 95422; (707) 263–9644.

The rolling countryside around the town of Clearlake is as green as Ireland in spring and winter, wildflower-y, dry, and warm in the summer and fall. Eleven routes for biking and walking are described in detail and mapped, from strenuous to easy, in a booklet available at the Visitor Center or by mail.

REAL GOODS
13201 Highway 101, Hopland 95449, (707) 744–2100; www.realgoods.com.

A destination in itself, Real Goods is an unusual retail showplace of renewable energy products—solar, recycled, biodegradable, nontoxic, energy-efficient items for sustainable living, including toys, clothing, and books. Even the building itself demonstrates "green" concepts; the north and east walls of the main building were constructed of straw bales. Just exploring the surrounding landscaping is an educational experience.

VICHY HOT SPRINGS

2605 Vichy Springs Road, Ukiah 95418; (707) 462–9515; www.vichysprings.com.

Since 1854, a family-oriented country resort famous for carbonated water springs. From 25,000 feet below the surface of the earth, the magical waters rush forth, sixty-five gallons a minute, filling a large swimming pool and several tubs. Simple, spacious rooms have verandas overlooking sweeping lawns, meadows, and gardens. You can hike on 700 acres of countryside. $–$$

GRACE HUDSON SUN HOUSE (all ages)

431 South Main Street, Ukiah 95418; (707) 462–3370.

An impressive complex housing American Indian baskets, artifacts, and paintings, this is a light, colorful place that children enjoy. The late Grace Hudson painted the faces and the domestic life of native Pomo Indians, while her ethnologist husband assembled the extraordinary collection, one of the most important in the Northern Hemisphere. Open to inspection, their home is a wonderful redwood Craftsman-style bungalow. A tree-shaded park surrounds the museum buildings. My granddaughters have found Native American–oriented toys, books, and games in the gift shop.

Where to Eat

Park Place. *50 Third Street, Lakeport 95453; (707) 263–0444.* In a comfy booth, or on the deck with lake views, everyone goes for the homemade pasta, Nancy's amazing vegetable soup, fresh fish, and steak. Veggies come from a local patch, and the blackberries in the sorbet are picked in the owner's backyard. You can motor here in your boat, and take a snooze in the park across the street. Open all day for breakfast, lunch, and dinner. $

Main Street Cafe. *14084 Lakeshore Drive, Clearlake 95422; (707) 995– 6450.* Indoors or outdoors, the locals' favorite for down-home cooking. Children like the burgers and sandwiches. $

Where to Stay

El Grande Inn. *15135 Lakeshore Drive, Clearlake 95422; (707) 994–2000.* On the lake, forty-five very nice rooms and suites, plus a pool, sauna, garden courtyard, and restaurant. $

B. J. Wall's Lakeside RV and Campground. *2570 Lakeshore Boulevard, Nice 95464; (707) 274–3315.* On Clear Lake, full hookups, campsites, shade trees, private beach, boat dock, showers, laundry. Walk to nearby restaurant and boat rentals. $

Bellhaven Resort. *3415 White Oak Way, Kelseyville 95451; (707) 279–4329; www.bellhaven.com.* On Clear Lake's Soda Bay, a nice beach, a fishing and swimming pier, and cabins with kitchens and private dock. $

Featherbed Railroad Company. *2870 Lakeshore Boulevard, Nice 95464; (707) 274–8378.* Irresistible, nine-car trains with cabooses are a sweet surprise overlooking the lake. The Rosebud Caboose has bunkbeds for two kids, and there is a small swimming pool. A hearty breakfast is served in the ranch house or on the front porch. $–$$

Harbin Hot Springs. *18424 Harbin Springs Road, Middletown 95461; (707) 987–2377.* Hot, warm, and cold mineral pools; sundecks; sauna and gym. Some 1,160 acres of nature trails. Camping, restaurant, store. $

For More Information

Lake County Visitor's Center. *875 Lakeport Boulevard, Lakeport 95453; (707) 525–3743; www.lakecounty.com.*

California State Park Campground Reservations. *(800) 444–7275.*

Calistoga

More than a century ago, people came to this little tree-shaded Victorian spa town in horse-drawn carriages to "take the waters." Steam rises from 200-degree mineral springs at a dozen or so health resorts—this is the place for rest and rejuvenation, for massages and mud baths. Children are not likely to go for a massage, or for wine tasting at the many wineries in the area. They will love the town's museum, the Calistoga Gliderport, a unique wildlife preserve, and biking down Mount St. Helena. Except for the busy few blocks of the main street, Lincoln Avenue, this is the quiet side of Napa Valley, making biking and hiking particularly serene. This is a walking town, a compact grid of streets that look suspended in time. Stroll up and down the streets perpendicular to Lincoln, on the west side, and look for the sweet gazebo and playground in creekside Pioneer Park on Cedar Street.

SHARPSTEEN MUSEUM (all ages)

1311 Washington Street, Calistoga 94515; (707) 942–5911. Admission is Free.

Kids love the unstuffy atmosphere of this place, which was built and donated by a thirty-year veteran of the Disney studios. His Disney memorabilia is on display, along with an elaborate diorama re-creating the 1800s resort town, plus a big collection of old photos and a stagecoach.

CALISTOGA GLIDERPORT

East end of Lincoln Avenue, Calistoga; (707) 942–5000. Glider rides are about $150 for two people, maximum combined weight 340 pounds, with a pilot.

Sit in the lawn chairs provided and watch gliders being lifted up by small plane and cut loose for rides on the upcurrents of air over the valley. For the thrill of a lifetime, try gliding! If you're hungry at the Calistoga Gliderport, you're already at **Big Daddy's Burgers;** picnic tables are on-site.

PALISADES MARKET

Next to the Calistoga Gliderport, 1506 Lincoln Avenue, Calistoga 94515; (707) 942–9549.

The best gourmet market and deli in town with miraculous sandwiches and salads, wonderful fresh produce, and locally made foodstuffs.

INDIAN SPRINGS HOT SPRINGS SPA AND RESORT

1712 Lincoln Avenue, Calistoga 94515; (707) 942–4913.

Founded in 1865, Indian Springs is one of the oldest spa resorts in town, and it still has an old-fashioned air about it. Filled with mineral water from three natural geysers, the Olympic-size pool is heated to 92 degrees in summer and 101 degrees in winter. Horseshoes and a clay (!) tennis court, bicycles and bike surreys, croquet, hammocks, and Weber grills are available here. From a studio cottage to a large house, accommodations are simple and comfortable, including fireplaces, robes, and air-conditioning. $$

CHÂTEAU ST. SHIRTS (all ages)

1355 Lincoln Avenue, Calistoga 94515; (707) 942–5029.

My favorite place to buy T-shirts, sweatshirts, shorts, and cover-ups. Top-quality clothing with a wide variety of Wine Country logos, in addition to darling children's cotton playclothes.

OLD FAITHFUL GEYSER (all ages)

A mile north of Calistoga, on Tubbs Lane; (707) 942–6463.

One of only three regularly erupting geysers in the world. Every forty minutes or so, a column of 350-degree water and steam roars more than 60 feet into the air. That's it.

 ## SAFARI WEST (all ages)

3115 Porter Creek Road, Santa Rosa 95404, ten minutes east of Calistoga; (707) 579–2551. Advance reservations required; call for reservations and schedule. Tickets are $48 for adults and $24 for kids 3 to 16; kids 2 and under Free.

Giraffes in Wine Country? Yes, at the far northern end of the valley, on open grasslands and rolling hills, sits a wildlife preserve with more than 400 exotic animals and birds, as well as African plains animals, including zebras, elands, giraffes, impalas, Watusi cattle, and rare endangered antelopes. Private half-day, narrated tours are conducted in safari vehicles. The beauty and number of the animals were surprising to me, and there is much to see around the base camp when the safari tour is over. It's hot and dry here in summer and early fall, so be prepared with hats and sunscreen. I don't recommend bringing toddlers along unless you know they can handle a two-hour, sometimes bumpy ride. The last time we went to Safari West, we saw a newborn zebra, and we loved it when the herd of Watusi cattle came pounding down the road and crowded up against the truck. What shoulders!

 ## ROBERT LOUIS STEVENSON STATE PARK (all ages)

Seven miles north of Calistoga, on Highway 29; (707) 942–4575.

 On the wooded slopes of Mount St. Helena, take forest trails for easy walks, or embark on the steep, 5-mile scramble to the 4,343-foot summit. Mountain bikers use the fire road, which starts about 0.25 mile north of the parking lot. Spyglass Hill in Robert Louis Stevenson's *Treasure Island* is based on the landscape of Mount St. Helena; see a museum devoted to Stevenson's life and works at the library in St. Helena (707-963-3757). No dogs are allowed in the park, and there is no water.

Giuseppe's Truck
865 Silverado Trail North, near Calistoga; (707) 942–6295. At the turn of the century, health addicts drove their horse-drawn carriages from San Francisco all the way to Calistoga to drink the waters. Bubbling up out of the ground with intense carbonation and more than sixty-five minerals essential for good health, Calistoga water has been bottled since the early 1900s and is now one of the premier bottled waters in the world.

To commemorate the founding of the Calistoga Mineral Water company, and to have some fun, a larger-than-life sculpture was erected on the roadside at the mineral water facility—and it makes a great photo. Six tons, 14 feet tall, and 35 feet long, it's a huge sculpture of the 1926 truck that founder Giuseppe Musante and his dog Frankie drove over the narrow, winding dirt roads to the California State Fair in Sacramento, where his water won gold medals year after year.

PETRIFIED FOREST (all ages)
4100 Petrified Forest Road, 5 miles west of Calistoga; (707) 942–6667; www. petrifiedforest.com. Admission is $4.00 for adults and $2.00 for children 4 to 11, Free *for younger kids.*

For an unusual one-hour side trip, walk on an easy, 0.25-mile path through a redwood forest turned to stone six million years ago by a volcanic eruption, a site you're not likely to see elsewhere. One-hundred-foot tree trunks are swirled in opalescent purple and pink. The gift shop sells colorful polished stones, semiprecious gems, and fossils. Wheelchair access is marginal but doable; pets are okay.

HURD BEESWAX CANDLE FACTORY (all ages)
Two minutes north of the Culinary Institute of America on Highway 29 at the FREEMARK ABBEY *sign in St. Helena; (707) 963–7211.*

Watch fanciful and weird candles of every description being handmade. The large shop flickers with hundreds of unusual candles, including storybook characters, gnomes, and seasonal figures.

Where to Eat

Restaurants in Napa Valley are some of the best in the world, no doubt about it. The advantage to families is that every restaurant in the valley, without exception, is casual in atmosphere. I doubt that you will ever see a coat and tie (except perhaps at the Silverado Country Club). Children are welcome everywhere. Prices tend to be high. To save money, pick up breakfast and lunch provisions at some of the fabulous bakeries and delis throughout the valley, and chow down by your motel pool or in one of the many parks.

Cafe Pacifico. *1237 Lincoln Avenue, Calistoga 94515; (707) 942–4400.* A Mexican motif is the backdrop for incredible breakfasts, lunches, and dinners. Try the blue-corn buttermilk pancakes, fresh enchiladas, and chiles rellenos. $

All Season's Cafe. *1400 Lincoln Avenue, Calistoga 94515; (707) 942–9111.* A classically trained chef invents American versions of Mediterranean foods with locally grown and produced ingredients. Home-smoked salmon and

chicken, grilled Petaluma duck breast, pizzettas, pasta, fresh fish, and killer pies are featured. Salads, such as warm spinach with smoked chicken and lemon dressing, are tops here. The greens come from fields just a few blocks away. $$

Calistoga Inn. *1250 Lincoln Avenue, Calistoga 94515; (707) 942–4101.* In a charming, circa 1880 building with a splendid outdoor dining terrace on the Napa River, the inn serves inventive sandwiches, meal-size salads, lots of appetizers to share, and grilled meats, as well as microbrews from the on-site brewery. $

Where to Stay

Scott Courtyard. *1443 Second Street (2 blocks from downtown), Calistoga 94515; (707) 942–0948.* Roomy, circa 1940 bungalows with kitchens, surrounded by lush gardens. Small swimming pool, hot tub, library with fireplace, fully equipped art studio for guest use. I like this place for the separate video/TV/exercise room and the art studio, where children would enjoy hanging out—unusual at a B&B. Full breakfasts, evening wine-and-cheese. $$

Carlin Country Cottages. *1623 Lake Street, Calistoga 94515; (707) 942–9102 or (800) 734–4624.* Nice, simple cottages in a wide courtyard, with Shaker-style furnishings. Some cottages have Jacuzzi tubs; some have one or two

separate bedrooms with kitchens. Spring-fed swimming pool. $$

Comfort Inn. *1865 Lincoln Avenue, Calistoga 94515; (707) 942–9400.* Reasonably priced, simple, modern rooms; pool and sauna; continental breakfast. $–$$

Calistoga Club RV and Camping Resort. *580 Lommel Road, off upper Silverado Trail in Calistoga 94515; (707) 942–6565.* Popular, rustic camping resort in an oak forest, with a creek, meadows, an Olympic-size pool, indoor/outdoor games, short hiking trails, and a small fishing lake. Tent and RV sites; basic cabins. Fewer people and greener surroundings can be found here in winter and spring. $

For More Information

Calistoga Chamber of Commerce. *1458 Lincoln Avenue, Calistoga 94515; (707) 942–6333.*

St. Helena

Families like the little town of St. Helena for its tree-shaded old-fashioned neighborhoods, for postcard-perfect Main Street lined with nineteenth-century stone buildings—each with a quaint shop or cafe inside—and for the biking and walking trails in the surrounding countryside and the nearby state park. Kids who like to cook will enjoy visiting the Culinary Institute of America at Greystone, and the West Coast annex of a famous gourmet store, Dean and DeLuca. It's best to park your car and walk around.

TAPIOCA TIGER

1224 Adams Street, St. Helena 95474; (707) 967–0608.

Great stuff for children, unique clothing, and handcrafted furniture and toys. Kids will enjoy the sand table with objects moved by magnets.

NATURE, ETC

1327 Main Street, St. Helena 95474; (707) 963–1706.

Puzzles, games, books, toys, music, T-shirts, and more, all with an environmental or nature theme.

FIDEAUX

1312 Main Street, St. Helena 95474; (707) 967–9935.

Don't forget Muffie and Spot. Pick up a lavish cat bed, a handmade dog collar, chew toys galore, a doggie futon, or some gourmet biscuits at this fun store.

DEAN AND DELUCA

601 Highway 29, just south of St. Helena 95474; (707) 967–9980.

Huge gourmet market, wine shop, produce mart, and deli—a welcome new offshoot of the famous New York store. You'll find here an incredible variety of cheeses and meats, rotisserie chicken, and wonderful salads and entrees to go, plus packaged gourmet foodstuffs of all kinds. I like the big glass jars of exotic dried mushrooms and marinating olives and the amazing array of vinegars and oils to taste, from fig balsamic vinegar to olive oil pressed in the most isolated, obscure orchard in Tuscany. You can enjoy your sandwiches, fresh fruit smoothies, and espresso drinks in the back on the sunny patio. $$$

BOTHÉ-NAPA VALLEY STATE PARK (all ages)

3801 Highway 29 at Larkmead Lane, St. Helena; (707) 942–4575 (campground reservations: 800–444–7275).

Wilderness trails in a pine and redwood forest, plus a sycamore-shaded campground in Ritchie Creek Canyon. Surprising in a state park is the small swimming pool here, with a lifeguard. Day-trippers picnic on the grass along the creek. It's a short walk from here into Bale Grist Mill State Park; both parks are home to the endangered spotted owl. The fifty-site campground has hot showers and laundry tubs.

BALE GRIST MILL STATE PARK (all ages)

3369 North St. Helena Highway, between St. Helena and Calistoga; (707) 963–2236.

A wooded glade with a 36-foot grinding wheel powered by a rushing creek. Costumed docents grind grain on the millstones and make bread during Old Mill Days in October and frequently on summer weekends.

NAPA VALLEY TRAIL RIDES (ages 6 and up)

P.O. Box 877, Glen Ellen 95442; (707) 996–8566.

One- and two-hour guided horseback rides in Bothé Park along Ritchie Creek and up along the ridges overlooking the valley. These are easy, slow rides, okay even for beginners.

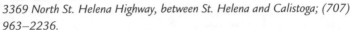

CULINARY INSTITUTE OF AMERICA AT GREYSTONE (CIA) (all ages)

2555 Main Street, just past Beringer Winery on Highway 29, St. Helena 94574; (707) 967–1010. Museum and grounds are Free*. Kitchen tours and demon-strations are a few dollars a person; call ahead for tours and for lunch and dinner reservations.*

A massive landmark guarded by towering palms, Greystone was built in 1889 with 22-inch-thick, hand-cut volcanic stone blocks. Today it's one of the nation's most prestigious culinary colleges, the Culinary Insti-tute of America at Greystone (CIA). Plan at least an hour to wander around, see the food and wine museum, and browse the school store—a blockbuster of a gourmet emporium, where CIA logo attire and 1,500 cookbook titles are just part of an unbelievable inventory of tools and gifts in an environment reminiscent of southern Europe.

The attractive, noisy restaurant and outdoor terrace, which overlook an ancient oak forest and rolling vineyards, are pricey for families, and the food often fails to measure up to top valley restaurants. Graduate chefs are on view, preparing Spanish tapas and Mediterranean cuisine. A drink and snack on the terrace is a pleasant experience.

Kids enjoy the medieval castle look of the interior. Restless youngsters, accompanied, of course, can run around on the beautiful grounds; paths wind through aromatic herb gardens. Take budding chefs on the teaching kitchen tour in the upper reaches of the building.

Where to Eat

Gillwoods. *1313 Main Street, St. Helena 94574; (707) 963–1788.* Home-style American food: tuna sandwiches, grilled cheese, homemade soup, burgers, fried chicken, chili, ribs, meatloaf, apple pie. Breakfast, lunch, and dinner. $

V. Sattui Winery. *111 White Lane, 11.2 miles south of St. Helena on Highway 29 94574; (707) 963–7774 .* A pretty, shady picnic grove on two acres of lawn around a stone-walled 1885 winery. The gourmet deli sells literally hundreds of varieties of cheeses and meats, fresh breads, juices, and drinks. One disadvantage is the sight of the busy highway. Don't be concerned if you miss the wine tasting here; there are better choices for wine. $

Model Bakery. *1357 Main Street, St. Helena 94574; (707) 963–8192.* A circa 1920 brick oven turns out sourdough and rustic breads, pizzettas, fruit tarts, and amazing desserts. The simple cafe serves wonderful soups, salads, and sandwiches for here or to take out. $

Tomatina. *1016 Main Street, on the south end of town, St. Helena 94574; (707) 967–9999.* Yummy brick-oven pizza and pasta are served at long wooden tables, and to go. And there is more: polenta, *piadines* (salad-sandwich-pizzas), and amazing desserts. $

The Spot. *Next to Dean and DeLuca, just south of St. Helena on Highway 29 94574; (707) 963–2844.* Grease is the word for the era but not the food. Superneat 1950s decor, a real family joint with a soda fountain and cool booths. Burgers, shakes, and sandwiches. $

Gail's Oldies and Goodies. *1347 Main Street, St. Helena 94574; (707) 963–3332.* An old-fashioned ice cream parlor, candy store, and cafe, with a jukebox, a player piano, and a fun, turn-of-the-century atmosphere. Breakfast and lunch. $

Where to Stay

Harvest Inn. *One Main Street, just south of St. Helena on Highway 29, St. Helena 94574; (707) 963–9463.* Somewhat pricey, but with great advantages: lush, rambling English gardens; a labyrinth of shady pathways, lawns, and bowers; and two nice pool terraces. If I had babies or toddlers, I would definitely choose this place and spend time walking, playing on the lawns, and lolling in the pools. Some suites have antiques, four-posters, fireplaces, and eclectic collections of elaborate furnishings; other rooms are simpler and more appropriate for a child or two. An expanded continental breakfast is served in a beautiful "great room." $$

El Bonita. *195 Main Street, just south of St. Helena on Highway 29, St. Helena 94574; (800) 541–3284 or (707) 963–3216.* Hidden behind the original 1930s Art Deco motel are new two-story motel units with private balconies looking into the trees and over the gardens. Large, two-room suites have microkitchens. Small pool, sauna, continental breakfast. $$

For More Information

St. Helena Chamber of Commerce. *1010 Main Street, St. Helena 94574; (707) 963–4456.*

Wine Country Reservations. *(707) 257–7757.*

Yountville

Yountville is a tiny Wine Country burg whose few streets are lined with vintage cottages in overgrown country gardens. Washington Street, the main drag, holds a blizzard of shops, restaurants, and inns. A nice half-day excursion here will include a little shop and gallery browsing, a walk on an idyllic country road, a picnic and playtime at a great playground, and exploration of a fascinating old cemetery. There are several family-oriented restaurants within walking distance of the main attraction, Vintage 1870.

VINTAGE 1870

6525 Washington Street, midtown Yountville 94599; (707) 944–2451; www.vintage1870.com.

The landmark building in Yountville, a warren of shops, galleries, and cafes in a huge former winery. A good place to rest or run around, a nice lawn in back is bordered by trees and benches. If you're wending your way from Napa up the valley and someone needs a bathroom, Vintage 1870 is quickly accessible from the highway; restrooms are around back.

PACIFIC BLUES CAFE

In front of Vintage 1870; (707) 944–4455.

Indoors or on the deck, a cafe serving breakfast burritos, biscuits and gravy, and hearty traditional breakfasts; for lunch and dinner, it's gourmet burgers and sandwiches, veggie specialties, fresh seafood, lots of appetizers, homemade soups, big salads, and microbrews on tap. A thoughtful kids' menu features grilled cheese, pizza, plain pasta, and more.

CHÂTEAU ST. SHIRTS
Vintage 1870; (707) 942–5029.

Best T-shirt store in the Wine Country. Top-quality, beautiful shirts, with a wide variety of logos and art; darling children's cotton clothes.

Wine Country Biking
Biking is big in Napa Valley. The advantages here are gorgeous scenery; miles and miles of easy, flat routes; and easy access to rest stops, food and restaurants, and sightseeing attractions along the way. In other words, you can bike your brains out and still be within a few minutes of civilization.

Twelve- to twenty-one-speed hybrid-, mountain-, and tandem-bike rentals and maps are available at several bike shops in the valley. They will deliver bikes to your hotel and pick you up later.

The mostly flat Silverado Trail, running 35 miles along the east side of the valley, is a main biker's route. Crisscrossing the valley between Highway 29 and the Silverado Trail are myriad leafy country roads. Bike shops will give you maps.

Each of these shops offers rentals, pickup service, equipment, and tours:

- **Bicycle Trax.** *796 Soscol Avenue, Napa 94558; (707) 258–8929.*

- **Napa Valley Cyclery.** *4080 Byway East, on the north end of Napa adjacent to Highway 29 94558; (800) 707–BIKE.* Conveniently located at the beginning of the frontage road between Napa and Yountville, which makes a nice, short trip.

- **Palisades Mountain Sports.** *130B Gerrard Street, behind the Fire Department in Calistoga 94515; (707) 255–3377.*

- **Gateway Bicycle Tours.** *1117 Lincoln Avenue, Calistoga 94515; (800) 499–BIKE); www.getawayadventures.com.* All the usual services and equipment, plus special Kids Treks tours for families with children ages 9 and older. Gateway also conducts an exciting Downhill Cruise from the top of Mount St. Helena, a speed-controlled ride with stops along the way to enjoy the views. It's perfectly safe, even for toddlers in bike trailers. The Downhill Cruise costs $39, including bike.

THE TOY CELLAR

Vintage 1870; (707) 944–2144.

A big store crowded with toys, dolls, and games, with a toy train zipping around the ceiling.

YOUNTVILLE PARK (all ages)

At the north end of town, on Washington Street.

An oak-shaded grassy commons, with a great children's playground and picnic tables.

PIONEER CEMETERY AND INDIAN BURIAL GROUND (all ages)

Adjacent to the playground on the north end of town on Jackson Street.

A wonderful cemetery, with fascinating tombstones from the 1800s, including the graves of George Yount, founder of the town, and early pioneers from New England, Canada, and Europe. While living temporarily in New England, I became fond of cemeteries whose stones tell haunting stories, from shipwrecks to fires and storms. My 5-year-old granddaughter and I strolled around the Yountville graveyard, a pretty, tree-studded place, discussing burials and cremations; now she is the family expert on what happens to people when they die.

YOUNT MILL ROAD WALK (all ages)

East of the playground on the north end of Yountville (park where the houses end).

An easy, 3-mile round-trip walk or bike ride, north to Highway 29 and back. Running along a tributary of the Napa River, the road is quiet, shady and bedecked with lovely views of the mountains and vineyards. Watch for a plaque about George Calvert Yount, the first white settler in the valley. Yount wangled from Mexico the huge land grant of Rancho Caymus in the 1850s—composing much of the heart of the valley, including Yountville—and built grist- and sawmills on the river. You will see the remains of one of his large wooden barns.

THE NAPA VALLEY MUSEUM (all ages)

55 Presidents Circle, Yountville 94599; (707) 944–0500; www. napavalleymuseum.org. Admission is $4.50 for adults, $2.50 for kids ages 7 to 17, and Free *for younger kids.*

Among old oaks and a redwood grove by a creek, an architectural surprise: a new museum of contemporary art and the history of the valley, with indoor and outdoor exhibits and garden terraces to roam.

The museum is on the beautiful grounds of the Veterans Home of California, where you can take a walk under magnificent, century-old trees and lounge on the sweeping lawns. Adjacent is the new **Yountville Golf Club**, a pretty 9-holer with a spectacular driving range and a casual indoor-outdoor cafe; this is a good place for beginning golfers (707–944–1992).

NAPA RIVER ECOLOGICAL RESERVE (all ages)

Yountville Cross Road at the Napa River; (707) 944–0500. Admission is **Free**.

A short walk beside the river, under oaks and sycamores. You can wade and fish here too. Watch out for poison oak.

Where to Eat

Compadre's. *6539 Washington Street, Yountville 94599, adjacent to Vintage 1870; (707) 944–2406.* Mexican food and a lively atmosphere, on delightful, palm- and oak-shaded patios. $$

Rutherford Grill. *1880 Rutherford Road, Rutherford, on Highway 29 (watch for the two huge palms) 94573; (707) 962–1782. No reservations.* Go for the smoky baby back ribs, for mountains of feathery onion rings, inventive pastas, grilled and spit-roasted poultry and meats, garlic mashed potatoes, jalapeño corn bread. Big booths inside; umbrella tables and a wine bar outside. This is a popular, fun place, and you may have to wait on weekends. It has the advantage of being pleasantly noisy inside, so kids go unnoticed. $$

The Diner. *6476 Washington Street, on the south end of Yountville 94599; (707) 944–2626.* Bountiful meals in a former Greyhound bus station diner. Booths and a counter, colorful 1950s decor, and *big* plates of food, such as Ameri-can and Mexican food, soups and sandwiches, and huge desserts. Try the Portabello mushroom burger and the potato chorizo burrito. Breakfast, lunch, and dinner. $$

Gordon's Cafe and Wine Bar. *6770 Washington Street, at the north end of Yountville near the park 94599; (707) 944–8246.* In a former stagecoach stop, the best place in town for California cuisine picnic fare to go and casual, quick meals served at individual tables or the communal table. A small, noisy, popular and fun cafe and deli. Breakfast (cinnamon buns, yes!) and lunch every day; prix fixe dinner on Friday. $$

Frankie, Johnnie and Luigi, Too. *6772 Washington Street, Yountville 94599; (707) 944–0177.* Indoor and outdoor dining on the main street, a comfortable, casual place for families. Reasonable prices, good, hearty pizza and pasta dishes. Voted one of the best family restaurants in the Wine Country.

Where to Stay

Napa Valley Lodge. *2230 Madison Street, Yountville 94599; (800) 368–2468 or (707) 944–2468; www.woodsidehotels. com.* In a great location near the city park, with a heated pool on a sunny terrace, fireplaces, complimentary breakfast, and some kitchenettes. An upscale lodge with spacious rooms in a garden setting. Ask here for an Historic Yountville Walking Tour Guide. $$$

For More Information

Yountville Chamber of Commerce. *6795 Washington Street, Yountville 94599; (707) 944–0904.*

Napa Valley Conference and Visitor's Bureau. *1310 Napa Town Center, Napa 94559; (707) 226–7459.*

Napa Valley Tourist Bureau. *6588 Washington Street, Yountville 94599; (707) 944–1558.*

Tourist Information. *(707) 265–1835; www.napavalley.com info@freeruntech.com.* **Free** information about wineries, lodgings, dining, events, recreation, and shopping.

Napa

For 35 miles, from Napa north to Calistoga, the Napa Valley is criss-crossed by quiet country roads where families discover places to bike and hike, play on the riverbanks, and do a little shopping and sightseeing.

Some of the popular family attractions are state and regional parks, a geyser and a petrified forest, a gliderport, and two wildlife parks; some of these are near the town of Napa.

 OLD TOWN NAPA (all ages)

On the west side of the Napa River.

Here charming Victorian neighborhoods are bounded by Franklin, Division, Elm, and Riverside Streets. Under construction downtown near the river are the American Center for Wine, Food, and the Arts, a new opera house, the upscale Napa River Inn, and Hatt Marketplace, a boutique shopping and restaurant center. Every Friday night the Napa Town Center mall is packed with families enjoying the live music, food and wine tastings, fresh produce, and locally produced gourmet foodstuffs—it's a party!

SKYLINE WILDERNESS PARK (all ages)

2201 Imola Avenue, on the east side of Napa; (707) 252–0481. A $4.00 parking fee is charged.

A regional park with hilly woodlands and meadows for hiking, horseback riding, picnicking, and RV and tent camping. Find the waterfalls for a summer splash. Picnic and fish on the shores of Lake Marie, a 2.5-mile walk from the parking lot.

Six Flags Marine World *At Highways 80 and 37, 2001 Marine World Parkway Way, Vallejo 94591; (707) 643–6722; www.sixflagsmarine world. com. Tickets $34 for adults, $17 for height 48 inches and under, Free for kids 3 years and under; ask about family pricing.*

What I like best about this oceanarium, wildlife, and amusement park is the chance to get close to animals and marine life, an enriching and educational experience for a child. My granddaughter Melati knows what a giraffe's blue tongue looks and feels like, because she fed one leaves and apples. She played tug-of-war with an elephant and hugged a chimpanzee. And butterflies are of great interest to her now, since a gleaming blue morpho touched down on her open hand. She's also very proud that she can walk through the tunnel of sharks without batting an eye.

Now that $40 million worth of roller-coasters and rides have been added, it is a challenge to get everything into one day. Among the highlights are the live shows: "Dolphin Harbor," the "Batman Waterthrill" show, the "Killer Whale" show (waves of cold water are splashed out of the pool by the animals onto people in the front rows—be ready!), "Tiger Splash Attack," and the sea lion, elephant and tropical bird shows. The most outrageous rides are the Boomerang and the Kong roller-coasters, and the DinoSphere TurboRide, the world's first motion simulator adventure ride with 3D. Rides for younger children are the ferris wheel, Monkey Business teacups, and the Shoreline Express railway.

There are cafes and food booths with some healthy choices. To avoid lines, arrive early and have lunch early. You can also enjoy your own picnic at tree-shaded tables on the grass by the lake. Rent a dolphin stroller for kids 4 and younger, as you will be walking your feet off! A carefree way to reach the park from the Bay Area is by ferry from San Francisco (707–643–3779). Ask about ferry packages and special event days.

CARNEROS WALK

Dealy Lane off Highway 12, on the west side of Napa.

If you're up for a walk on a quiet country lane, park across the road from Carneros Creek Winery and walk west for a couple of miles until you reach a PRIVATE PROPERTY sign, then return. Along the way you'll hear the alarming call of peacocks, and as you approach the peacock farm, a gaggle of guardian geese may appear.

 LAKE BERRYESSA (all ages)

Seventeen miles east of Napa, at Highways 128 and 21; (707) 966–2111.

 One of the state's most popular recreation lakes, with 165 miles of hilly, oak-covered shoreline. On the west shore, Knoxville Road gives access to marinas, park headquarters, a resort, beaches, and campgrounds. Oak Shores Park day-use area has the best beach and picnic sites, with lifeguards on weekends. Spring is ideal for bass fishing; fall, for trout. Marinas rent fishing, patio, and ski boats and other watercraft. This is a mild environment in which to learn windsurfing.

NAPA VALLEY WINE TRAIN

1275 McKinstry Street off Soscol, Napa 94559; (800) 427–4124 or (707) 253–2111; www.winetrain.com.

Elegant, restored Pullman railroad dining and observation cars take passengers on a relaxing ride up the valley, a three-hour chug from Napa to St. Helena and back, with a gourmet lunch or dinner included—a pricey and rather confining experience for youngsters, although a la carte snacks and meals are offered in a separate deli car, and there are Family Fun Nights when children 3 to 12 ride 𝕱𝖗𝖊𝖊; a supervisory staff keeps the kids happy with games, movies, and food.

Where to Eat

Alexis Baking Company. *1517 Third Street, Napa 94559; (707) 258–1827.* Where the locals go for breakfast and coffee breaks, Sunday brunch, lunch, and dinners. Homemade pastries and desserts are remarkable. $$

Pasta Prego. *3206 Jefferson Street in the Grapeyard Center, Napa 94559; (707) 224–9011.* A friendly trattoria frequented by winery families. Served here are northern Italian food, seafood, pasta, and grilled fresh fish. For the most fun sit at the counter and watch the cooks. Lunch and dinner; indoors or on the tiny patio. $$

Downtown Joe's Restaurant and Brewery. *902 Main Street, Napa 94559; (707) 258–2337.* Breakfast, lunch, or dinner on the patio overlooking the Napa River, adjacent to a small, grassy park where little ones can run while waiting for their dinners. Salads, sandwiches, pastas, and a microbrewery. $

Gillwood's Bakery and Cafe. *1320 Town Center, Napa 94558; (707) 253–* 0409. Luscious pastries and desserts, great old-fashioned breakfast, lunch and dinner. $

Villa Corona. *3614 Bel Aire Plaza, Napa 94558; (707) 257–8685.* A fresh little cafe tucked away behind a bank. The best Mexican food in town, from enchilada plates to burritos bursting with juicy fillings and a pastry bakery, to eat here or take out. $

Where to Stay

Embassy Suites Napa Valley. *1075 California Boulevard, adjacent to Highway 29, Napa 94559; (707) 253–9540; www.embassy-suites.com.* Upscale Mediterranean-look hotel, with spacious suites, separate living room and sofa bed, small kitchens; conveniently located at the highway. Complimentary full breakfast and two-hour cocktail/snacks hour in the pleasant cafe by the lovely gardens. Indoor and outdoor pools, sauna, complimentary passes to nearby health club. Guest laundry. $$

Tall Timber Chalets. *Between Napa and Yountville, at 1012 Darms Lane 94559; (707) 252–7810.* Circa-1940 cottages in a grove of trees; fresh, bright decor; sitting rooms, kitchens, continental breakfast; room to run around. $

For More Information

Napa Valley Conference and Visitors Bureau. *1310 Napa Town Center, Napa 94559; (707) 226–3610.*

Napa Valley Reservations. *1819 Tanen Street, Napa 94559, on the north end of town just off the highway; (707) 252–1985 or (800) 251–6272; www.napavalleyreservations.com.*

Sonoma

On the west side of the Mayacamas Mountains, Sonoma Valley comprises a patchwork of vineyards and farmlands, with a fascinating early California history, best displayed in the town of Sonoma, which was laid out by a Mexican general in 1834. The site of many annual fiestas, parades, and art, wine, and food events, Sonoma Plaza is surrounded by the past, including a small California mission, a military compound from the days of the Mexican conquest, thick-walled adobe and Victorian homes, and a blizzard of upscale shops and restaurants.

 SONOMA MISSION AND SONOMA BARRACKS (all ages)
First and Spain Streets, Sonoma; (707) 938–1519.

The commandant who held sway in the Sonoma area when Mexico owned California, General Mariano Vallejo built a barracks compound for his soldiers, and it is now a state park and a museum on the plaza. The museum is an easy walk-through for children, offering re-created rooms and costumes of the early days. The museum shop is a great place to find educational and entertaining items for children, from paper dolls in period dress to small toys. In May, a special Children's Day is held at the mission. The last of the California missions built, this one has a beautiful small chapel and museum.

 SONOMA WALKING/BIKING PATH (all ages)
Fifty yards north of East Spain Street, Sonoma. From Fourth Street East, west to Sonoma Highway 12; (707) 996–1090.

A paved path for walking, biking, and Rollerblading winds 1.5 miles from one end of Sonoma to the other, passing through parks and playing fields and ending on the west side at a big park with a playground. A block from Sonoma Plaza on the walking path, Depot Park has a playground, barbecues, and picnic tables under the trees: a good choice when the plaza is crowded. My granddaughter Laurel learned to Rollerblade on the trail, and her little sister, Melati, pedaled shakily along on her first "big girl's" bike ride.

 DEPOT PARK MUSEUM (all ages)
270 First Street West, on the Sonoma Walking/Biking Path, Sonoma 95476; (707) 938–1762. Open afternoons (hours vary) Wednesday through Sunday; gift shop.

If you get hooked on local history, make a stop here to see a restored stationmaster's office, re-creations of Victorian households, and photos of early Sonomans.

 GENERAL M.G. VALLEJO HOME (all ages)
About 0.5-mile northwest of the plaza off Spain Street, Sonoma; (707) 938–1519. The home is part of the state park property, so one admission ticket is good at the mission, the barracks compound, and the Vallejo home.

Accessible by the walking path and by car, a beautiful yellow-and-white, "Yankee-style" Gothic Revival house that was shipped around the

Horn and erected in 1851 by the Mexican General Vallejo. Called *Lachryma Montis,* meaning "Tears of the Mountain," the house is shaded by huge magnolias and twined with rambling yellow roses.

My granddaughters love to wander through, looking at the original and period furnishings, and daydream about the days when Vallejo and his several daughters lived here before the turn of the century. There are tintypes of the daughters, their hair below their waists, wearing long, elaborate dresses; black stockings; and high-button shoes. Their bedrooms are as they were, with a tiny dollhouse, a miniature stove, tin bathtubs, lace coverlets, and cut velvet couches. The general's son had his own private pad, where his rifle, a narrow bed, and keepsakes are carefully preserved.

ZIMBABWE SCULPTURE GALLERY

452 First Street on the plaza, Sonoma 95476; (707) 935–6254.

Kids in an art gallery? Yes, this is something different. Dramatic African Shona stone sculpture, interesting oversize photographs of Africa, and a video to watch.

NATURE ETC

450 First Street East in a shopping alley off the plaza, Sonoma 95476; (707) 938–5662.

Animal and nature-oriented toys and games, books and music, and a great collection of T-shirts. My little friends go directly to the animal hand puppets, from jagged-toothed sharks to furry lambs.

HALF PINT (ages 1–8)

450 First Street East on the plaza, Sonoma 95476; (707) 938–1722.

Kids' clothes of your dreams, beautiful European imports, trendy hats and shoes, a few toys.

SONOMA TRAINTOWN (ages 2–8)

20264 Broadway, 1 mile south of the plaza, Sonoma 95476; (707) 938–3912. Open daily in summer and weekends during the rest of the year. Tickets are $3.75 for adults and $2.75 for children; the carousel ride is $1.50.

Younger children love this: an open-air steam train ride through a redwood forest to a tiny farm that has a petting zoo, a vintage carousel, and a snack shop.

SEBASTIANI TROLLEY RIDE AND A SECRET PICNIC SITE (all ages)

Sonoma Plaza, Sonoma; (707) 938–5532.

On a replica of a San Francisco cable car, **Free** rides from Sonoma Plaza around town to and from Sebastiani Cellars, a few blocks away. Pick up picnic provisions, hop on the trolley, hop off at the winery, and walk 1 block to behind the winery to shaded picnic tables next to a vineyard with dazzling vineyard and hillside views. For an easy, twenty-minute stroll, walk north from the picnic area a few hundred yards and take the first left turn (Gehricke Road) past vineyards; take the first left, turn left again, turn left yet again, and you're back where you started.

SEBASTIANI THEATER

476 First Street, Sonoma 95476; (707) 996–2020.

A wonderful, classic vintage movie theater showing foreign flicks and film festivals, and likely the only movie house where you often get live entertainment before the film. Held here and at outdoor venues—a great way for families to spend a summer evening. The Wine Country Film Festival shows both adult and family-oriented films (707–996–2536; wcfilmfest@aol.com).

SONOMA VALLEY SHAKESPEARE FESTIVAL (ages 5 and up)

July and August at Gundlach Bundschu Winery, 3775 Thornsberry Road off Napa Road, Sonoma 95476; (707) 575–3854.

A painless way to introduce children to Shakespeare: Lively, colorful comedies are performed on an outdoor stage at this small country winery. Bring a picnic and a blanket and lie about on the lawn in front of the stage—lots of children, lots of fun on a warm summer night. Snacks, wine, and soft drinks are available. $$

JACK LONDON STATE PARK (all ages)

2400 London Ranch Road off Arnold Drive, Glen Ellen 95442; (707) 938–1519. A $5.00 day-use fee per auto is charged.

This area is called the Valley of the Moon, named for famous (some say infamous) resident, Jack London, author of the classic children's adventure tales *Call of the Wild* and *The Sea Wolf.* London's globe-trotting life early in this century is portrayed in photos and haunting artifacts in a wonderful Craftsman-style lodge, the "House of Happy Walls." Once

London's ranch, the park comprises 800 acres of trails, crisscrossed by creeks winding through magnificent groves of oaks, madronas, fir, redwoods, and fern grottoes. You can picnic here in a wildflowery meadow and see the ruins of Wolf House, London's eccentric stone mansion, found at the end of a 0.25-mile path through the trees (handicapped accessible by golf cart). Only walls and chimneys remain of the elaborate home that burned to the ground a few days before London and his wife, Charmian, could move in. Intrepid hikers will enjoy the steeper trails on the hillsides on the east side of the parking lot, and will be rewarded with wide-open views of the valley.

 SONOMA CATTLE COMPANY (ages 6 and up)
P.O. Box 877, Glen Ellen 95442; (707) 996–8566.
Guided horseback rides in Jack London State Park and in Sugarloaf Ridge State Park.

 BENZIGER FAMILY WINERY (all ages)
1883 London Ranch Road, Glen Ellen 95442; (707) 935–3000 or (800) 989–8890.
Located here are beautiful valley oaks and gardens, an art gallery and picnic grounds, and a tasting room. This is the only winery in the valley to offer a motorized tram tour of the vineyards, and children are welcome. Call ahead for reservations.

 MORTON WARM SPRINGS (all ages)
Between Glen Ellen and Kenwood, 1651 Warm Springs Road; (707) 833–5511.
My high school mates and I spent many a hot summer day here, and later, my children loved it. A family-owned, country day-use swimming resort, Morton Warm Springs offers three heated pools, a wading pool, sweeping lawns under giant trees, picnic sites, and a snack bar. Horseshoes, boccie, basketball, baseball, and volleyball are available too.

  SUGARLOAF RIDGE STATE PARK (all ages)
Adobe Canyon Road off Highway 12, just north of Kenwood; (707) 833–5712 (campground reservations: 800–444–7275).
A 3,000-acre green and golden jewel of hillsides, redwood groves, creeks, wildflower-strewn meadows, and views. Take a short walk or a strenuous hike, picnic in the pines, park your RV overnight, or camp out in your tent.

Winery Fun For Kids

A winery tour may last an hour or more, and youngsters can get restless. Choose your wineries well!

- **Niebaum Coppola Estate Winery.** *1991 St. Helena Highway, Rutherford; (707) 963–9099.* My choice for "if you have time for only one winery," this winery has unique interest for young people because of the Hollywood movie connection. Renowned moviemaker Francis Ford Coppola restored to its former glory one of the oldest winery estates in the valley (Inglenook) and had his Hollywood designers create an extravaganza of a winery, gift store, museum, and park complete with bubbling fountains, promenades, and lawns.

  Ever see real Oscars up close? Here they are, Coppola's golden beauties, along with photos and other cool stuff from his movies, including the *Tucker* auto, the boat from *Apocalypse Now,* and costumes from *Bram Stoker's Dracula.*

- **Chateau Montelena.** *1429 Tubbs Lane, Calistoga; (707) 942–5105.* Exotic ducks and swans glide around two red-lacquered gazebos in a small lake. Young children love to stand on the bridges and toss feed to attract the ducks and the koi fish. On the winery grounds a few picnic tables beneath weeping willows are within sight of the mossy, crenellated castle of French limestone where the wine is made.

- **St. Supery Winery and Wine Discovery Center.** *8440 St. Helena Highway at Rutherford; (707) 963–4507.* Besides lawns and picnic sites here, there is a lot to see that may be interesting to school-age children: A Victorian farmhouse wine-growing demonstration area, and relief maps of the valley are here too. You can easily leave the winery tour at any time; it's fun to walk on catwalks above the giant storage tanks.

- **Rutherford Hill Winery.** *200 Rutherford Hill Road, off the Silverado Trail, Rutherford; (707) 963–7194.* Cool, delightfully spooky underground caves are fun to see on a thirty-five-minute tour. You can buy juices and picnic goodies here to enjoy at tables under the oaks or in the olive grove with wide valley views.

- **Sterling Vineyards.** *1100 Dunaweal Lane, Calistoga; (707) 942–3300.* Tram tickets $6.00 for all ages over 10. Free for kids under 10. Take a thrilling, four-minute gondola ride to a sky-high terrace for bird's eye views. The winery tour is self-guided, and there are outdoor tables up here for picnicking—with your own provisions or you can buy simple deli items on-site. Children are given an activity bag with juice, raisins, crayons, cards to color, and stickers!

SONOMA VALLEY REGIONAL PARK (all ages)

Across the road from the Garden Court Cafe, Highway 12 between Arnold Drive and Madrone Road, near Glen Ellen; (707) 539–8092. There is a $2.00 parking fee.

A mostly flat, paved path winding about 1 mile one-way through an oak forest, with a pretty creek along the way. You can bike and picnic; dogs must be leashed. My little granddaughter and her buddies like to pick up sticks and branches, drag them along on the walk, and build a fort on a fallen tree trunk.

FAMILY WINERIES OF SONOMA VALLEY

9200 Sonoma Highway, Kenwood 95452; (707) 833–5504.

Car full of kids, and parents want to taste wine? Right on the highway, this is an easy place to stop, taste wines, and let the kids and the designated driver play in the picnic area. Seven of the valley's finest small wineries offer wines unavailable for tasting elsewhere.

Where to Eat

Cucina Viansa. *400 First Street at Spain Street, Sonoma 95476; (707) 935–5656.* The prettiest vintage building in town, and the best of all for a quick gourmet deli lunch here or to take to the plaza, across the street. $

Sonoma Cheese Factory and Deli. *2 West Spain Street, Sonoma 95476; (707) 996–1931.* An excellent array of cheeses and deli foods to go, or eat here at picnic tables, with the disadvantage of its being the place where the tour buses stop and thus often impossibly crowded. $

Basque Boulangerie Cafe. *60 First Street on the plaza, Sonoma 95476; (707) 935–7687.* French and Basque-style salads, pastries, muffins, cakes, and tarts; home-baked breads and rolls; espresso drinks. Sit at the counter or at a sidewalk table. Open from breakfast through late afternoon. $

Piatti. *405 First Street West on the plaza, Sonoma 95476; (707) 996–2351.* Beautiful dining room and gracious tree-shaded patio, wood-fired pizza ovens, rotisserie roasting, contemporary Northern Italian food. $$

Rob's Rib Shack. *18709 Arnold Drive, on the west side of Sonoma 95476; (707) 938–8520.* A small, very informal cafe at the golf practice range, offering ribs and barbecue specialties to die for, killer fries, a really good Caesar salad, and microbrews. Fun roadhouse decor; outdoor tables. There is a less spicy kids' menu. $

Pizzeria Capri. *1286 Broadway, Sonoma 95476; (707) 935–6805.* Fantastic pizza and pasta—a family place with live weekend entertainment and sports on TV. $

Breakaway Cafe. *19101 Highway 12 in the Albertson's shopping plaza, Sonoma 95476; (707) 996–5949.* The best family place in town, with big booths, a toy corner, and all-American food, such as pork chops and mashed potatoes, roast chicken, burgers, salads, comforting soups, huge omelets, veggie specials, smoothies, and a kids menu. They know kids here, and they like them. Breakfast, lunch, and dinner. $

Mary's Pizza Shack. *452 First Street East, Sonoma 95476; (707) 938–8300.* Sit outdoors near the town plaza, across from the sticker store and next to the ice-cream parlor, and have really good pizza. Grown-ups like the roasted garlic and chicken pizza with garlic-shallot butter. Ask for pizza sticks while you wait. $

Where to Stay

Sonoma Valley Inn. *550 Second Street West, Sonoma 95476; (707) 938–9200.* Nice motel rooms around a courtyard with pool; some rooms with fireplace and microwave. Guest laundry. Across the street from a shopping center. $$

Lodge at Sonoma. *1325 Broadway, Sonoma 95476; (707) 935–6600.* A large luxury hotel, brand new and beautiful, within several blocks of the plaza and a block from Train Town, with cottages and spacious hotel rooms with sitting areas, a swimming pool, terrace, gardens, and a full-service spa; child care is available. $$$–$$$$

For More Information

Sonoma Valley Visitor's Bureau. *In the plaza, 4532 First Street East, Sonoma 95476; (707) 996–1090.*

Sonoma Reservations. *(800) 576–6662.* Motels, inns, spas, condos, homes.

Healdsburg

The small town of Healdsburg sleeps peacefully under a canopy of trees. On most summer weekends, band and jazz concerts and outdoor festivals are held in the classic Spanish-style town plaza, which is ringed with cafes and shops. On the west side of town, the Dry Creek Valley is prime biking and wine-tasting territory. For an easy, scenic 20-mile loop on gently rolling hills, start at the town plaza, head south to Mill Street, cross under the highway and join Dry Creek Road heading north. Endless vineyards and rows of low, forested mountains remain in view throughout the ride.

DRY CREEK GENERAL STORE
3495 Dry Creek Road, Healdsburg 95448; (707) 433–4171.

Buy sandwiches and picnic goodies to eat here, or bring them along in your bike baskets for a picnic by the side of the road.

SPOKE FOLK CYCLERY
249 Center Street, Healdsburg 95448; (707) 433–7171.

Bike rentals and maps.

HEALDSBURG VETERANS MEMORIAL BEACH
Just on the edge of town, Old Redwood Highway on the Russian River; (707) 433–1625.

A very popular swimming spot, with a sandy beach, picnic areas, and lifeguards.

TROWBRIDGE CANOE TRIPS (ages 4 and up)
20 Healdsburg Avenue, Healdsburg 95448; (707) 433–7247.

Canoe rentals, with all equipment included and transport to the Russian River for a paddle from Healdsburg to Monte Rio.

TREE WALK (all ages)
Map at the Visitor's Bureau, 217 Healdsburg Avenue, Healdsburg 95448; (707) 433–6935.

With the descriptive booklet provided, take the kids on a tree walk around the plaza and on nearby "Old Town" streets. Some of the highlights are a dawn redwood from China, once thought to be extinct; coast redwoods, magnificent palms, oaks, magnolias, maples, and many more.

HEALDSBURG MUSEUM (all ages)
221 Matheson Street, Healdsburg, 95448; (707) 431–3325.
Free *admission.*

In the beautiful Carnegie Library building, circa 1910, displays of Pomo Indian basketry, artifacts from the Mexican rancho and pioneer eras, great old photos, and a fun shop with educational toys and books for kids.

CALIFORNIA RIVER PADDLE SPORTS (ages 4 and up)

10070 Old Redwood Highway, Windsor 95492; (707) 838–8919.

Kayak and canoe rentals, guided or self-guided paddles on the Russian River, and transport to the river.

OCTOBER ON THE FARM (all ages)

Westside Farms, 7097 Westside Road, Healdsburg 95448; (707) 431–1432. Admission is $5.00 per car.

Weekends in October, climb the straw mountain, take a hay ride, choose pumpkins, and have a fun fall day.

 JIMTOWN STORE (all ages)

 7606 Highway 126, Healdsburg 95448; (707) 453–1212; www.jimtown.com.

In the idyllic Alexander Valley a few minutes from Healdsburg, Wine Country gifts, antiques and collectibles, and gourmet deli food for here or to go. Kids' menu includes peanut butter sandwiches and other simple stuff. Fresh homemade lemonade! Lots of neat things for kids, such as paper dolls, gliders, and small toys. Picnic tables on the patio.

SNOOPY'S REDWOOD EMPIRE ICE ARENA (all ages)

1667 Steele Lane, Santa Rosa 95404; (707) 546–7147. Adults and children ages 12 and up $5.50, ages 11 and under $4.50. Skate rental $2.00. Puppy Practice: kids 12 and under and their parents receive a twenty-minute lesson with Free *skate rental (adults $5.50, children $4.50).*

A great stop in the Wine Country right off Highway 101, the ice arena has a cafe overlooking the ice, and a large shop and museum devoted to the Peanuts gang—Snoopy, Woodstock, Charlie Brown, Lucy, and their buddies. Founder of the arena, the late *Peanuts* cartoonist, Charles "Sparkie" Schultz, worked in his studio nearby and spent many an hour chatting with kids and parents.

Where to Eat

Costeaux French Bakery and Cafe. *A block from the plaza, 417 Healdsburg Avenue, Healdsburg 95448; (707) 433–1913.* Award-winning breads and pastries, scrumptious sandwiches, and picnic items to stay or go; breakfast and lunch. $

Flying Goat Coffee Roastery Cafe. *324 Center Street, Healdsburg 95448; (707) 433–9081.* Hang out with the locals and read the paper; have a Goat Bar (chocolate, oats, nuts) or some coffee cake. Simple bistro food. $

El Farolito. *128 Plaza Street, Healdsburg 95448; (707) 433–2807.* In a town with a large Mexican population, really good Mexican food. $

Oakville Grocery. *124 Matheson Street on the square, Healdsburg 95448; (707) 433–3200.* At this welcome offshoot of the famous Oakville Grocery in the Napa Valley, an outdoor fireplace makes the terrace a cozy spot for pizza from the brick ove, rotisserie chicken, sandwiches, and wonderful pastries. The pricey, gourmet grocery sells top-quality seasonal local produce and local cheeses, charcuterie, and wines. $

Where to Stay

Vineyard Valley Inn. *178 Dry Creek Road, Healdsburg 95448; (800) 499–0103.* Simple hotel with sauna and whirlpool, coffee shop, free continental breakfast. $

Alexander Valley Campground *Alexander Valley Road near the Healdsburg Bridge, Healdsburg 95448; (707) 431–1453.* A large tent and RV campground on the banks of the river, with swimming beaches and canoe rentals.

For More Information

Healdsburg Chamber of Commerce. *217 Healdsburg Avenue,* *Healdsburg 95448; (707) 433–6935; www.hbg.sonoma.net.*

Russian River

Anchored by the town of Guerneville (see map of **North Coast**), the Russian River Valley cradles the river as it flows through forest canyons and past sandy beaches and vineyards. The river is generally slow-moving and calm, with quiet coves and sandy beaches along the way. Canoeing, kayaking, and tubing are popular activities; try them on the scenic, 10-mile stretch from Forestville to Guerneville, where there are nice beaches and stopping points for fishing and picnicking. Osprey, blue herons, deer, turtles, and more wildlife will accompany your trek. Canoe and kayak companies shuttle you back to the starting point (see rentals in Healdsburg section). Bring plenty of water, secure your car keys with a safety pin in your pocket, wear hats, and beware of sunburn on the tops of your legs.

On the way out to the coast from Guerneville, stop at **Duncan's Mills**, a charming village on the river with an old-fashioned general store, cafes, and boutique shops. Children can run around and take a short walk on the quiet country road that runs alongside the village.

GUERNEVILLE

A laid-back summer vacation town since the mid-1800s, Guerneville is draped lazily along the bank of the Russian River. The town is primarily souvenir shops, a few galleries and casual cafes, and a supermarket or two where you can stock up on provisions for camping and day-tripping on the coast, on the beaches, and in the redwood park.

ARMSTRONG GROVE REDWOOD STATE RESERVE

In Guerneville, go north off Main Street on Armstrong Woods Road; 2.2 miles to the park entrance; (707) 869–2015.

Easy forest trails wind through magnificent stands of old-growth redwoods, some more than 300 feet tall. Picnic sites are cool and shady on the warmest summer days. Available are wheelchair access, a Braille trail, restrooms, a visitor center, no-reservation campsites, and mountain-biking and equestrian trails.

AUSTIN CREEK STATE RECREATION AREA

Accessed through the Armstrong Redwood Reserve entrance; (707) 865–2391.

Located here are relatively undeveloped 5,000 acres of grasslands and hills, river glens and canyons, open forests, a hike-in campground, and a horse camp (carry your own water). You'll find wildflowers in the spring, good birding, and bluegill and black bass fishing in Redwood Lake. Hot and dry in the summer, glorious green in the winter and spring, the preserve is abundant with wildlife, from great blue herons, woodpeckers, and ravens to deer, foxes, and, occasionally, bobcats.

BULLFROG POND CAMPGROUND

Austin Creek State Recreation Area; (707) 869–2015.

The popular family campground here is accessed by a steep, narrow road that cannot be negotiated by RVs more than 20 feet long. Reservations by phone are advised, but you can also drop in and check the bulletin board at the campground for open sites.

ARMSTRONG WOODS PACK STATION

Armstrong Grove; (707) 887–2939.

Even beginning riders will enjoy the lunch ride, which meanders gently out of the redwood forest through a variety of wildlife habitats to ridgetops overlooking the Russian River Valley. On top of the world with a 360-degree view of five counties, a gourmet lunch is laid out on white tablecloths in a wildflower-strewn meadow. You can also ride your own horses on the guided pack trips and bring your own food.

JK'S AMUSEMENTS (ages 3–15)

16101 Neeley Road, Guerneville 95446; (707) 869–3102.

Look for the 20-foot T-rex to announce cartoon-character themed pee-wee golf. There are "go-karts" and bumper cars, a water slide, and more activities for younger kids. In business for over two decades, this is a slightly frowsy but fun roadside attraction with reasonable prices.

Where to Eat

Sweet's Cafe and Bakery. *16251 Main Street, Guerneville 95446; (707) 859–3383.* The best place for Belgian waffles, omelets, homemade croissants, espresso, lunches. $

Topolos at Russian River Vineyards. *5700 Gravenstein Highway 116, Forestville 95436; (707) 887–1562.* A perfect stop for lunch or dinner on the way to or from the Russian River or the Sonoma Coast, built in an interesting hop-kiln-style reminiscent of a century ago. Greek and California cuisine is served in a circa 1870 rustic estate home, in the dining room by the wood-burning stove or outside on the garden patio (there is space outside for toddlers to cruise around while waiting for lunch): local seafood, duckling in black currant Madeira sauce, souvlaki, spanakopita, pork in raspberry Riesling sauce, seasonal specialties. The winery owners are the restaurant owners, and the bottle of wine you order may be opened by one of the winemakers, Jerry or Michael Topolos. Wheelchair access. $$

Main Street Station. *16280 Main Street, Guerneville 95446; (707) 869–0501.* Good for a lunch stop while driving to the coast; hearty Italian meatball sandwiches and sausage sandwiches, country-style pizza, salads, smoothies, and great desserts. $

Where to Stay

Casini Ranch Family Campground. *22855 Moscow Road, Duncans Mills 95430; (707) 451–8400.* On the Russian River, adjacent to a small village of shops and restaurants, twenty minutes from the Sonoma Coast. More than 200 RV and tent camping sites, some on the river. It's just a few steps to good fishing. Grocery, Laundromat, showers, boat rental; pets okay. $

Fern Grove Cottages. *16650 Highway 116, Guerneville 95226; (707) 869–8105; www.ferngrove.com.* A short stroll from town, classic 1920s cottages are scattered beneath the redwoods; kids like the "Cowboy Cottage" best. Choose from one- or two-bedroom units with wood-burning fireplaces, a **Free** continental breakfast, and a nice swimming pool. $$–$$$

For More Information

Russian River Chamber of Commerce. *16200 First Street, Guerneville 95446; (707) 859–9000; www.russianriver.com.*

Redwood Empire Association and North Coast Visitor Center. *2802 Leavenworth, San Francisco 94133–1117; (415) 394–5991; www.redwoodempire.com.* Comprehensive brochures and other materials covering all of the Wine Country, the North Coast, and Redwood Country.

Sonoma County Tourism Program and Visitor's Bureau. *2300 County Center Drive, Santa Rosa 95403; (800) 5–Sonoma; www.visitsonoma.com; info@ visitsonoma.com.* Maps, booklets, guidebooks, and a friendly staff to offer advice and directions.

High Sierra North

A sapphire gem sparkling across the California and Nevada borders, Lake Tahoe lies above 6,000 feet in the icy embrace of the Sierra Nevada Range. In a dreamlike setting of snow-frosted peaks and evergreen forests, the lake is "clear enough to see the scales on a cutthroat trout at 80 feet," as Mark Twain put it. Families return year after year to the summer vacation towns, campgrounds, and ski resorts of the Tahoe region.

The choice of summer sightseeing and recreation is phenomenal: hiking and mountain biking on forest trails; fishing, swimming, and boating; exploring old logging towns. Some families head for state park campgrounds in the woods or on the lakeshore. Others rent a cabin at the beach, or they stay at a big resort with a pool and lots of organized activities.

Get an overview of the dazzling mountain landscape by taking the family on a slow cruise on one of the big paddlewheeler tour boats, across the lake to Emerald Bay. You'll see row after row of jagged granite peaks reflected in the deep blue water: 1,600 feet deep, and cold, very cold. Legends tell of Indian chiefs in full regalia and women in Victorian garb floating motionless and frozen at the bottom of the lake. Children love to hear the old Tahoe stories, especially tales of Tahoe Tessie, the Loch Ness–style monster whose spiny back is occasionally seen rippling above the surface. Watch for Tessie!

The sun shines an average of 274 days a year. Soft spring days are clear and wildflowery; fall is brisk, with aspen colors glittering through the pines. Winter days are lively at sixteen alpine ski resorts and as many cross-country ski areas. More ski resorts are concentrated here than anywhere else in North America.

The 72-mile-long Tahoe lakeshore is roughly divided into the South Shore, the West Shore, and the North Shore, each with unique attractions. Anchored by Tahoe City, the West Shore has an "Old Tahoe" feel, with log cabins from

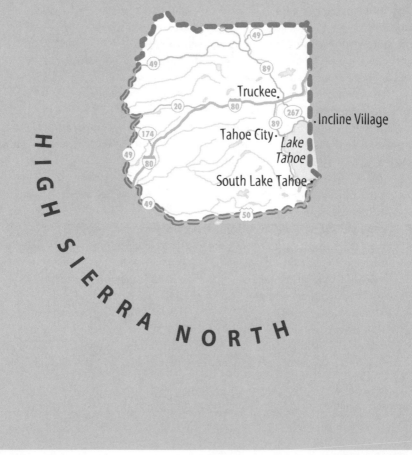

Truckee

Incline Village

Tahoe City

Lake
Tahoe

South Lake Tahoe

HIGH SIERRA NORTH

the 1920s and 1930s and old-fashioned cottage-style resorts. The Truckee River is a good reason to headquarter on the West Shore. You can spend a day rafting—it's exciting but not at all dangerous—and hike and bike on a paved trail that runs along the river and the lakeshore.

The North Shore is primarily the Incline Village area, the least developed and quietest part of the lake. On the South Shore, the only real city on the lake, South Lake Tahoe is famous for casinos, although families head for the historical sights and a chain of beautiful beaches. Outdoor fun is nearby in the Tahoe and El Dorado National Forests and in Desolation Wilderness.

TAKING CARE

It's wise to remember that Lake Tahoe is at high elevation—6,227 feet at the lakeshore. For the first day or two of your visit, everyone in the family, and particularly the children, may feel more tired than usual. If someone feels nauseated for no apparent reason, it is likely to be altitude sickness; extra rest and limited physical activities are the cures. If you are not experienced skiers or hikers, you will do well to plan an easy first day. If someone in the family continues to feel sick, sleepy, and disoriented, discuss it with a doctor; the only way to get over persistent altitude sickness is to descend to a lower altitude.

High altitude also means greater risk of sunburn, especially in winter. Use sunscreen every day, no matter how cold it feels outdoors.

During the summer and on winter weekends, avoid driving to Tahoe on Friday afternoons or returning on Sunday afternoons, to elude heavy traffic. A snow-storm can transform Highways 50 and 80 into parking lots for hours. Every month of the year, check the weather and road conditions, and keep a bag of jackets, blankets, and dry provisions in the car, year round.

South Lake Tahoe

Between Lake Tahoe and a magnificent wall of Sierra Nevada peaks, the city of South Lake Tahoe appears at first glance to be a canyon of neon and casinos, honky-tonk bars and flashy motels. Get off the main highway that bisects town, however, and you will see why families spend their vacations here. Beautiful beaches and family oriented resorts are located all along the lakeshore. From here it's a short drive to a tremendous variety of outdoor recreation and sightseeing destinations in the Tahoe Basin.

Three public beaches in town—El Dorado, Regan, and Connelly—have extensive facilities, including playing fields and swimming pools. At Nevada Beach and Zephyr Cove, you can rent every imaginable type of watersports equipment and take lessons: take a boat tour of the lake, try parasailing, go fishing, or just lie in the sun.

The city is undergoing major redevelopment on the main street and the lakefront to include two large resort hotels, an outdoor ice rink, a movieplex, new shops, restaurants, and a gondola that zips passengers from town to the mountaintop. And there is now nonstop airline service from L.A., Las Vegas, San Jose, Fresno and San Diego.

Highlights of your visit to South Lake Tahoe might be a sleigh ride behind a team of beautiful blond Belgium horses, or a summer sail across the lake on a huge catamaran. Watch for road signs announcing snow play areas (usually $3.00 per car), public beaches, and trailheads.

Virginia City If you have an extra day, take a drive to Virginia City, about 30 miles east of South Lake Tahoe on Highway 341. Tread the boardwalks of this picturesque, nineteenth-century town on the side of a steep mountainside, site of the discovery of the Comstock Lode, where the largest silver strike in the world was made. You can take a train ride, explore an old cemetery, and visit mines and museums. Watch taffy and chocolate being made, and shop for antiques and old-time souvenirs. This makes for a great outing, although you'll want to take it easy on the narrow, winding mountain road.

HEAVENLY VALLEY TRAM (all ages)

Off Highway 50 on the east end of Ski Run Boulevard, South Lake Tahoe; (775) 586–7000. Open Memorial Day to mid-October. Tickets are $5.00 for adults and $3.00 for children; kids 2 and under ride Free.

Right in the middle of town, an exciting 1-mile ride into the sky on the Heavenly Aerial Tram for a bird's-eye view of Lake Tahoe on one side and Nevada's Carson Valley on the other, along with hundreds of miles of high desert stretching out into the distance. On the 10,100-foot summit, an easy 2-mile trail loops the mountaintop, and there is a restaurant serving good but pricey meals. From the sundeck, take a guided nature, sunset, early evening birding, full moon, or stargazing hike.

HEAVENLY VALLEY SKI RESORT

4004 Ski Run Boulevard, South Lake Tahoe 96150; (775) 586–7000 or (877) 243– 0003; www.skiheavenly.com. Lift tickets for ages 13 and up are about $55, ages 6 to 12 are about $25, and kids 5 and under are Free*; multiday discounts are available. Sightseeing tram rides are $14 for ages 13 and up, $9.50 for ages 6 to 12.*

One of the largest ski resorts in the western states, Heavenly Valley has an average of 360 inches of snow, covering more than eighty ski runs. On the summit you have the phenomenal experience of feeling like you are skiing right into the lake. If your legs can take it, start from the top of Sky Express and ski 5 miles nonstop downhill.

Ski Explorers is the program for children ages 4 to 12, from new little skiers in the Enchanted Forest to hotdoggers taking "Shred-Ready" snowboard lessons. Besides all-day care and lessons, there are special presentations for kids by the ski patrol, demos by grooming vehicles, appearances by the avalanche dogs, and even cooking lessons.

Cruises

- *MS Dixie II* **Paddlewheeler.** *Five miles north of South Lake Tahoe on Highway 50, Zephyr Cove; (775) 588–3508. Several Emerald Bay cruises a day. Tickets $9.00 adults, $5.00 children, under 2 are* Free. In the wintertime, the *Dixie* becomes a ski shuttle, taking skiers from South Lake Tahoe to ski resorts on the West Shore. The paddlewheeler was a cotton barge on the Mississippi in 1927, then a floating casino at Tahoe, when it sank and was raised and converted into a tour boat.

- *Tahoe Gal* **Paddlewheeler.** *850 North Lake Boulevard, Lighthouse Mall, Tahoe City 96145; (800) 218–2464 or (530) 583–0141; www.tahoegal.com. Tickets for adults $17.00, children $7.00.* Breakfast, lunch, shoreline and evening cruises.

- *Tahoe Queen* **Paddlewheeler.** *9090 Ski Run Boulevard, South Lake Tahoe 96150; (530) 541–3364; www.hornblower.com/laketahoe. Tickets $18 adults, $8 children, kids under 2 are* Free. *Off-season family discounts.* Huge, beautiful paddlewheeler makes day and evening trips to Emerald Bay. Besides summertime cruises, you can ride the *Queen* in the winter to Tahoe City and meet shuttle buses for major ski resorts; there is a big breakfast buffet in the morning, and live music and food on the afternoon return cruise.

- *Woodwind II* **Sailing Cruises.** *Zephyr Cove Marina, South Lake Tahoe; (888) 867–6394 or (775) 588–3000. Tickets $20 adults, $10 children, under 2 are* Free. This fifty-passenger, 41-foot trimaran with a glass bottom and indoor/outdoor seating is a comfortable boat, but a breezier experience without the indoor space of the paddlewheelers, so it's probably not a good choice if you have toddlers.

SUGAR BOWL SKI AREA

750 Mule Ears Court, Norden 95734; (530) 426–9000 (snow phone: 530–426–3847); www.sugarbowl.com.

The other large ski resort at South Lake Tahoe, Sugar Bowl, is on the slopes of 8,383-foot Mount Judah. New express lifts, more trails and a new lodge make this one of the best medium-size ski resorts at the lake, and it's closer to the Bay Area by as much as an hour than most ski areas. A new beginning quad chair and learning area is located right next to the lodge. Ask about winter and summer accommodations packages.

In Summit Adventure Camp, kids ages 6 to 12 get an all-day lesson, lunch, mountain touring, and a gift.

Emerald Bay

West from South Lake Tahoe on Highway 89, also called Emerald Bay Road, around the south end of the lake are a number of sightseeing, cultural, and recreation destinations. Mount Tallac towers above them all.

Emerald Bay is the most photographed place at Tahoe, a scintillating piece of water surrounded by dense pine forests and decorated with an island that is topped by a teahouse. Campgrounds are extremely popular in this area because of the easy accessibility to trailheads into Desolation Wilderness.

Built in 1928, Vikingsholm, the treasure of Emerald Bay, is a cross between an eleventh-century castle and an ancient church. Reached by a steep, downhill, 1-mile paved trail (or by tour boat), the thirty-eight-room mansion is considered the finest example of Scandinavian architecture in North America. The **Free** ranger's tour of the fancifully furnished estate is well worth an hour of your time. This is a beautiful spot to have a picnic, swim and sunbathe, take a short hike, then take your time climbing back up to Highway 89.

From the highway it's an easy 2-mile loop hike to Eagle Falls and Eagle Lake, which are surrounded by the sheer walls of Desolation Wilderness, a glorious outback of rugged, alpine territory crisscrossed by trails and dotted with hundreds of lakes. Desolation Wilderness is best in the off-season, as easy accessibility makes it extremely popular for hiking and backpacking in high season. For an 11.4-mile loop day-trip, take the Glen Alpine trailhead at the end of Fallen Leaf Lake Road and hike to Lake Aloha.

Near Emerald Bay, Baldwin, Pope, and Kiva Beaches are accessible by bus from South Lake Tahoe. The popular Emerald Bay State Park Campground has 100 tent and RV sites and boat-in campsites (closed from mid-September until mid-June).

U.S. FOREST SERVICE LAKE TAHOE VISITOR'S CENTER

Emerald Bay Road, Baldwin Beach; (530) 573–2600. Open 8:30 A.M. to 8:30 P.M. during summer.

Here are exhibits of geology, animal habitats, and history. You can get maps and advice as to trail conditions and campground availability, and sign up for a ranger-led interpretive walk. A children's program called "Woodsy Rangers" is presented each day.

A four-hour, 5-mile, rather strenuous loop hike from here to the summit of Mount Tallac rewards trekkers with magnificent views at 9,700 feet. For casual strollers and for the handicapped, the **Rainbow Trail** is a paved path wandering past signs that explain the natural habitat; over 100 species of wildflowers bloom alongside the trail. The Stream Profile Chamber is a cross section of a real stream habitat filled with rushing water, fish, rocks, plants and other wildlife. Children can get a peek at the underwater world of a mountain stream through floor-to-ceiling viewing windows and in 12-foot-high murals. In the fall, thousands of visitors come to watch brilliant red spawning salmon wiggle their way from Lake Tahoe up Taylor Creek.

CAMP RICHARDSON AND STABLES

Five miles south of the "Y," Emerald Bay Road, South Lake Tahoe; (530) 541–1801.

Camp Richardson has been a favorite family summer vacation resort for decades. Rooms in the cavernous main lodge are small and simple. There are a marina, a sandy beach, riding stables, restaurants, cottages to rent, a 230-unit campground, and a general store. The camp makes a convenient headquarters from which to set off on horseback or on foot into Desolation Wilderness. Paddleboats, Jet Skis, and other water-toy rentals are available at the Marina.

The historic post office is a 1920s-style trading post, with locally crafted vintage toys, apple dolls, Native American art, scenic paintings of the lake, and logo items.

A new children's activity camp for kids ages 5 to 13 offers supervised winter snow play and cross-country ski lessons and summertime outdoor play and arts-and-crafts activities; the camp is only for guests at Camp Richardson and Harrah's Casino Hotel.

Breakfast and steak dinner guided horseback rides from Camp Richardson to Fallen Leaf Lake are a thrill for youngsters and the whole family. They take about three hours and are very popular, so reserve ahead. Children must be 6 years old; guided rides for children only are also available.

Fallen Leaf Lake is accessible by road off Highway 89 and makes a wonderful day-trip from Camp Richardson. You can hike around the lake, swim, picnic or barbecue, and launch a boat.

TALLAC HISTORIC SITE (all ages)

5 miles south of the "Y" at Camp Richardson, Highway 89; (530) 542–4166.

The rich and famous kicked up their heels in the 1920s at this beautiful, lakeside compound of formerly private estates, an old casino, the Valhalla Boathouse and a hotel. The buildings are restored and open for tours, and many musical and art events are held here in the summer (see sidebar).

KAYAK TAHOE (ages 4 and up)

Camp Richardson, P.O. Box 11129, Tahoe Paradise 96155; (530) 544–2011. Day tours, camping trips, lessons, rentals.

Rent kayaks here or take a guided kayak tour. Today's new kayaks are lighter and easier to use than those you may remember from years past. Smaller children can ride with parents on most boats, and children from about 7 years old can manage easily by themselves.

SORENSEN'S RESORT

14255 Highway 99, Hope Valley 96120; (800) 423–9949 or (530) 694–2203. Cabins; cafe; guided fishing, hiking, and cross-country ski tours. $$

In a pine and aspen grove on the West Fork of the Carson River, Sorensen's Resort was a rest stop for emigrants in the 1800s. Rustic log cabins here have a homespun country decor, brass beds, wood stoves, and some kitchens. At night, lights twinkle around the cabin doors and wood smoke is in the air. This is a popular place for families, and reservations need to be made weeks or even months in advance.

You can sit in a rocker on your cabin porch while the kids fish in the small stocked pond for trout. An old logging road adjacent to the resort leads right into the Toiyabe National Forest.

Ask about the guided hike on the Emigrant Trail. Worn smooth by pioneers on their way west, it's a fascinating route, with evidence of how wagons and animals were hauled up and down steep grades and cliffsides.

The fishing is great on the Carson, which winds through the valley beyond the resort. You can buy guidebooks and fishing licenses here and get advice on where to catch the big ones. Fishing and cross-country ski instruction and rentals are available.

Cozy with a woodburning stove, Sorensen's Country Cafe serves hearty breakfasts, lunches, and dinners, indoors and outside under the trees. Your family can sit with others at a big wooden table and tuck into beef stew, fresh fish, homemade bread, and fruit cobbler. Breakfast is all-you-can-eat waffles or bacon and eggs. A drive to Sorensen's just for a meal makes a nice getaway from South Lake Tahoe.

nnual Events at the Tallac Historic Site

- **Valhalla Renaissance Festival.** *June.* A step into Renaissance England: An old English country fair is re-created with knights in combat, archery contests, jugglers, magicians, dancers, plays, period music, and dozens of vendors of food, crafts, and psychic readings. It's fun to put together simple costumes to wear to the festival.

- **Reggae Sunday on Valhalla Lawn.** *August.* Held from 1:00 to 4:00 P.M.; barbecue.

- **Valhalla Festival of Arts and Music.** *July–August.* Concerts, exhibits, and children's events.

- **Wa-She-Shu Way Native American Festival.** *July.* **Free.** Indian dancers, historic reenactments, lots of children's activities.

- **Great Gatsby Festival.** *August.* **Free.** Costumed celebration of the 1920s.

- **Tuesday Potpourri Concerts,** *Valhalla, July–August.* Country western, steel drums, Irish jigs, swing—take your pick.

- **Boathouse Theater Productions.** *June–August.* Comedies, children's theater.

KIRKWOOD RESORT

601 Kirkwood Road, Highway 88, at Carson Pass 95646; (209) 258–6000 or (800) 967–7500; www.skikirkwood.com. $$–$$$.

A half-hour east of Sorensen's, Kirkwood is a year-round destination resort, headquarters for fly-fishing, cross-country and downhill skiing, and high-altitude hiking and backpacking. You can stay in a lodge room or rent a condo or a house. Brand new are the Mountain Club, a deluxe condo hotel with one- and two-bedroom units with lofts, and Snow-crest, a condo complex at the base of the lifts. Snazzy boutique shops and restaurants are new additions, too, that have helped transform Kirkwood into a major destination resort, adding glitter to a formerly backcountry atmosphere. The surrounding wilderness setting, however, remains as glorious as ever.

At 7,800 feet elevation, Kirkwood has the highest base elevation of any ski resort in the Tahoe Basin, with a long ski season and dependably top snow conditions. In a Tyrolean-style village atmosphere, laid-back Kirkwood is less commercial and more like ski mountains used to be, where you can ski in your jeans and dare to be seen with equipment more than five years old. The Mighty Mountain Ski Center offers child care, lessons, and a kids-only lift. Kamp Kirkwood entertains nonskiing kids, and there is an evening program for 6- to 12-year-olds. A new Children's Center is located at Timber Creek Lodge, near a terrain garden and a beginner and intermediate chair. On hundreds of acres of alpine meadows, Nordic skiing is perfection.

Among the unique adventures to be had here are horse-drawn sleigh rides, outdoor ice skating, and snowshoeing after dark with headlamps. Nearby, at the summit of Carson Pass, Caples Lake attracts trout fishermen, canoers, windsurfers, and swimmers. Trails lead into the Mokelumne Wilderness.

Where to Eat

Cantina Los Tres Hombres. *711 Emerald Bay Road, South Lake Tahoe 96158; (530) 544–1233.* Good Mexican food, lively atmosphere. $$

Ernie's. *Near the "Y," 1146 Emerald Bay Road, South Lake Tahoe 96158; (530) 541–2161.* Casual atmosphere; American breakfasts and lunches. $

Strawberry Lodge. *Highway 50, Kyburz 95720; (530) 659–7200.* Good, simple American food and soda fountain specialties in a restored 1940s lodge. Stop here on the way in and out of South Lake Tahoe. Walking trails are nearby. $

Hot Pepper Grill. *3490 Lake Tahoe Boulevard, South Lake Tahoe 96158; (530) 542–1015.* Wonderful tacos and fresh Mexican food, for here or to go. $

The Red Hut. *2723 Highway 50, 3.5 miles south of Stateline, South Lake Tahoe 96158; (530) 541–9024.* A popular retro cafe with comfy booths, a big counter, and an American comfort food menu. $

Where to Stay

The variety of places for families to stay in the South Lake Tahoe area is staggering, from condos and motel rooms to suite hotels and campgrounds. A call to the Lake Tahoe Visitor's Authority (800-AT-TAHOE) will get you advice on long- and short-term accommodations.

Embassy Suites Resort. *4130 Lake Tahoe Boulevard, South Lake Tahoe 96158; (800) 362–2779.* A contemporary mountain lodge, with two-room luxury suites that are a bargain for families: two double beds, a sofa bed, two TVs, a microwave, a coffeemaker, and in-room movies. Indoor pool and spa, sundeck, workout room; seasonal packages; **free** shuttle to the airport and the Heavenly Valley ski area and to casinos. Room rate includes full breakfast and a two-hour, early-evening party of snacks, drinks, and alcoholic beverages. $$

Tahoe Keys Resort. *999 Tahoe Keys Boulevard, South Lake Tahoe 96158; (530) 544–5397.* Homes and condos for rent; indoor and outdoor swimming pools, health club, bicycles, outdoor games,

playground, private beach, ski shuttles, power-boat rentals, parasailing, Jet Skis, boat launching—in other words, vacation central. $$

Lakeland Village. *3535 Lake Tahoe Boulevard, South Lake Tahoe 96158; (800) 822–5969 or (702) 785–2424; e-mail: lakeland@sierra.net.* Spread out along the lake in nineteen acres of pines, with a private, sandy beach, two heated swimming pools, a wading pool, and tennis courts. Condo or lodge units, some with fireplaces and kitchens. Convenient shuttle buses connect the resort with nearby ski areas and downtown. $$

Forest Inn Suites. *1 Lake Parkway, South Lake Tahoe 96158; (800) 822–5950 or (530) 541–6655.* One- and two-bedroom suites with equipped kitchens in five acres of forest, with pools, spas and a health club, and a shuttle to the Heavenly Valley ski area. $$

Lake Tahoe Accommodations. *2048 Dunlap Drive, South Lake Tahoe 96158; (800) 544–3234 or (530) 544–3234.* Condo and home rentals. $–$$$

For More Information

California State Campgrounds Reservations. *P.O. Box 942896,*

Sacramento, CA 94296-0001; (800) 777–0369 or (916) 653–6995;

www.cal-parks.ca.gov. Call or write for the "Camping Reservation Guide," a complete explanation of how to make campsite reservations with a complete directory of campgrounds, facilities, and costs.

Ski Lake Tahoe. *P.O. Box 10797, South Lake Tahoe 96158; (530) 541–2462 or (800) 588–SNOW; www.SkiLake Tahoe.com.* Represents six major ski resorts; ask about packages and family discounts.

Road Conditions and Ski Reports. *(530) 577–3550, (800) 427–7623, or (415) 864–6440.*

Lake Tahoe Visitor's Authority. *1156 Ski Run Boulevard, South Lake Tahoe 96151; (800) AT–TAHOE.* Use this number to book reservations, get tickets to events, obtain airline tickets, and hear about weather and road conditions.

Tahoe City/West Shore

Summers have that "vacation in the mountains" feeling on the West Shore of Lake Tahoe, when families return to their cabins at the beach and to favorite campgrounds and cottage resorts in the pines. The small town of Tahoe City, whose main street is right on the lakeshore, is headquarters for restaurants and shopping. Two of the largest ski resorts are nearby, Squaw Valley USA—site of the 1960 Winter Olympics—and Alpine Meadows. Both resorts have condos and houses to rent.

On the south end of town at the junction of Highways 89 and 28, you can't miss Fanny Bridge. Here where the Truckee joins the lake, people are always lined up, leaning over to watch and feed the fish in the trout ladder—a line of fannies—hence the name Fanny Bridge. Bring bread or fish food for a fun half-hour.

The largest winter carnival in the western states, **Snowfest**, takes place in March and is based in Tahoe City, Truckee, and at ski resorts. Fireworks and a torchlight parade at Squaw Valley start off a weekend of parades, ice carving, ice-cream eating, and live comedy and musical performances. More than 100 events include the Great Ski Race—a 30K Nordic event between Tahoe City and Truckee—a Snow Dog contest, celebrity races, and the Snowboard Spectacular. It's wall-to-wall people and lots of fun. Many children's events are scheduled, such as the dress-up-your-dog contest and snow sculpture.

The Old West in Carson City *About 45 minutes from South Lake Tahoe, by way of Highway 50. For information about events, museums, and attractions in Carson City, call 800–NEVADA.*

Carson City makes a great day-trip, particularly during one of the annual festivals and celebrations. The town is rooted in the Old West, with ties to Kit Carson and pioneer times. The 2.5-mile Kit Carson Trail is a walk past Victorian homes, the Governor's Mansion, the Nevada State Museum, and the Krebs Peterson House, where John Wayne's last movie, *The Shootist*, was filmed. On your portable tape player or your car radio, you can tune in to recorded descriptive anecdotes.

The **Nevada State Railroad Museum** here displays more than two dozen restored railroad cars and locomotives. On "steam-up" weekend, visitors can hop aboard one of the historic trains and take a twenty-minute, 1-mile ride with a conductor who spins tales of early railroading days. The facility, at 400 Carson Road in Carson City (702–333–4550), is open daily; admission is $2.00 for adults, with children under 18 admitted Free.

For kids ages 3 through 12, the Children's Museum of Northern Nevada offers 8,000 square feet of interactive fun, such as a giant kaleidoscope to walk through, the giant piano from the movie *Big*, and more neato stuff (783 Carson Road in Carson City; 702–887–5436).

TRUCKEE RIVER

One of the loveliest places to walk and bike a good distance is the paved Truckee River Bike Path, which winds 4 miles along the river into Tahoe City, then heads south along the lakeshore for 9 more miles through forested neighborhoods and parks. The path is flat enough for baby strollers and wheelchairs. This is a beautiful path in fall, when the days are crisp and aspens turn gold. In the low-water days of late summer and fall, the river slides quietly along; in winter and spring it boils and crashes past ice-decorated trees and snowy islands.

Rafting the Truckee is a "must" on at least one of your Tahoe trips. It's a Class 1 river, meaning it's quite safe most of the year. Even if you've never rafted before, after a short lesson you can easily manage. If you have children under 5, be sure to call ahead to ask if the rafting company allows younger kids.

You rent six-person rafts and life jackets and paddle merrily along downriver about 5 miles, stopping along the way to play and swim if you wish and maybe to picnic on a sand spit. Some people bring their fishing rods along. Paddling without stopping, it takes about two hours to reach your destination, which is River Ranch, where a shuttle bus takes you back to your car. Rentals are about $25 per person at the Truckee River Rafting Center (530–583–RAFT) and Fanny Bridge Raft Rentals (530–583–3021), both on the southern end of Tahoe City.

RIVER RANCH

Highway 89 at Alpine Meadows Road, Tahoe City 96145; (530) 583–4264.

A small, charming hotel with a very popular indoor/outdoor restaurant and bar, River Ranch is on the south end of the Truckee Bike Path. The river-rafting trips end here, and rafters invariably hang out for a while in the sun, eating burgers and salads and watching other rafters and bikers arrive.

BLACKWOOD CANYON

Off Highway 89, 9.5 miles south of Tahoe City, just north of Tahoe Pines 96145; (530) 573–2600 or (916) 573–2600.

A few minutes south of Tahoe City, just north of Tahoe Pines, this is one of the most accessible but least known wilderness areas at Tahoe. The road into the canyon is perfect for easy walks, Rollerblading, and biking. The paved road is the only development and has almost no traffic, making a good add-on to the shoreline bike path. On the leafy banks of Blackwood Creek and in the forests and meadows here are idyllic picnic spots. You can hike on the flat valley floor or drive up the road to the steep trails of 8,000-foot Barker Pass, hooking up with the Pacific Crest Trail.

SUNNYSIDE RESTAURANT AND LODGE

1850 West Lake Boulevard, 2 miles south of Tahoe City 96145; (530) 583–7200.

With one of the most breathtaking blue-water and high-mountain views on the lake, the deck at Sunnyside is the place to be on a summer afternoon. Boats of every description come and go in the marina, French-fried zucchini and onion rings are tops, and once you and the kids get settled outside on the deck, you'll find it hard to move from the spot. Kids can run around a bit, staying away from the boats.

Here you can rent Jet Skis, sailboats, and power boats and take a sailing lesson. Winter evenings are warm and friendly in the lounge in front of a giant river rock fireplace. Sunnyside's lodge rooms are small and very nice, though rather pricey and not set up for families.

HOMEWOOD MOUNTAIN RESORT

5145 West Lake Boulevard, 6 miles south of Tahoe City, Homewood 96141; (530) 525–2992 (snow phone: 530–525–2900); www.skihomewood.com. Lift tickets are about $40 for adults, $25 for ages 13 to 18, and $10 for ages 11 to 12, kids under 10 are Free, *and there are multiday and ski school packages.*

One of the most accessible and most reasonably priced ski areas for children and beginning skiers, Ski Homewood offers nine lifts on a small mountain with big views of Lake Tahoe. Parking is easy, and licensed day care and a "Ski and Play" program are available. On "Wild Wednesdays" after January 1, adult lift tickets are sold on a two-for-one basis. Call ahead to book the Homewood shuttle from sites on the West Shore.

CHAMBERS LANDING

One mile south of Homewood, on Highway 89; (530) 525–7672. Day-use fee is $5.00. Restrooms; no lifeguard.

A good place to plunk down on the beach for the day is at Chambers Landing, which has a short pier with a bar at the end where locals hang out. On one side of the pier is a private beach for people staying in the Chambers Landing condos and on the other side is a public beach, one of the nicest on the West Shore. It's a good beach for small children, because there are enough boating and water sports activities to keep them interested in the passing scene but not so many people that you feel overwhelmed. The upscale restaurant here has a glass-enclosed, heated terrace.

Tahoe Rim Trail *Maps and information: (530) 577–0676.* From Fairway Drive in Tahoe City, you can connect with the 150-mile Tahoe Rim Trail, a hiking and equestrian path that follows the ridgetops surrounding the entire lake, passing through six counties in Nevada and California and incorporating about 50 miles of the Pacific Crest National Scenic Trail. The Tahoe Rim Trail is also accessible from several other trailheads around the lake, as shown on the map you can get by calling the number above.

SUGAR PINE POINT STATE PARK (all ages)

Five miles south of Tahoe City on Highway 89; (530) 525–7982. The facility has 175 campground sites (reservations: 800–444–7275).

This is a place to spend a whole day, tour a vintage mansion, walk in the woods, swim and sunbathe, and picnic and play in a spectacular lakeside setting.

One of the grandes dames of Tahoe, a spectacular three-story, 12,000-square-foot Queen Anne–style summer home, the Ehrman Mansion, once a privately owned estate, is now owned by the National Park Service. The mansion is surrounded by sweeping lawns shaded by tall pines. Rangers give daily **Free** tours of the house and the charming boathouse, while they impart stories of halcyon old days on the lake. Even little kids enjoy the tour because the house is full of interesting stuff and you clamber up wooden staircases, looking into family bedrooms. After the tour wander around the grounds, spread a blanket on the beach, or take a walk on flat, easy trails along the lakeshore. A longer hike is accessible from the large campground across the road.

MEEKS BAY RESORT AND MARINA (all ages)

Ten miles south of Tahoe City, Highway 89; (530) 525–7242 or (530) 573–2600.

Owned by the U.S. Forest Service, Meeks Bay is a popular Jet Ski and water-ski beach, with an unparalleled view of the lake. This is a good place for beachy activities such as rowing, canoeing, paddleboating (all rentable), and hanging out in the sun, though all the motors create plenty of noise during summer. My granddaughters and I have canoed from here around the coves and shorelines on either side of the bay. In just a few minutes, you are away from the fracas on the beach. Just watch the boat traffic when you are paddling in and out of the bay. A little cafe here serves snacks and burgers, and there are a 150-unit campground and a few cottages. $

SQUAW VALLEY USA

Between Tahoe City and Truckee on Highway 89, Olympic Valley, 96146; (800) 401–9216 or (800) 545–4350 (snow phone: 530–583–6955); www.squaw. com. Lift tickets for adults about $50.00, ages 13 to 15 $25.00, ages 12 and under $5.00.

A huge summer and winter recreation area, Squaw Valley is spectacular in every season. Waves of wildflowers—or snowfields—roll across open meadows below a jagged circle of snowcapped peaks. Lodges, hotels, rental condos, and homes are scattered in forested areas.

To get an overall view of the valley, take the 150-passenger aerial cable car to the High Camp complex, a thrilling, 2,000-foot ascent to an 8,250-foot summit. Up here on the top of the world, you can ice skate, hike, mountain bike, swim, picnic, play volleyball and tennis, bungee jump, or just blink in amazement at the surrounding mountains. For the sports-oriented family, Squaw Valley offers facilities unmatched in the western states.

A nice 4-mile hike from the floor of Squaw Valley is the Shirley Lakes trail, starting behind the Olympic Village Inn. Younger children like it, because they can stop to wade or swim in the creek, roll around in grassy meadows, or take naps under the pines.

One of the world's largest and best ski mountains—actually five peaks—Squaw Valley USA Ski Resort, where the 1960 Winter Olympics were held, has thirty lifts accessing more than 4,000 acres of skiable terrain. A new high-speed six-person chair operates even during storm conditions.

At night until 9:00 P.M., ride the heated cable car to High Camp, the midmountain restaurant and ice-skating complex, and have dinner before you glide down Mountain Run, a 3.5-mile, illuminated run.

Après-ski, sip hot cocoa or ice skate; all-day and half-day lift tickets are valid for night skiing.

You can choose from combinations of child care and ski lessons at "Children's World," for 2- to 12-year-olds, including rentals, meals, lift tickets, and lessons. A licensed day-care facility cares for 2- to 3-year-olds, with meals, music, snow play, and plenty of quiet time. If your 3-year-old is ready to ski, he or she can have a lesson just for tots.

The "Fun in the Sun" program introduces those 13 and up, including adults, to skiing for the first time and features a **Free** cable car ride, **Free** rentals, and demonstrations. Kids under 13 and adults over 65 ski for only $5.00 every day. That's a *deal*.

The Squaw Valley Nordic Center consists of 20 miles of groomed track and wilderness trails, plus a telemark downhill area accessed by lifts.

SQUAW VALLEY USA MOUNTAIN BIKE PARK (ages 7 and up)

Tram ride and trail pass cost $19.00; rentals $17.00–$40.00; helmets, $5.00. Tracks and roads are open from 10:00 A.M. to 5:00 P.M., and you can rent new bikes. Packages are available.

As soon as the snow melts, the High Camp tram starts transporting mountain bikers and their bikes to the Squaw Valley USA Mountain Bike Park. Because of the phenomenal access to alpine-level trails, mountain biking is wildly popular at Tahoe. Annual biking events at Squaw include the Fat Tire Fest in August and the Downhill Mania and American MB Championship, both in September.

ALPINE MEADOWS SKI AREA

Six miles northwest of Tahoe City on Highway 89, P.O. Box 5279, Tahoe City 96145; (800) 441–4423; snow phone: (530) 581–8374; www.skialpine.com. Lift tickets for adults about $50, ages 13 to 15 about $40, ages 7 to 12 and under $10; grandmas and grandpas over 75 ride and ski Free. *Stay and Ski packages at nearby condos save families money (800–949–3296).* Free *shuttle buses connect skiers with lodgings on the West and North Shores.*

Priding itself on the longest ski season, Alpine is known for its laid-back, casual atmosphere. Intermediate and advanced ski runs have scary names like Chute That Seldom Slides, Promised Land, and Our Father.

Kids are VIPs at Kid's School and Ski Camp. On the new Sun Kid beginner surface lift, children just step onto a slow conveyor belt with their equipment on, avoiding the sometimes intimidating chair lift until they are ready for it. Programs for all ages are offered for racing, snowboarding, telemark, freestyle, and just plain skiing; and there is ski instruction for people with mental and physical disabilities. Sled dog tours from here are an exciting way to get out into the beautiful forest and snow-covered meadows.

Where to Eat

Fire Sign Cafe. *1785 West Lake Boulevard, Tahoe City 96145; (530) 583–0871.* Home-style cooking, cozy country atmosphere, breakfast and lunch. $

Rosie's Cafe. *571 North Lake Boulevard, Tahoe City 96145; (530) 583–8504.* Reasonable and relaxed, serving breakfast, lunch, and dinner. $

Fast Eddie's Texas BBQ. *690 North Lake Boulevard, Tahoe City 96145; (530) 583–0950.* The best barbecue in the Tahoe Basin. Lunch and dinner. $

Rubicon Deli. *In the Tahoe Tree Nursery, 401 West Lake Boulevard, 2 miles north of Tahoe City 96145; (530) 583–0577.* Super-yummy sandwiches to have here or take away, within a beautiful plant nursery and gift shop. $

Where to Stay

Cottage Inn. *1690 West Lake Boulevard, 2 miles south of Tahoe City 96145; (530) 581– 4073.* Fifteen mountain-style cottages with Scandinavian decor, fire-

places, hearty breakfasts, sauna, private beach. Ask for a unit away from the road. This is a popular place. $$

Tahoe Taverns. *300 West Lake Boulevard, near Fanny Bridge in Tahoe City 96145; (530) 583–3704.* Large complex of nice condos in a pine grove, on the waterfront; pool, lawns, quiet, ultra-convenient location. $$

Tavern Inn. *203 Squaw Valley Road, Olympic Valley 96146; (800) 435–9467.* Luxury condos, all with fireplaces, sleep four to ten. $$$

Norfolk Woods Inn. *6941 West Lake Boulevard, Tahoma 96142; (530) 525–5000.* Across the road from the bike trail and the lake, small rooms in the lodge, plus rustic, remodeled cottages with two bedrooms and kitchens. Pool and hot tub. Rates include big breakfasts. $$

Chinquapin Resort. *Three miles north of Tahoe City, 3600 North Lake Boulevard, Tahoe City 96145; (800) 732–6721.* Spacious, one- to four-bedroom townhouses and condos with wonderful lake views. Fireplaces, fully equipped kitchens, pool, and tennis courts. $$$

Squaw Valley Lodge. *201 Squaw Peak Road, Olympic Valley 96146; (800) 922– 9970 or (530) 583–5500; www. squawvalleylodge.com.* A sprawling, all-suite lodge with one or two bedrooms and lofts, equipped kitchens, and luxurious amenities such as down comforters. You can park your car here and get to outdoor recreation, restaurants, and sites on foot, by cable car to High Camp, and valley shuttles. Enjoy the tennis courts and big pool, and unlimited use of a nearby health club with Nautilus. Ski right out the door to the lifts! $$–$$$

Resort at Squaw Creek. *400 Squaw Creek Road, Olympic Valley 96146; (800) 327–3353.* A luxurious, 400-room destination resort in a lovely mountain setting overlooking the meadows of Squaw Valley, with three swimming pools, a 120-foot water slide, a championship golf course, elegant shops, a tennis complex, and a chair lift to ski runs and to High Camp.

Mountain Buddies daytime camp for ages 3 to 13; special excursions for teens. Cross-country ski, hike, and bike right from the hotel. $$$–$$$$

Granlibakken Resort. *P.O. Box 6329, just north of Tahoe City 96145; (800) 543–3221; www.granlibakken.com.* A perfect headquarters for families in summer or winter, a 160-room condominium resort with a beginners ski and snowboard hill, Nordic skiing, developed snow play area, and a big swimming pool. Some units have fireplaces, kitchens, lofts, and decks or patios. The complimentary hot breakfast is huge! $–$$

For More Information

North Lake Tahoe Resort Association. *P.O. Box 1757, Tahoe City 96145; (888) 434–1262 or (530) 583–3494; www.tahoe-4-u.com.*

Truckee Donner Chamber of Commerce, *12036 Donner Pass Road, Truckee 96161; (530) 584–2757.*

Incline Village/North Shore

A small community on steep, forested hillsides above the North Shore of Lake Tahoe, Incline Village has three private beaches with breathtaking views. Lots of outdoor recreation is within a few minutes' drive. If you have small children, you'll like the quiet, family residential atmosphere here. With the kids in tow, you can get in beach time and take walks around town, visit a western theme park nearby, and plan a few half-day outings to easily accessible mountain meadows, lakes, and streams.

Tahoe Tessie's Lake Tahoe Monster Museum
8612 North Lake Boulevard, Kings Beach; (530) 546–8774. Open weekends from 10:00 A.M. to 5:00 P.M. (till 6:00 P.M. June 15 to Labor Day). Admission is Free *for all.*

What's that swimming in the lake? It's a USO—an Unidentified Swimming Object! It's green, it's scaly, it's bumping into boat docks and terrorizing water-skiers. Is it a sea serpent or a giant fish?

Part of the folklore of Lake Tahoe, a notorious creature has been seen and feared for centuries by the Indians, the silver miners, and Tahoe's old-timers. The 1960s, 1970s, and 1980s brought a rash of mysterious sightings by tourists and residents, including two policemen, some nuns, and a clutch of postal employees.

Some say it's a huge sturgeon planted in the lake by accident; sturgeon can grow to 1,500 pounds and live to be one hundred years old. There's also the Mackinaw theory, the giant trout theory, the boa constrictor theory, and the brontosaurus theory.

Researchers from UCLA came to study the monster in the 1980s, testing the theory that since Lake Tahoe is one of the deepest, highest, and coldest lakes in the world—similar geologically to Scotland's Loch Ness—perhaps a prehistoric marine reptile from an extinct species still exists. Tessie declined to appear for the scientists.

Concerned that tourists would be frightened away, the South Tahoe Visitors' Bureau confiscated videotapes of an alleged monster sighting.

In recent years thousands of young readers and their delighted parents and grandparents have become pals with the gregarious green creature in the pages of the book *The Story of Tahoe Tessie*. According to the local author, Jim McCormick, Tessie frolics in the lake, saves drowning children, and teaches Tahoe history and Indian lore.

Tahoe Tessie's Lake Tahoe Monster Museum in Kings Beach is a tiny, somewhat touristy but fun place to see a life-size Tessie, read eyewitness accounts of Tessie sightings, see "real" photos of her, and buy Tessie T-shirts, souvenirs, and toys.

Incline's private beaches, and a beautiful recreation center with a pool, playground, and tennis courts are available only to those who rent, own, or stay at selected hotel and motel accommodations in Incline. Renting a condo or house is the way to come here, and it can be as cost-effective as a resort or a motel. When you make your arrangements for accommodations, be sure to ask about getting an IVGID card, which will admit you and the family to the beaches and the rec center.

A paved sidewalk on Lakeshore Drive runs along the lake for several miles, past the beaches and lovely homes—perfect for jogging, baby carriage–pushing, walking, and biking. Giant sugar pine cones are scattered liberally about, free for the taking. The gardens and the architecture are interesting sights in themselves.

BURNT CEDAR BEACH

300 Lakeshore Drive, Incline Village 89451; (775) 831–1310. Open daily year-round from 7:00 A.M. to sunset. Restrooms, lifeguard, pool.

My grandchildren love the beaches at Incline. Their favorite, Burnt Cedar Beach, has a big heated pool with a lifeguard, a playground, lawns shaded by tall sugar pines, and a sandy beach with shallow water for wading, deeper water for swimming, and a killer view! The kids use coat hangers and small nets to fish for crawdads in the rocks. Sometimes we buy lunch at the snack bar, or we bring a picnic to have on the lawn. The facility also has nice picnic tables and barbecues.

SKI BEACH AND INCLINE BEACH

500 Lakeshore Drive, Incline Village 89451; (775) 831–1310. Open daily year-round from 7:00 A.M. to sunset. Restrooms, lifeguard, boat and water-toy rentals.

Ski Beach, in front of the Hyatt Regency Lake Tahoe, and Incline Beach are busier than Burnt Cedar—and a little noisier, with Jet Skis and boats—but they have the advantage of being more fun for older children and long enough for a half-hour's stroll.

SAND HARBOR STATE PARK

Highway 28, ten minutes south of Incline Village; (775) 831–0494. (For tickets to Music and Shakespeare at Sand Harbor, call 530–583–9048). Restrooms, barbecues, boat launch, lifeguard.

This is one of the most beautiful beach parks at the lake, with giant boulders, boat launch sites, pine groves, and white-sand beaches with lifeguards.

Families return year after year to the annual Sand Harbor Music and Shakespeare Festival, held July and August in the outdoor amphitheater overlooking the lake. Bring the kids, a picnic, and blankets, and lie stargazing while you listen to one of the Bard's comedies.

Concerts at Sand Harbor may be reggae or Dixieland, country western or rock-and-roll. Excitement builds as the sun sets, turning the lake from blue-green to bronze. As the play or the music begins, the kids settle down, the water goes deep ultramarine, and distant pines are inky-black against a dramatic mountain backdrop. Get your tickets early, as these events sell out, and remember to bring jackets and extra blankets for chilly evenings. Light sprinkles have been known to dampen the pines but not the spirits of play- and concertgoers. A "dance corral" separates the sand-kickers from quiet family groups on their blankets.

PONDEROSA RANCH (ages 4 and up)

100 Ponderosa Road, on the east side of Incline Village off Highway 28, Incline Village, NV 89451; (775) 831–0691. Open May through October, with limited winter operations, from 9:30 A.M. to 5:00 P.M. daily. Admission for adults $10.50, ages 5 to 11 $5.50, and **Free** *for kids under 5.*

Your kids don't remember the TV show *Bonanza,* but if they are about 12 or younger, they will love Ponderosa Ranch, a re-created western town and theme park based on the original set used to film *Bonanza.* Start with a haywagon breakfast, explore a mine, pan for gold, eat Hossburgers, and have sundaes in an old-fashioned ice cream parlor. Kids can pet farm animals, have a **Free** pony ride, pretend to be cowboys and cowgirls in a shooting gallery, and more.

SPOONER LAKE

Highway 28, 12 miles south of Incline Village; (702) 831–0494.

Spooner Lake nestles among pine and aspen forests crisscrossed by easy hiking trails. You can have a picnic in a meadow and can fish for trout in the small lake. In winter, Spooner Lake becomes a small cross-country ski area; rent equipment here and cruise the groomed trails, or bring snow saucers and slide around.

Here is the trailhead for a moderately strenuous, uphill, 10-mile hiking and mountain-biking trail to Marlette Lake. Spectacular views of the lake and surrounding mountains are the reward at the top, especially in fall when the aspens are blazing yellow. You can see vestiges of a huge system of wooden flumes that were built in the mid-1800s to move water from the lake to the booming silver-mining towns of Virginia City and Carson City, on the eastern side of the mountains.

MOUNT ROSE

Seven miles northeast of Incline Village on Highway 431. Hiking trails and undeveloped cross-country ski trails and sledding hills. No restrooms. Roadside parking.

Above Incline Village at 10,800 feet, Mount Rose is the highest peak in the area. From the scenic overlook on Highway 431, almost the entire 22-mile-long lake gleams below, rimmed by the Sierras on the west and the Carson Range on the east. Seven miles beyond the lookout point, on the east side of the road, is Tahoe Meadows, a scattering of glorious alpine meadows where you can enjoy cross-country skiing and summertime hiking, easy or strenuous. Tahoe Meadows Whole Access Trail is a wide, 1.3-mile loop designed for those in wheelchairs and baby strollers.

The 12-mile loop hike to the summit of Mount Rose is a half-day trip that starts on an old jeep road, near the cinder-block building close to the highway on the west side. Even if you can't make it to the top for the view that awaits, you might want to start up this trail; there are a pond with a frog chorus in residence and wildflowers galore. At the top you'll see the whole lake basin and the Carson Valley sweeping away into the distance—and even Lassen Peak, in Lassen National Park, on a clear day. Just beyond Tahoe Meadows, Mount Rose Campground is nice and cool in midsummer and often has tent and RV sites available when campgrounds near the lake are full *(775–882–2766)*. Stop here for fresh water and restrooms. You can walk from the campground to the top of the mountain and the Tahoe Meadows trail system.

TRUCKEE

Highway 80 at Highway 267; (530) 587–2757; www.truckee.com.

A popular stop on the way to the West Shore, the tiny town of Truckee was a rollicking railroading, logging and ice-harvesting headquarters in the 1800s. The picturesque main street is lined with Western wear and outdoor equipment stores, restaurants, and saloons in brick and stone, false-front buildings facing the railroad tracks and the 1869 depot where Amtrak trains blast into town daily. In May, Truckee steps back in time with gunslinger reenactments, gold panning, strolling musicians and storytelling.

NORTHSTAR-AT-TAHOE

Highway 267 between Truckee and Lake Tahoe; (800) 466–6784 or (530) 562–1010; www.skinorthstar.com.

One of the largest resorts at the lake, Northstar is a self-contained family-oriented complex laid out in a spectacular mountain and forest setting. It includes a golf course; equestrian, mountain biking, and hiking trails; shops, a deli, and a grocery; several bars and restaurants; and a plethora of nice condos, lodge rooms, and beautiful homes to rent.

You can park your car and get around entirely on foot and on the frequent resort shuttles. In the summer, chairlifts take hikers and bikers up to beautiful mountain-top trails, and there is a busy schedule of activities and events all year. Guided nature hikes include a lift ride and a chat with a naturalist about the plants, trees, animals, and the geology of the Sierras.

Older kids head for the teen center and the workout rooms. Parents love the lap pool. Little kids can play in the wading pool and the shallow end of the main pool, under the watchful eye of a lifeguard. Licensed child care is available.

The Northstar ski resort great for families, with a large number of intermediate- and beginning-level downhill and snowboarding runs. Minor's Camp cares for kids 2 to 6, with ski lessons optional. **Free** half-hour ski lessons are offered to all ages; and, skiers and boards ages 13 and up are offered **Free** intermediate and advanced lessons with the purchase of a lift ticket. Ask about the special First Tracks program, which gives early risers a head start before the lifts open to the public, and includes breakfast.

Parents looking forward to years of family fun on the slopes can attend a **Free** one-hour clinic on how to enjoy skiing with children. What a good idea!

As at virtually every ski resort at Tahoe, there are half-pipes and terrain parks for snowboarding and aerobatics. One of the many annual wintertime events at Northstar is the exciting Inverted Aerial Freestyle Ski Competition in February. Snow play is state of the art here, with snowscoots, snowbikes, snowsliding toys, tubing, and the Zorb, a 9.5-foot clear plastic sphere that rolls downhill with a passenger inside! At night on weekends and holidays, Polaris Park is an illuminated snow playground with music.

The sunny Summit Deck on the top of Mt. Pluto is twice as big now and twice as lively and fun for casual lunches and snacks.

DONNER LAKE (all ages)

Between Soda Springs and Truckee off Highway 80; (530) 582–7892.

Families who want a quiet, old-fashioned vacation in the mountains love Donner. On the 7.5 mile shoreline, you can camp, launch a boat, rent a cabin, fish, hike, ski and enjoy the crystal-clear, blue waters.

There are nearly thirty public piers on the north side for fishing and boating. Shoreline Park offers bank fishing and a pier, boat launching, picnic sites, and swimming. On the west end, a swimming area is supervised by lifeguards.

Above the lake on Highway 80, the Emigrant Gap viewpoint on Donner Summit, at 7,135 feet, is a must stop. Your family will get a dramatic geology lesson when you look out over hundreds of miles of high country to see the tremendous tilted block of the Sierras sloping toward the west. Glacial canyons are gouged out of the granite, and the Yuba and Bear Rivers have cut their own valleys.

On the west end of the lake is a trailhead for the Pacific Crest Trail. From here, you can take a fifteen-mile strenuous hike along the ridge of the Sierra crest, descending down into Squaw Valley's Shirley Canyon.

DONNER MEMORIAL STATE PARK (all ages)

3 miles west of Truckee, off Highway 80; (530) 544–3053.

Spend a half day's pleasant outing here on the way to Tahoe, and get a history lesson, too. Beneath towering evergreens, at 5,950 feet, walking paths and picnic groves are cool and shady. The Emigrant Trail Museum depicts stories of the Donner Party, a group of pioneer families who were trapped here during the violent winter of 1846–47. A monument rests on a stone base 22 feet high—the snow level of that fateful winter. In the museum are artifacts and displays on the building of the railroad through the Sierras in the 1800s. In the distance, you can see train tracks, mostly covered with snow buildings, running along the rugged mountainsides above Donner Lake; the tracks are still in use by Amtrak today.

Rangers guide interpretive walks throughout the summer, explaining local flora and fauna, and the history of the Donner Party.

DIAMOND PEAK SKI AREA

1210 Ski Way, on Highway 431 above Incline Village; (775) 832–1177; e-mail: ivgid@sierra.net; www.diamondpeak.com. Full-service ski resort, restaurants, ski school, equipment rental, child care.

Diamond Peak Ski Area at Mount Rose is a medium-size ski resort with spectacular lake and mountain views, and downhill and cross-country skiing. Intermediates and beginners are happy here; expert skiers will head for larger resorts. Snow conditions are less dependable than at higher-elevation resorts, but when the snow is primo, Diamond Peak is a good choice for families who prefer uncrowded ski runs and a casual, family-oriented atmosphere. Ask about discounts for the beginner lifts, twilight tickets, and family rates. There is an extensive shuttle network from area lodgings.

The Donner Party

One of the most notorious events of the pioneer era, the story of the Donner Party is taught to every California schoolchild. Kids find the grisly, cannibalistic aspects of the story quite fascinating. In July of 1846, eighty-seven emigrants—almost half of them children—started out in a wagon train from the Midwest on their way to a new life in California. They made the mistake of leaving a few weeks late with overloaded wagons. Encountering 22-foot snows and nonstop storms on the eastern side of the Sierras, they became trapped at high elevation for several months of the long winter, and almost half of the group died. Those who survived did so by resorting to making maximum use of the bodies of their deceased companions.

From the Emigrant Gap viewpoint area, on Highway 80 at Donner Summit, the starving travelers winched their wagons down into the Bear Valley, then dragged themselves back up to Washington Ridge on the opposite side, the most difficult part of their nightmarish journey.

An hourly slide show at Donner Memorial State Park is a good introduction to the Donner Party story.

TAHOE DONNER SKI AREA

897 Donner Pass Road, Truckee 96161; (530) 587–9484. Trail pass for adults $15, children 2 to 16 $9, under 2 **Free**. *Day lodge with restaurant, lessons, equipment rentals.*

A small, friendly, reasonably priced Nordic ski resort with a day lodge and lots of flat meadow trails for beginners.

BOREAL SKI AREA

Highway 80 at Donner Summit; (530) 426–3666. Lift tickets for adults about $25, children less than $20; small charge for snow play area.

A reasonably priced, nonintimidating choice for new skiers. The Nugget chairlift for beginners is **Free**, and there is a snow-play area with rental saucers, or you can bring your own. Night skiing is popular at Boreal, especially with teenagers, who like the illuminated terrain park with its huge half-pipe, table-top jumps, and rolls. The view from the top of the Sunset Boulevard run is dazzling. (All day-lift tickets are valid for night skiing.) Admission is **Free** at Boreal's Western American Ski Sport Museum, where ski history from the 1850s to the present is depicted in photos, displays, and vintage movies.

ROYAL GORGE USA (ages 7 and up)

Off Highway 80, Soda Springs 95728; (530) 426–3871; www.aminews.com/ royalgorge. Trail pass for adults about $20, children about $15.

Royal Gorge is the largest Nordic ski resort in the nation, and has been voted the best in North America by ski magazines. Spend the day here sledding, or tour forest trails on skis or snowshoes. The network of trails is so vast and so varied that even on weekends you will encounter few other skiers.

For a memorable experience, arrange for the family to be wrapped in fur robes and ferried in a horse-drawn sleigh to the European-style wilderness lodge, built in the 1930s. You can stay in one of the family bunk rooms, chow down on hearty meals in the main dining room, ski and play in the snow, and share experiences with others who come in at the end of the day. This is an especially good place to introduce children to the sport, because eleven cozy warming huts are scattered through the trail network. Hot chocolate and hot tea are complimentary, and you can buy snacks. Moonlight ski tours are unforgettable.

Where to Eat

Azzara's. *930 Tahoe Boulevard in the Raley's Center, Incline Village 89451; (702) 831–0346.* Everything Italian, such as Sicilian artichokes, turkey with mozzarella and tomatoes, and pizza and pasta. Reservations are definitely required for dinner. $$

Gar Woods Grill and Pier. *5000 North Lake Boulevard, Carnelian Bay 96140; (530) 546–3366.* Indoors or on the glassed-in deck, year-round, a wonderful spot to have a long lunch or sunset dinner with the children while watching boating activity on the lake. Restless kids can play around on the small pier and the pathways along the water below the deck; those about 5 and under will need supervision. Sunday brunch at Gar Woods on a sunny day—it doesn't get any better. Reservations recommended. $$

Hacienda de la Sierra. *931 Tahoe Boulevard, across from Raley's, Incline Village 89451; (702) 831–8300.* Mexican food; warm, colorful atmosphere; booths. $

Original Old Post Office. *5245 North Lake Boulevard, Carnelian Bay 96140; (530) 546–3205.* You may see people waiting on the porch for their turn at monster-size, all-American breakfasts. No reservations. $

Steamer's Beachside Bar and Oven. *8290 North Lake Boulevard, Kings Beach 96143; (530) 546–2218.* One of the most popular pizza restaurants on the North Shore, with a great outdoor patio on the lakeside and indoor seating by the windows for when the weather turns cool. If your family likes calzones and pizza, they'll love

Steamer's. The kids can run around on the beach while they wait for lunch or dinner. $

Where to Stay

Vacation Station Lake Tahoe. *P.O. Box 7180, 110 Country Club Drive, Incline Village 89451; (800) 841–7443.* Agency for rental of homes and condos. $–$$$

Hyatt Regency Lake Tahoe. *Lakeshore and Country Club Drive, Incline Village 89451; (702) 832–1234.* Highrise hotel and lakeside units, vacation packages. Camp Hyatt day and evening child care. $$$–$$$$

Inn at Incline. *1003 Tahoe Boulevard, Incline Village 89451; (702) 444–6758.* Motel units in a forest setting; indoor pool, sauna, spa. Continental breakfast, some kitchens. $$

BRAT Resort Properties. *120 Country Club Drive, Incline Village, NV 89452; (888) 266–3612; www.bratresort.com.* Rental condos and houses, with ski and vacation packages.

Truckee Tahoe Inn. *11331 Highway 267 between Truckee and Northstar, Truckee 96161; (530) 587–4525; www.bestwesterntahoe.com.* Reasonably priced, newish motel with simple, fresh rooms and suites with sofa beds and complimentary continental breakfast, sauna, and spa. Ask about ski packages and off-season rates. $–$$.

For More Information

Incline Village Crystal Bay Visitors Bureau and Convention Bureau. *969 Tahoe Boulevard, Incline Village, NV*

89451; (800) GO–TAHOE or (775) 832–1606; e-mail: gotahoe@sierra.net.

Shasta Cascade

Where the Sierra Nevada Range ends and the Cascade Range begins, two colossal glaciated volcanoes are visible for hundreds of miles. Dormant 14,162-foot Mount Shasta and still active 10,457-foot Lassen Peak loom like misty ice gods above the forested recreation lands of northernmost California.

Families who crave recreation in the great outdoors, high-country scenery, and sightseeing in historic towns can spend a lifetime of vacations in the Shasta Cascade area. Roughly the size of Ohio, the region contains seven national forests, eight national and state parks, five mighty rivers, and hundreds of lakes.

Fishing is legendary on the McCloud, Sacramento, Klamath, Salmon, and Scott Rivers. Lush woodlands along the riverbanks are precious ribbons of wilderness that shelter birds, waterfowl, and other wildlife in great numbers.

One of the largest recreational lakes in the country, Lake Shasta is encircled by 370 miles of wooded shoreline that spreads out into four main arms fed by three rivers and a creek. Houseboating is one of the most popular ways for families to vacation on the lake.

On the fringes of the wild, dark forests of the Trinity Alps are sprinkled a handful of tiny towns favored by antiques hunters and trout fishers. The forty-niners, pioneers, and Chinese immigrants in the area left a rich cultural heritage that can be seen in the charming old buildings and museums of Weaverville.

A unique geophysical crossroads, mountainous Lassen Volcanic National Park boils and bubbles with mudpots and sulfury hot springs. On the slopes of both Mount Lassen and Mount Shasta are developed areas for downhill and Nordic skiing, as well as snow play.

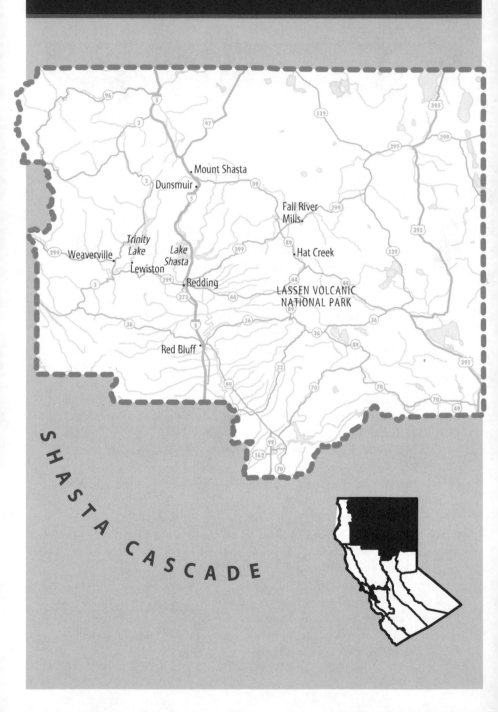

SHASTA CASCADE

Anchoring Highway 5, the main route to the Northwest, the city of Redding is the jumping-off point for adventures in the Shasta Cascade. A wide variety of motels, restaurants, recreation opportunities and fishing outfitters, plus easy access to the Sacramento River, make this an important stop.

Mount Shasta City

At the foot of Mount Shasta, the laid-back small town of Mount Shasta City is where many families headquarter, heading out every day to explore the national forests in the summertime and to ski when the snow falls.

MOUNT SHASTA SKI PARK (all ages)

Located 10 miles east of Mount Shasta City, at 104 Siskiyou Avenue; (530) 926–8600 (snow phone: 530–926–8686); www.skipark.com. Lift tickets in winter are $30.00 for adults and $3.00 for kids under 7; cross-country ski trail passes are $11.00 for adults, $7.00 for kids ages 4 to 12, and $3.00 for kids 3 and under. In the summer lift fees are $8.00 for adults and Free *for kids under 12.*

A good-size winter resort, with mostly intermediate and beginner downhill runs at 5,000 feet, a ski school, Nordic and night skiing, and a nice day lodge with a restaurant. "Powder Pups" is the supervised ski program for kids ages 4 to 7; across the road from the ski park, Snowman's Hill is a snow-play area. At the Nordic skiing center are 16 miles of groomed trails and skating lanes, with a lodge, a warming hut, and shuttle service. The advantage of family skiing here is the reasonable cost, child-oriented staff, the lack of lift lines and crowds, and a carefree drive on Highway 5, which is seldom encumbered with enough snow to require chains.

Thar She Blows At 14,162 feet, Mount Shasta is the fourth highest peak in the continental United States and the largest volcano by volume—80 cubic miles.

Shasta is near the southern end of the Cascade Range, which begins with the active volcano Mount Lassen and runs north to British Columbia, with volcanoes about every 50 miles—quite a sight from a plane. The Cascades are part of the notorious "Ring of Fire" that surrounds the Pacific Ocean.

The last recorded eruption of Mount Shasta was in 1786.

In summer take the forty-minute round-trip up the chairlift for the view of a lifetime. Hike around up here, picnic, and take the lift back down. Or bring your mountain bikes up (or rent them here) and pedal the excellent trails, ending up back at the lodge. In the summer and fall, the wildflowers in the meadows on top and at the base of the mountain are truly spectacular. There are frequent concerts and festivals in the beautiful outdoor amphitheater, and you can buy hot food to eat on the sunny deck, or cold picnic fare to carry back to blanket. In response to the climbing craze, a 24-foot tower has climbing routes for all ages and abilities. Really. There is also a **Free** multimedia exhibit about the formation of Mount Shasta.

MORE CROSS-COUNTRY SKIING
Off Highway 89 beyond Mount Shasta Ski Park in the Shasta-Trinity National Forest; (530) 926–4511. **Free**.

Watch for signs to Bunny Flat and Sand Flat, marked cross-country trails for beginners and intermediates and maintained by the U.S. Forest Service. Restrooms and parking are available only at Bunny Flat, which is also a snow-play area.

MOUNT SHASTA RESORT
1000 Siskiyou Lake Boulevard, Mount Shasta City 96067; (800) 958–3363 or (530) 926–3030; www.mountshastaresort.com.

In a pretty wooded setting near walking trails and lakes, families settle into beautiful one- and two-bedroom chalets with fireplaces, sofa beds, fully equipped kitchens, spacious living rooms, and decks. The golf course here is spectacular and challenging; spend an hour on the practice range with budding golfers. There is an outdoor dining deck and a comfortable restaurant with views of the mountains, plus a snack bar with outdoor tables. Ask about ski and golf packages. $$–$$$

BACKPACKING AT SHASTA-TRINITY NATIONAL FOREST
Wilderness permits and maps are available at Mount Shasta Ranger District office, 204 West Alma, Mount Shasta City 96067; (530) 926–4511.

The Shasta-Trinity National Forest offers exceptional backpacking. The Pacific Crest Trail can be accessed west of Mount Shasta City at Parks Creek, South Fork Road and Whalen Road, and at Castle Crags State Park.

CASTLE CRAGS STATE PARK (all ages)

Forty-five miles north of Redding, off Highway 5; (530) 235–2684 (campground reservations: 800–447–7275 or 916–235–2684).

A fortress of 6,000-foot granite pillars and monster boulders, with 2 miles of the Sacramento River gleaming below and good trout fishing in the streams. At this spectacular park you can swim, hike, rock climb, and camp in one of sixty-four developed sites. Get maps at the park office and amble up the sun-dappled **Indian Creek Nature Trail**, a 1-mile loop. The Crags Trail to **Castle Dome** is 5.5 strenuous miles up and into the **Castle Crags Wilderness**, connecting with the **Pacific Crest Trail.** People often stop at the park just to fill up jugs with natural soda water. The road is plowed all winter for ice fishing on Castle Lake.

LAKE SISKIYOU CAMP RESORT

Three miles from Mount Shasta City, take Hatchery Road to a left onto Old Stage Road, then turn right at W. A. Barr Road; (530) 926–2618; www.merrymac. com/mspage/lscr/index.htm.

One of the prettiest multiuse camping and RV facilities in the state, the resort is located at a large reservoir in a fresh, clean, pine-scented setting at the headwaters of the Sacramento River. You can rent a fully equipped trailer on-site or bring your own tent or RV. Day-trippers are welcome: Walk around the lake, lounge on the 1,000-foot-long sandy beach, swim, or launch a fishing boat. Available to rent are water toys, kayaks, canoes, paddleboats, sailboats, and fishing equipment. Also here are a store, a snack bar, outdoor movies, and a playground.

CASTLE LAKE (all ages)

Passing the Lake Siskiyou Camp Resort entrance on W. A. Barr Road, go left on Castle Lake Road to the parking area; (530) 926–4511.

This is one of the most easily accessible alpine lakes in Northern California. The parking lot is within a few yards of the lakeshore, and within a short easy stroll, you can be in an idyllic, seemingly isolated wilderness setting. Walk in either direction along the lakeshore through beautiful forest, putter around in the creek, fish in the lake, launch your skiff or kayaks, or have a picnic. The water here is wonderfully pure and clear, and the fishing and (chilly) swimming are great. For a 3-mile-round-trip, moderately strenuous hike, take the trail to the left of the lake near the stream, along the lakeside, and up above the lake to 5,900 feet. Bear to the right up 100 feet more to **Heart Lake**, a small lake that warms up in summer and is popular for swimming. One of the best photo ops of Mount Shasta is on Castle Lake Road, about 0.5 mile before the parking lot.

SISSON MUSEUM/MOUNT SHASTA FISH HATCHERY

1 North Old Stage Road, Mount Shasta City 96067; (530) 926–5508. Admission is **Free** *at both facilities.*

In the small museum are displays of the history, geology, and climate of the mountain. Walk around to see the hatching and rearing ponds. Established in 1888, the hatchery produces millions of rainbow and brown trout to stock rivers and streams statewide.

Where to Eat

Michael's. *313 North Mount Shasta Boulevard, Mount Shasta City 96067; (530) 926– 5288.* Italian specialties and continental dishes, homemade pasta, soups, sandwiches, burgers. Lunch and dinner. $

Where to Stay

Tree House Best Western. *111 Morgan Way at Highway 5 and Lake Street, Mount Shasta City 96067; (530) 926–3101.* Large, nicely landscaped motel, with some two-bedroom units and refrigerators; large heated indoor pool; casual dining room with fireplace. $$

Mount Shasta Ranch. *1008 W. A. Barr Road, five minutes from Lake Siskiyou, Mount Shasta City 96067; (530) 926– 3870; www.travelassist.com/reg/ca121s. html.* In a beautiful country setting, a B&B with spacious rooms, suites, and a carriage house; a gigantic common living room and game room; and a full breakfast. Children are quite welcome in the carriage house. There are games, Ping-Pong, and pool tables. $$

Railroad Park Resort. *100 Railroad Park Road, Dunsmuir 96025; (530) 235–4440; www.rrpark.com.* One of the best places in the region for families to stay. Stop here for a meal and take a look at the collection of old railcars and railroading paraphernalia. Accommodations include an RV park, a campground, cabins, and motel rooms in railcars, plus a swimming pool. $$

Mount Shasta KOA Campground. *900 North Mount Shasta Boulevard, Mount Shasta City 96067; (530) 926–4029.* A grassy, gardeny place with RV and tent sites, animal corrals, camping cabins, a store, a swimming pool, and a playground. $

Strawberry Valley Inn. *1142 South Mount Shasta Boulevard, Mount Shasta; (916) 926–2052.* Lovely landscaped grounds and shade trees make this reasonably priced motel a winner; some rooms have two beds, and there are two-room suites. A huge breakfast buffet is served on a sunny patio or by the fireplace. $–$$

For More Information

Shasta Cascade Wonderland Association. *1619 Highway 273, Anderson 96007; (530) 365–7500 or (800) 474–2782; www.shastacascade.org.*

Mount Shasta Visitor Pavilion. *300 Pine Street, Mount Shasta City 96067;* *(800) 926–4865.* Two blocks east of the Highway 5 central exit at Lake and Pine Streets.

U.S. Forest Service. *204 West Alma, Mount Shasta City 96067; (530) 926–4511.*

Lake Shasta

They call it California's Water Wonderland, a huge warm-water lake at the confluence of several major rivers. The surface waters reach eighty degrees in summer, perfect for swimming and waterskiing. Attracting avid anglers are sixteen species of fish, from bass to trout, sturgeon, salmon, and channel catfish.

With a filigreed shoreline of 370 miles, Shasta is very popular for all kinds of water sports and houseboating. Houseboats range from 15 to more than 50 feet long and sleep from four to twelve people. These boats are easy to navigate, even for first-timers. You can get air-conditioning, TV, and washers and dryers, among other amenities. Rentals at the dozen or so houseboat marinas on Lake Shasta cost $1,000 per week and up. The houseboats come completely equipped except for linens and food. You motor slowly along, exploring hidden inlets, fishing, and stopping at beaches and marinas. (See "Houseboating Tips for Families" on page 45.)

The U.S. Forest Service operates developed and boat-in campgrounds at Shasta. More than two dozen private campgrounds and marinas are scattered along the river arms of the lake, primarily on the Sacramento near Lakehead and on the McCloud. You can sleep overnight in a boat anywhere on the lake. There are even floating restrooms!

HIKE LAKE SHASTA

Hiking around the lake can be a hot, dry experience in summer, but trails are green and gorgeous all other times of year. From Packer's Bay Road take Waters Gulch Trail through an oak forest (about 3 miles) up to great views of the Sacramento arm of the lake. Eastside Trail, also at Packer's Bay, is a 0.5-mile, easy walk to swimming and fishing spots. From the Bailey Cove parking lot, a trail runs for almost 3 miles through a pretty, wooded area with lake views, and you can swim at several places along the way.

LAKE SHASTA CAVERNS

Fifteen miles north of Redding off Highway 5, take the O'Brien/Caverns exit; (530) 238–2341.

One of the most dramatic natural wonders in the western states, the caverns constitute a fantasy of multicolored columns, 20-foot-high stone draperies, stalactites and stalagmites, brilliant crystals, and unusual limestone and marble formations, all subtly lit for maximum effect. A fifteen-minute boat ride ferries you across the lake to a wooded island, where you go by bus 800 feet up a steep road through aromatic bay, oak, and manzanita. Groups of about twenty people are guided up and down hundreds of stone steps through a series of giant chambers. The atmosphere is damp and drippy and a constant fifty-eight degrees, which is refreshing in the summer, when outside temperatures can reach more than one hundred.

SHASTA DAM

Off Highway 5, just north of Redding, on Shasta Dam Boulevard; (530) 275–4463.

Walk out on the rim of the second-tallest concrete dam in the United States. Take a look at historic photos and watch a short film in the visitors center. The guided tour into the dam involves an elevator ride that kids under age 8 may find scary.

BRIDGE BAY RESORT

12 miles north of Redding, Bridge Bay exit off Highway 5, 10300 Bridge Bay Road, Redding 96003; (530) 275–3021 or (800) 752–9669; www.sevencrown.com.

Under a big bridge over the lake, this full service marina has houseboat rentals, cabins, ski boats, patio boats, personal watercraft, and a clean, simple motel with a swimming pool and some kitchens—a great headquarters for plying the lake or trying out a houseboat. The house-boat rental company Seven Crown Resorts (1–800–752–9669) is one of the largest and oldest of its kind. They also have rental operations at Digger Bay on Shasta, and in the California Delta and other states.

THE BLUE GOOSE (all ages)

P.O. Box 6600, Yreka 96097; (530) 842–4146.

This circa 1910 train hauls lumber, freight, and passengers daily between Yreka and Montague, a 7-mile trip. Climbing onboard the steamers at 10:00 A.M., you'll cruise past cattle ranches, sawmills, and great scenery. The train may be attacked by bandits (I'm not kidding) as it approaches the historic town of Montague, where you'll have an hour or so to picnic on the village green or take a horse-drawn tour; then it's back to Yreka.

Where to Eat

Tail of the Whale. *Twelve miles north of Redding, at the Bridge Bay exit off Highway 5; (530) 275–3021.* Dependable American food in a setting overlooking an arm of the lake and Bridge Bay Resort; seafood, prime rib, Cajun shrimp, a hearty, all-American menu. $

Where to Stay

Holiday Harbor. *Eighteen miles north of Redding, on Shasta Caverns Road; (800) 776–BOAT.* Complete resort facilities, RV hookups, and waterskiing lessons. $

Lakeshore Villa RV Park. *20672 Lakeshore Drive, Lakehead 96051; (530) 238–8688.* Rent a cabin, a houseboat, a ski boat or a fishing boat. Enjoy the pool, or just have lunch and watch the action. $

Antlers Resort and Marina. *P.O. Box 140, Lakehead 96051; (530) 238–2553.* Another source for houseboat rentals, cabins, and water sports equipment. $

For More Information

Shasta Cascade Wonderland Association. *1619 Highway 273, Anderson 96007; (530) 365–7500 or (800) 474–2782; www.shastacascade.org.*

Lassen Volcanic National Park

The largest "plug dome" volcano in the world, Lassen Peak last blew its top in 1921. Hot springs, boiling mudpots, and sulfury steam vents remind us that sometime in the next few hundred years, a drive through Lassen Volcanic National Park may not be a good idea. For now it's one of the wonders of the world.

You can drive through the park in half a day, including stops along the 35-mile route up and over the 8,000-foot summit, viewing the snow-covered peaks and crystalline lakes from a distance. Better yet, settle into a camp-ground for a week of fishing on a few of the fifty lakes and of hiking on some of the 150 miles of interconnecting wilderness trails. Several lakes allow non-powered boating. Seventeen miles of the Pacific Crest Trail twist through aro-matic conifer forests, magnificent stands of aspens and cottonwoods, and wildflower-washed meadows.

In the fall, the entire mountain and lake region seems to burst into flame—the aspen, birch, and oaks are spun gold; eastern maples, chokecherry, and dogwood (and poison oak!) turn red along the highways and hiking trails, and are reflected in the many mountain lakes. In winter, cross-country skiers, snow-shoers, and snow campers take off into the spectacular backcountry. The snow may fly as early as September and as late as May (be advised to carry chains). Campgrounds are all located above 5,650 feet and are open from Memorial Day to the end of September, depending on road and snow conditions.

Anglers from all over the world come to the Lassen area for wild trout fish-ing in the cold, clear waters of Hat Creek and the Fall and McCloud Rivers on the north side of the park. Nonfishing members of the family will enjoy wildlife viewing in the Hat Creek area, where osprey, bald eagles, elk, and a variety of waterfowl are commonly seen.

VISITOR CENTER

The main park headquarters is at 38050 Highway 36, just east of Mineral, near the park; (530) 595–4444; www.nps.gov/lavo.

At one of the three park entrances, stop for the Lassen Park road guide and the current schedule of naturalist-led tours and kids' story hours. More than sixty points of interest and trails are indicated in the guide and are numbered to correspond to road signs. The park road winds around three sides of the park, past woodlands, meadows, streams, and lakes.

Saddle Up *Wild Horse Sanctuary. Thirty miles east of Red Bluff, at the junction of Highways 44 and A6, Shingletown; (530) 474–5770.* For a rare and unforgettable experience, consider spending a weekend at this perfectly beautiful ranch that shelters wild horses on 5,000 acres within view of Black Butte and Mount Lassen. Two- and three-day horseback rides in the tree-studded foothills track the wild herds. Imagining wild horses to be scrawny refugees, I was surprised to find them vibrating with spirit, muscle, and shiny coats; in fact, the herds are a spectacular sight, each a small group of mares, fillies, and colts led by a spirited stallion. The horses are agitated when they see riders, and curious, so they hang around for a few minutes watching, sometimes as close as 40 or 50 feet—while riders snap photos like mad—then they gallop off. Wild turkey, deer, bald eagles, coyote, fox, owls, and bobcats are also commonly sighted.

Some previous riding experience, though not required, makes this more enjoyable. You ride slowly through brush, over creeks and gullies, and across meadows; the pace is quite leisurely. Riders and their guides stay overnight at a charming encampment on a small vernal lake, in basic frontier-style cabins. Hearty meals are prepared while guests rest, swim, help groom and feed the horses, and explore. Two- and three-day trips cost about $235 per person, with family packages available. You can also spend a day hiking to see the horses, if horseback riding is not your forte, and it costs just $25 per person. A very popular annual Longhorn Cattle Drive blazes the trail for two days.

The owners of the ranch, Jim and Dianne Clapp, have provided sanctuary for wild horses and burros for more than two decades. They and their cowboy and cowgirl staff are charming, welcoming hosts. Believe me, your children will beg you to let them stay and live here.

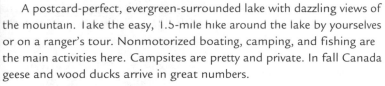

MANZANITA LAKE (all ages)

In the national park, near the north entrance.

A postcard-perfect, evergreen-surrounded lake with dazzling views of the mountain. Take the easy, 1.5-mile hike around the lake by yourselves or on a ranger's tour. Nonmotorized boating, camping, and fishing are the main activities here. Campsites are pretty and private. In fall Canada geese and wood ducks arrive in great numbers.

BUMPASS HELL
Near the southwest park entrance.

A 3-mile, easy walk into the park's most active thermal area. Walk on boardwalks over hot springs, steam vents, mudpots, and other eerie manifestations of the earth's hot insides.

DEVASTATED AREA INTERPRETIVE TRAIL
Road Marker 44.

One of several trails that are handicapped accessible, a 0.25-mile trail leads you through lodgepole pines and aspens, particularly lush and breathtaking in fall.

KINGS CREEK FALLS
Road Marker 32

A 700-foot descent and 1.5 miles one-way to a beautiful, 30-foot cascade, with streams, meadows, and forests along the way.

LASSEN PARK SKI AREA

Located 3 miles southwest of Chester on Highway 36, just inside the southwest park entrance; (530) 595–3376.

The entire main road through the park is available for cross-country skiing, with unending views of snow-bound mountains, valleys, and lakes. Equipment can be rented for sledding, snowshoeing, snowboarding, and downhill and cross-country ski-

*S*nowmobiling in Lassen National Forest

In the national forest are six designated trail areas for snowmobiling, each with parking and Free admission; for information call (530) 335–7575.

- **Ashpan:** Nine miles southwest of the junction of Highways 44 and 89; 39 miles of trails; warming hut.

- **Swain Mountain:** Nine miles north of the junction of Highways A21 and 36; 47 miles of trails.

- **Jonesville:** Two miles east of Cherry Hill Campground on Butte Meadows; 43 miles of trails.

- **Fredonyer:** Ten miles west of Susanville; 80 miles of trails.

- **Morgan Summit:** Five miles east of Mineral on Highway 36; 77 miles of trails; warming hut.

- **Bogard Rest Stop:** Thirty miles west of Susanville on Highway 44; 75 miles of trails.

ing. The small downhill skiing hill has four runs, all beginning and intermediate, with a warming hut. Ski lessons are Free on Saturdays, and a Free two-hour, guided snowshoe hike is offered at 1:30 P.M. on Saturdays, too, for ages 8 and up; snowshoes are Free. There are 7 miles of groomed ski trails near Manzanita Lake, with no attendant facilities.

BUTTE LAKE

From Old Station go 10.5 miles east on Highway 44, go south on Butte Lake Road, and drive 7 miles on a rough dirt road; (530) 595–4444.

A beautiful campground sits at lakeside, surrounded by ponderosa pines and rugged volcanic outcroppings. Motorized boats are not allowed, and the fishing is phenomenal. Interesting cinder cones and other volcanic formations, plus two more lakes nearby and backcountry trails, make this a great destination.

LAKE ALMANOR

Some 40 miles southeast of Lassen Peak, off Highway 89 near Chester; (530) 274–4739.

At this pine-fringed lake at 4,500 feet, the snowy peak of Lassen and surrounding mountains are mirrored in clear, calm waters. Families who like to swim, boat, fish, and water-ski enjoy the sandy beaches, small lodges, and campgrounds on the western shore; summer lake surface temperatures reach seventy-five degrees. The Lake Almanor Recreation Trail, an easy, flat, paved route for biking, walking and cross-country skiing, follows the west shore of the lake.

The small town of Chester caters to vacationers with simple lakeside resorts, motels, and campgrounds.

Where to Eat

Stover's St. Bernard Lodge. *Mill Creek, 10 miles west of Chester 96061; (530) 258–3382.* Knotty pine walls, stained glass, and antiques in a casual dining room; hearty American food, such as huge hamburgers, fresh fish, steak, and fried chicken. Take a walk around the trout pond. $

Creekside Grill. *278 Main Street, Chester 96020; (530) 258–1966.* In a charming country setting by a creek, with a fireplace and an outdoor dining deck, a fine chef produces sophisticated California cuisine and comfort food, too. $–$$

Peninsula Station Bar and Grill. *401 Peninsula Drive, Lake Almanor 96137; (530) 596–3538.* Fresh trout and reasonably priced, excellent meals with good selections for children. $

Where to Stay

Drakesbad Guest Ranch. *End of Warner Valley Road, Lassen Volcanic National Park; mailing address: Drawer K, Chester 96020; phone: Drakesbad #2 via Susanville operator (if no answer, 530–529–9820); calguest@mci.com.* Secluded within the southeastern corner of the national park, a century-old hot springs resort in spectacular scenic surroundings at 5,700 feet. The old-fashioned western ranch experience brings families back year after year—it's the kind of place where you can just let the kids go to participate in the many activities: trail rides, a little kids' program, hikes, crafts, swimming, badminton, horseshoes, Ping-Pong, volleyball, and fishing. Rustic, comfortable lodge rooms, cabins, and bungalows, with kerosene lamps for light (cabins and bungalows have no electricity). Make reservations months in advance; for high-season weekends and holidays, a year ahead. $$–$$$

Lassen Mineral Lodge. *Highway 36, Mineral 96063; (530) 595–4422.* A simple motel, well located near the national park. Cross-country ski from the door; equipment rentals here. Swimming pool, tennis, restaurant, general store. $

Spanish Springs Guest Ranch. *P.O. Box 70, Ravendale 96123; (800) 272–8282.* Family ranch vacations, cattle drives, buckaroo camp, horseback riding on a big working cattle ranch. Accommodations vary, from a log cabin to a vintage ranch house. The fishing for trout is easy in stocked ponds. Family-style, hearty meals are served in the ranch house. $$–$$$

Lake Almanor Resort. *2706 Big Springs Road, Lake Almanor 96137; (530) 596–3337; www.Homestead.com/lakealmanorresort/Lakealmanorresort.* A multifaceted, lively, nice lakefront resort on the north shore, with boat dock and fully equipped cabins and lodge units, and tent and RV sites. A three-bedroom, one-bath lakeside house has a sleeping porch, boat slip, and washer and dryer. The marina and playground areas are busy in summertime, and you can rent boats and kayaks, and lounge and swim at the lawn/beach area. $–$$

For More Information

Plumas County Visitors Bureau. *P.O. Box 4120, Quincy 95971; (800) 326–2247 or (530) 283–6345; www.plumas.ca.us.* Call for booklets: "Family Bike Tours," "Mountain Bike Trail Guide," and "Hiking Guide," with trail descriptions and maps.

Fall River Valley Chamber of Commerce. *P.O. Box 475, Fall River Mills 96056; (530) 336–5840.*

Redding

A regional hub at the junction of Highways 5, 299, and 44, Redding has attractive motels, as well as fishing and camping outfitters. A refuge for the last mature riparian woodland left in the state, the Sacramento River runs along the edge of town, bordered by a great walking path. Most of the attractions of the Shasta Cascade are within a short drive of Redding.

East of Redding, in the southeastern corner of the Klamath National Forest, McArthur-Burney Falls Memorial State Park in the McCloud River Valley offers waterfalls, swimming holes, great fishing, and campgrounds. Within the park Lake Britton is one of several lakes in the area, a trout-fishing mecca for trophy-size brown, rainbow, and Eastern brook trout.

PAUL BUNYAN'S FOREST CAMP/TURTLE BAY

At the Turtle Bay Museums, 800 Auditorium Drive, Redding 96001; (530) 243–8850. Admission is $2.00 for adults; kids ages 16 and under are admitted **Free**.

On a bend of the Sacramento River, indoor and outdoor activities focus on forest resources. Follow Paul's huge footprints to hands-on interpretive sites, climb the fire lookout tower, and play on child-size earth-moving equipment and on the Spar Swings and the Log Slide. Admission includes entry to the **Redding Museum of Art and History** and the **Carter House Natural Science Museum.**

SACRAMENTO RIVER TRAIL

In Redding, drive north on Market Street to Riverside Drive on the south side of the Sacramento River, go west to the parking lot where the trail begins; (800) 874–7562.

A tree-shaded, 7.7-mile path along the riverbanks, through a residential area, and crossing over the river on a unique pedestrian bridge, then continuing to Caldwell Park. Interpretive signs and benches are found along the way.

SACRAMENTO RIVER DISCOVERY CENTER

From Highway 5 take the second Red Bluff exit onto Antelope Boulevard and turn right onto Sale Lane, Red Bluff; (530) 527–1196.

Interpretive trails through native riparian habitats, grasslands, wetlands, and woodlands.

THE FLY SHOP

Off Highway 5, on the south end of Redding; (530) 222–3555.

Look for a weathered gray building with a big fish visible from the highway. Available here are equipment, tours, and advice on which fish are biting, where to catch 'em, and what the water conditions are.

WATERWORKS PARK (ages 4 and up)

151 North Boulder Drive, Redding 96001; (530) 246–9550.

Ride a giant water slide and tube the 400-foot Raging River. Little kids like the watery playground designed just for them while teens head straight for the beach volleyball.

PARK MARINA RAFT RENTAL (ages 4 and up)

2515 Park Marina Drive, Redding 96001; (530) 246–8388.

Everything you need to raft the Sacramento River, including life jackets. In three or four hours, rafters and canoers float south down the Sacramento River from Redding to Anderson River Park. Beneath over-hanging sycamores, cottonwoods, oaks, and willows, you can slide quietly along or stop to fish the salmon-spawning riffles. Raft-rental companies pick you up at the park and shuttle you back to Redding.

OSPREY EXCURSIONS

8587 Future Drive, Redding 96001; (530) 246–1740.

Exciting, scenic jet-boat tours on Northern California rivers and on Lake Shasta and Whiskeytown Lake. In a boat carrying up to six passengers, this is a nice way to see the Sacramento River from Redding to Anderson or Red Bluff, skimming over the water only inches deep, racing through rapids, and exploring the river. Swimming, picnicking, and fishing stops are made, with all equipment and food provided.

MCARTHUR-BURNEY FALLS MEMORIAL STATE PARK

11 miles northeast of Burney, off Highway 89; (530) 335–2777.

In the Shasta-Trinity National Forest, the big attraction here is two million gallons of water a day tumbling over a misty, fern-draped, 129-foot cliff. Take a short hike down into the forest gorge to the base of the falls, where wild tiger lilies, maples, dogwood, black oak, and pines decorate the streamside. The walk is about a half-hour for the fit and fast, an hour for amblers and photographers, and two hours for walkers who take side trails. Good trout fishing can be had in the deep pool at the base of the falls and in the 2-mile stream above and below. Pleasant hikes in and near the park in evergreen forests include a 1.5-mile flat route to Lake Britton Dam, then 3 miles farther to **Rock Creek**.

LAKE BRITTON

In McArthur Burney Falls Memorial State Park, off Highway 89; (530) 335–2777 (campground reservations: 800–444–7275).

Located here are 18 miles of shoreline amid evergreen forests near the Pit River. Camping and RV sites are not too private but are nice in the off-season. Accessible by boat (rentals here), with a terrific swimming hole at its foot, **Clark Creek Falls** is a jet of frigid water crashing into the lake. Crappie, bass, and catfish bite all season.

IDE ADOBE STATE HISTORIC PARK

21659 Adobe Road, Red Bluff 96080; (530) 529–8599; www.rbuhsd.k12.ca.us/ adobedocs/index.html. Admission is $3.00 per car.

On the way to the Shasta region, a lovely rest stop on the river. The park is cool and shady, with giant oaks, lawns, picnic tables, and historical displays. You can fish here, but swimming in the fast current is not advisable. Crafts demonstrations are presented most weekends.

Where to Eat

Westside Deli French Bakery. *1600 California Street, Redding 96001; (530) 222– 0787.* Sandwiches and pastry treats. $

Jack's Grill. *1743 California Street, Redding 96001; (530) 241–9705.* In a casual, noisy, hometown atmosphere, sixteen-ounce steaks, deep-fried prawns, big plates of good old American food. Dinner only. $

Wild Bill's Rib-Steakhouse and Saloon. *500 Riverside Way, Red Bluff 96080; (530) 529–9453.* A casual place with a deck on the river; steaks, pasta, and fish. $

Where to Stay

Hilltop Inn. *2300 Hilltop Drive, Redding 96001; (530) 221 6100.* A large, very nice motel, with simple, spacious rooms, swimming pools, a wading pool, and complimentary continental breakfast. Two reasonably priced restaurants. $

Red Lion Motor Inn. *299 Hilltop Drive, Redding 96001; (530) 221–8700.* A big garden court with a swimming pool, a wading pool, a putting green, and lots of trees. Rooms are large and very nice. One coffee shop, one upscale restaurant. Pets allowed with advance notice. $$

Lava Creek Lodge. *1 Island Road, 12 miles north of Highway 299, east of Redding in Fall River Mills 96028; (530) 336–6288.* A small, rustic fishing lodge with cabins in a wooded setting on a lovely piece of the Fall River, adjacent to Ahjumawi Lava Springs State Park. Hearty American fare is served in the dining room. $

River Inn. *1835 Park Marina Drive, Redding 96001; (530) 241–9500.* Located at the edge of town on a small lake, with mountain views, nice motel rooms, a pool, barbecue, and a boat launch into the Sacramento River. $–$$

For More Information

Redding Convention and Visitors Bureau. *7777 Auditorium Drive, Redding 96001; (800) 874–7562.*

Fall River Valley Chamber of Commerce. *P.O. Box 475, Fall River Mills CA 96056; (530) 336–5840.*

Weaverville/Trinity

Glaciers chiseled the jagged peaks of the Trinity Alps aeons ago, then melted away, leaving more than fifty sparkling alpine lakes among the brooding conifers of the **Trinity Alps Wilderness,** part of the **Shasta-Trinity National Forest.** Black bears, mountain lions, Roosevelt elk, mink, river otters, eagles, and spotted owls inhabit the upper reaches of one of the wildest and least visited national forests in the country.

Thousands of feet below snowy peaks, Trinity Lake snakes several miles through a rugged valley, where a few small summer resorts and villages attract families who like the quiet side of the Shasta Cascade region. More than two dozen U.S. Forest Service campgrounds are scattered on the west side of the lake. Call (530) 623–2121 for information.

Sometimes a stretch of calm water, sometimes rapids raging in a gorge, the Trinity River leaps with salmon and steelhead, yielding fish of ten pounds or more. Wildflowers run riot in the spring, and fall foliage is brilliant all along the river.

Surrounded by a dramatic mountain backdrop, Weaverville's original structures were destroyed by fire and replaced in the mid-1800s by brick buildings with wooden overhangs and exterior spiral staircases. A circa 1900 bandstand and the second oldest courthouse in California contribute to an Old West atmosphere.

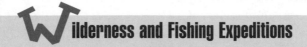

Wilderness and Fishing Expeditions

- **W.O.A. Float Tours.** *Horse Creek; (530) 496–3652.* Scenic float trips on 6 miles of the Klamath River; oar-powered drift boat; quiet, dry, and safe for all ages, even babies. Streamside picnic, gold panning, bird-watching.

- **Turtle River Rafting Company.** *(530) 926–3223.* Guided raft trips on the Klamath, Rogue, Trinity, and Sacramento Rivers.

- **Trinity River Rafting.** *P.O. Box 572, Big Bar; (530) 623–3033.* Whitewater rafting on the Trinity River, guided and self-guided. Raft and kayak rentals.

- **Bigfoot Rafting Company.** *P.O. Box 729, Willow Creek; (800) 722–2223.* One- to three-day whitewater trips on the Trinity; also scenic floats for beginners.

- **Trinity Trail Rides.** *HC2 Box 4940, Trinity Center; (530) 266–3343.* Horseback pack trips into the Trinity Alps.

JOSS HOUSE STATE HISTORIC PARK (all ages)

Oregon and Main Streets, Weaverville 96093; (530) 623–5284. Admission is $2.00 for adults, and $1.00 for kids 6 to 13.

Remnants of the Gold Rush remain at the colorful Joss House, the "Temple Amongst the Forest Beneath the Clouds," built in forty-niner days for the Taoist worship of those Chinese who built the California railroads and sought gold on the river. Carved altars, tapestries, and elaborate artifacts are restored to their former glory. Shady picnic sites lie beside a creek in the park.

JAKE JACKSON MUSEUM AND TRINITY COUNTY HISTORICAL PARK

408 Main Street, Weaverville 96093; (530) 623–5211. Admission is Free.

Gold Rush and pioneer days are re-created in a stamp mill, a miner's cabin, a blacksmith shop, and other displays.

TRINITY LAKE (all ages)

Accessed off Highway 3 between Weaverville and Coffee Creek; main campground and resort area is 10 to 15 miles north of Weaverville; (530) 623–2131 or 623–6101.

More than 1,507 miles of rugged shoreline and hundreds of coves seem to absorb and hide houseboats, water-skiers, Jet Skis, and fishing boats. The west side is dotted with campgrounds, resorts, and boat launch ramps, while the east side, with somewhat restricted auto access, is largely undeveloped. Try your luck at fishing for trophy-size largemouth bass, trout, kokanee salmon, and catfish.

SOUTH FORK TRINITY RIVER NATIONAL RECREATION TRAIL

Maps and information: Shasta-Trinity National Forest, 2400 Washington Avenue, Redding, CA 96001; (530) 246–5222.

The beautiful trail follows the South Fork Trinity River for 21 miles, from Scott Flat Campground near Forest Glen to Wildwood Road, and for 4 miles from a trailhead near Hyampom to Forest Glen.

LEWISTON

Twenty-nine miles west of Redding off Highway 299; (530) 623–2131 or 623–6101.

A half-hour from Weaverville, and so tiny that you can see all of it in a glance, the country village of Lewiston is strung out prettily along the rushing Trinity River. A 1903 landmark is the Old Lewiston Bridge, one of the last one-lane bridges still in use. Buildings from the 1860s are on the National Register of Historic Places. Several antiques shops have literally thousands of square feet of collectibles of all descriptions.

Cold, constantly moving water flows into Lewiston Lake from Trinity Lake, an ideal situation for large rainbow, brook, and brown trout. Salmon and steelhead show up below the Lewiston Dam, below the bridge, and in the smaller streams.

COFFEE CREEK GUEST RANCH

Coffee Creek Road, HC2 Box 4940, Trinity Center 96091; (530) 266–3343 or (800) 624–4480; www.coffeecreekranch.com.

Not much changed since the 1920s, this is a great place for families. Offered are rustic housekeeping cabins and weekly activities such as square dancing, trail rides, bonfires, movies, tennis, tubing, badminton, and more. Situated on 127 acres, with Coffee Creek rushing through, the resort is within 2 miles of trailheads into the Trinity Alps Wilderness

Area. You can have three hearty, family-style meals a day here. There are a heated swimming pool, a rifle range and trapshoot, flyfishing in Coffee Creek for rainbow and German brown trout, guided hikes, and archery. Also available are babysitting for ages 3 and under, supervised play and organized games and activities for ages 3 to 17, and even overnight camping and riding lessons. This is summer camp for everyone in the family! Bring your cowboy hats and your fishing poles. Open in the wintertime, too—dogsled and sleigh rides!

SCOTT MUSEUM (all ages)
Airport Road, Trinity Center; (530) 266–3367.

Indian artifacts, covered wagons, stagecoaches, and artifacts from old pioneer and Gold Rush days.

Where to Eat

Pacific Brewery. *Across from the Joss House, 401 Main Street, Weaverville 96093; (530) 623–3000.* Hearty American fare in a circa 1850 brick building. Breakfast, lunch, and dinner. $

Mustard Seed. *210 Main, Weaverville 96093; (530) 623–4432.* Home-style breakfast and lunch in a yellow Victorian house, featuring Belgian waffles, quiche, tacos and burritos, and homemade apple pie under the elm. $

Allan's Oak Pit Bar-B-Q. *1324 Nugget Lane off Main, at the edge of Weaverville 96093; (530) 623–2182.* Barbecued chicken, beef, and pork dinners, plus sandwiches. $

Sam's Eclectic Kitchen and Serendipity Bookstore. *Turnpike and Deadwood Road off Trinity Dam Boulevard, Lewiston 96052; (530) 778–3856.* Pizza, sandwiches, light dinners, coffeehouse. $

Where to Stay

Weaverville Victorian Inn. *1709 Main, Weaverville 96093; (530) 623–4432.* A very nice place for families, offering spacious motel rooms, a swimming pool, a woodsy setting, and guest laundry facilities. $

Ripple Creek Cabins. *Off Highway 3, north of Coffee Creek 96091; (530) 266–3505.* Old-fashioned housekeeping cabins on the Trinity River, with a nearby swimming hole and trails leading to

alpine lakes. Borrow inner tubes and bikes here. No TV or phones, except at the office. Well-behaved, leashed pets okay. Open in the wintertime for cross-country skiing. $

Wyntoon Resort. *Highway 3 just north of Trinity Center, P.O. Box 70, Trinity Center 96091; (530) 266–3337.* RV, trailer, and tent campgrounds on ninety wooded acres; a marina; boat, water sports; and bike rentals. $

Lakeview Terrace Resort. *HC 01 Box 250, Trinity Dam Boulevard off Highway 3, Lewiston 96052; (530) 778–3803; www.campgrounds.com/lakeview.* On Lewiston Lake, one- to five-bedroom simple, clean cabins about 20 to 30 yards apart under the trees, completely equipped, and, thankfully, with no TVs or phones. There are also an RV site with lake views, hot showers, and laundry facilities. You can rent 14-foot fishing boats and patio boats holding up to eight people. Cabins rent for about $80–$100 per night for four to six people, and pets are okay.

For More Information

Trinity County Chamber of Commerce. *317 Main Street, Weaverville 96093; (800) 487–4648 or (530) 623–6101; www.trinitycounty.com.*

Shasta Trinity National Forest. *2400 Washington Avenue, Redding 96001; (530) 246–5222.*

Redwood Country

The largest and oldest trees in the world live in a narrow band along the Northern California coastline and a few miles inland, with magnificent groves clustered in the "Redwood Empire" of Northern California. Walking beneath a 300-foot redwood forest canopy among these silent giants from the age of the dinosaurs will be an unforgettable experience for your family, ranking right up there with Yosemite and the Grand Canyon. The deepest, oldest groves have a truly prehistoric look: in fact, *The Lost World, Jurassic Park* was shot in Humboldt County redwood parks.

Beaches, birdwatching, camping, fishing, and country pleasures are more reasons to spend vacations in Humboldt County. Eureka, Ferndale, and Arcata are charming, walkable "all-American" towns, each chockablock with Victorian buildings. And, there is much new in the way of family-friendly restaurants, shops, museums, and outdoor recreation.

Eureka

The hub of Redwood Country, Eureka is home port to more than 500 fishing boats in Humboldt Bay. The town's founding coincided with the birth of Victorian architecture, and blocks and blocks of elaborate 1850–1904 houses remain. A stunning example is the **William Carson Mansion** at Second and M Streets, a mixture of several styles that took one hundred workers more than two years to build. The house is said to be the most photographed Victorian home in America. You don't need to drag the kids on a sightseeing tour of the Victorians, because these structures are everywhere you look.

Use Eureka as your base for exploring the redwood parks. If your family likes to fish, head for the Mad River, the Van Duzen, the Eel, and other rivers. Recently named the "Best Small Art Town in America," Eureka is a uniquely

REDWOOD
NATIONAL
PARK

Trinidad

REDWOOD
NATIONAL PARK

Arcata

Eureka

Ferndale

AVENUE OF
THE GIANTS

Garberville

REDWOOD COUNTRY

creative community, as demonstrated in many art-, music-, and culture-related events, festivals, and galleries. Take note of the flamboyant murals around town: ask for a mural walk map at the chamber of commerce.

 ## HUMBOLDT BAY MARITIME MUSEUM (all ages)

1410 Second Street, Eureka 95501; (707) 444–9440. Admission is **Free**.

A favorite haunt for kids. In a replica of the oldest home in Eureka, the museum displays nautical relics, old navigation equipment, an early radar unit, a lighthouse lens, and fragments of wrecked ships.

 ## INDIAN WEST EMPORIUM

326 Second Street, Eureka 95501; (707) 442–3042.

Native American art and artifacts; western memorabilia, and vintage clothing. Kids are not always happy to shop and browse in art galleries, but this shop and the Many Hands Gallery at Second and Seventh Streets are chock-full of cool things of interest to youngsters.

 ## CLARKE MEMORIAL MUSEUM (all ages)

Third and E Streets, Eureka 95501; (707) 443–1947. Admission is **Free**.

This 1920s Italian Renaissance former bank with a glazed terra-cotta exterior houses an extraordinary collection of Indian basketry and ceremonial regalia, antique weapons, maritime artifacts, and photos of early Humboldt days.

 ## GEPPETTO'S

416 Second Street, Eureka 95501; (707) 443–6255.

A toy store offering costumes, dolls, games, and hundreds of stuffed bears.

 ## MOON'S PLAY AND LEARN

3022 Broadway, Eureka 95501; (707) 442–5761.

In the largest toy store north of the Bay Area, you'll find bright kites, windsocks and wind toys, puzzles, craft kits, science and nature items, books and kinetic yard art kits.

*E*asy Wildlife Walks

- **Eureka Waterfront.** *Park at the Carson Mansion on the north end of town.* Enjoy glimpses of the mansion gardens, then walk 1 block south on Second Street and turn right into the Adorni Center parking lot. A paved waterfront path offers beautiful views of the bay and boats.

- **Sequoia Park.** *Park near the Duck Pond.* Take a 1-mile loop trail in redwood and alder groves.

- **Woodley Island.** *Take Highway 255/R Street across the Samoa Bridge, and park at the Samoa Cookhouse or along the road.* From here you can walk or bike along the edge of Humboldt Bay, 6 miles north to Arcata. The birdlife is extraordinary, from marbled godwits to curlews, dowitchers, falcons, and many more.

- **Humboldt Bay National Wildlife Refuge.** *1020 Ranch Road, Loleta, just south of Eureka; (707) 733–5406. Take Hookton Road exit from Highway 101 and follow it 1.2 miles to the Hookton Slough trailhead, a 1.5-mile path along the south edge of Humboldt Bay.* Thousands of birds and ducks migrate through these beautiful grasslands, freshwater marshes, and mudflats, including 25,000 black brants, which fly from their nesting grounds in the Arctic to Baja. Look for herons, owls, ospreys, mallards, egrets, terns, and more. Restrooms.

- **Russ Park.** *On the south end of Main in Ferndale: go left on Ocean Street.* Three miles of pleasant, wildflowery trails and good birdwatching in a 110-acre, closed-canopy spruce and redwood forest. Restrooms.

- **Ferndale Bottoms.** *On the east side of Ferndale.* The bottoms are great for walking and biking; a network of country lanes between lovely meadows lead to the Eel River Estuary. You can launch a canoe or kayak at the end of Morgan Slough Road and/or take a guided boat tour of the estuary (Eel River Delta Tours; 707–786–4187). Loons, cormorants, harriers, egrets, and over 150 feathered species live in or pass through these wetlands. Where the Eel meets the sea, watch for sea lions, seals, and river otters.

- **Loleta Bottoms.** *From Loleta drive (or bike) west on Cannibal Island Road to Crab Park, at the mouth of an arm of the Eel River.* You can scramble around the edge of the estuary, and walk back east on the quiet road, watching for plovers, tundra swans, and curlews. Go right on Cock Robin Island Road, where mudflats attract masses of shorebirds. Continue back to your car or on toward Loleta, where the Loleta Cheese Factory is a good place to stop for sandwiches, snacks, and cheese tasting (fabulous organic cheese).

HUMBOLDT STATE UNIVERSITY (HSU) NATURAL HISTORY MUSEUM AND STORE (all ages)

1315 G Street, Arcata 95518; (707) 826–4479. 𝐅𝐫𝐞𝐞 *admission.*

Kids can touch a dinosaur tail, millions-year-old fossils, and the inhabitants of a tide pool; see live native animals, identify sea shells; and learn about the natural history of the region. When you're in Trinidad, visit the **Humboldt State University Marine Lab and Aquarium,** where you'll find touch tanks and ocean exhibits.

SEQUOIA PARK

Glatt and W Streets, downtown Eureka.

Fifty-two delightfully green acres of virgin redwoods are home to a little zoo, a playground, formal gardens, walking paths, and a duck pond.

HUM BOATS

At the foot of F Street, Eureka; (707) 443–5157.

Rent boats here or arrange to take a tour of Humboldt Bay: sea kayaks, sailboats, water-taxi rides.

BLUE OX MILLWORKS HISTORICAL PARK (all ages)

At the foot of X Street, Eureka 95501; (800) 248–4259; www.blueoxmill.com. Admission is $5.00.

A museumlike sawmill and job shop that makes custom trim for Victorian buildings, using the same machines that created the originals. Take a self-guided tour on catwalks overlooking the artisans and watch them turn columns, carve rosettes, and form wooden gutters and gewgaws, or call ahead to ask about scheduled tours. Surrounded by an enchanting wetlands wildlife sanctuary, the Blue Ox has set up a re-creation of a loggers' camp, a school, a bird-viewing station, and other attractions.

FIRE AND LIGHT

1499-B Tenth Street, Arcata 95518; (707) 825–7500.

In a town committed to sustainable environmental practices, a fabulously successful line of tabletop accessories and dinnerware is manufactured from recycled glass. Call ahead for a tour to see the spectacular operation of transforming, by hand, 4,200-degree molten glass into luminous, jewel-colored dinnerware. From bins of broken jars to the beautiful end products, it's a fascinating process. For information on the White House Task Force on recycling, where Fire and Light is one of the featured companies, go to www.ofee.gov.

SAMOA COOKHOUSE
Across the Samoa Bridge from downtown Eureka, on Samoa Boulevard; (707) 442–1659.

Built on Woodley Island in 1885, this is the last surviving lumber camp cookhouse in the West. Giant American breakfasts are served from 6:00 A.M., including biscuits with sausage gravy, platters of pancakes, and scrambled eggs. Lunch and dinner are served family-style at long oilcloth-covered tables with charmingly mismatched chairs. Huge loaves of bread, cauldrons of soup, big bowls of salad and vegetables, baked ham, and roast beef are followed by wedges of homemade pie. Prices are quite reasonable and kids 4 and under eat **Free**.

Even if you don't eat here, stop in to see the **Free** museum of logging equipment, artifacts, and fantastic photos of early days. A short walk from the restaurant is a quiet bayside village and a nice playground.

M.V. MADAKET
At the foot of C Street, Eureka; (707) 444–9440.

Cruise the bay on a fantastic wooden steam-driven ferry built in the 1920s, an exciting way to get a new perspective on the harbor and the shoreline. The historical and natural sights are explained as you pass oyster farms, fishing and pleasure craft, the third largest colony of harbor seals in the West, and zillions of fresh- and saltwater birds.

About Redwoods

- A coastal redwood can live to be more than 2,000 years old.
- The tallest living things on Earth, some redwoods grow to exceed 300 feet in height.
- The world's tallest tree is a coastal redwood in Redwood National Park, at 367.8 feet.
- Redwoods' ecosystems contain up to ten times the living matter of tropical forest ecosystems.
- Humboldt Redwoods State Park shelters the largest remaining stand of ancient redwoods in the world.
- Winter rainfall in the northern redwoods can reach 100 inches a year.

AVENUE OF THE GIANTS (all ages)

Off both sides of Highway 101 just north of Garberville; (707) 946–2311.

The highlight of your visit is likely to be the sight of the 2,000-year-old Coastal Redwoods in the Eel River Valley. A 30-mile scenic drive called the Avenue of the Giants, within Humboldt Redwoods State Park, is well marked, with turnouts and parking areas accessing short loop trails into the forest. Begin your tour at the visitor center, 2 miles south of Weott, where a movie, exhibits, and trail maps will help get you oriented (restrooms here too). Ask for advice on the length and type of walks and drives you can take. At the south end of the avenue, accessed via the Phillipsville exit off the highway, you will find small grocery stores.

HUMBOLDT REDWOODS STATE PARK (all ages)

Off Highway 101, visitor center 2 miles south of Weott on the Avenue of the Giants; (707) 946–2409.

The largest and one of the least visited state parks, in part because it encompasses several small towns, the park is divided by the highway and has no main entrance. Most visitors do not realize that most of the park lies to the west and is reached by leaving the Avenue of the Giants and taking Mattole Road.

Not to be missed is the **Rockefeller Forest** in the Big Trees area, a 5-mile drive in on Mattole-Honeydew Road. Since the former champion sequoia Dyerville Giant, 362 inches in diameter, fell in rain-saturated ground in spring 1991, the new champ is a 363-inches-in-diameter behemoth in the Rockefeller Forest. Tiptoeing along boardwalks and spongy pathways in the damp, cool stillness at the foot of these magical giants, you'll hear only the bustle of chipmunks. A short trail leads to a sandy riverbank, for sunbathing, wading, picnicking, and fishing.

A hundred miles of trails in the park are frequented by hikers, back-packers, mountain bikers, and horseback riders. Meanderings will turn up old homesteaders' cabins and several campgrounds, some for RVs and others consisting of simple sites in the backcountry. Apple blossoms bloom in orchards planted by early settlers. In fall big-leaf maples, alders, and buckeyes turn red and gold. Sighted in the farthest reaches of the park are bobcats, black-tailed deer, foxes, ring-tailed cats, and even black bears.

Having survived aeons of ice ages and climate changes, only fragments of the original redwood forests now survive their greatest threat—logging companies. From the late nineteenth century to today, the virgin stands have been largely decimated, primarily by clear-cutting, which destroys not only the trees but many of the creeks, rivers, and hillsides as well as wildlife habitats. Established in 1918 for the purpose of rescuing the Eel River Valley from the lumbermen, the Save-the-Redwoods League is credited with the establishment of the California parks that shelter most of the old-growth redwoods remaining in the world.

At the visitor center are a museum and exhibits, a native plant garden, a slide show, and bookstore. Guided walks and talks are available.

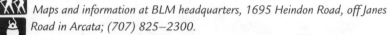

KING RANGE NATIONAL CONSERVATION AREA

Maps and information at BLM headquarters, 1695 Heindon Road, off Janes Road in Arcata; (707) 825–2300.

Rugged and largely inaccessible, the "Lost Coast" between Mattole Point and Shelter Cove is 24 miles of shoreline, mountain streams, trails, and forests for camping, hiking and fishing, with five campgrounds. Two-lane Mattole Road is a corkscrew called Wild Cat, which winds through spectacular mountainous countryside. It's scenic, but not fun for backseat passengers or little kids. The easiest route in is from Redway to Shelter Cove, where you can wander on a black-sand beach, have lunch in a cafe, camp in your RV or tent, and fish off the shore.

Where to Eat

Cafe Waterfront Oyster Bar and Grill. *Corner of First and Seventh Streets, Eureka 95501; (707) 443–9190.* Enjoy Eureka's famous seafood and sea views—fish burgers, clams, and oysters in a casual Victorian setting. Breakfast, lunch, and dinner. $–$$

Cafe Marina. *Woodley Island, Eureka 95501; (707) 443–2233.* Overlooking the docks of Humboldt Bay on a deck with umbrella tables: fresh seafood and typical American fare. Breakfast, lunch, and dinner. $–$$

Sea Grill. *316 E Street, Eureka 95501; (707) 443–7187.* Voted "Best Seafood Restaurant" in the county for several years, and a noisy, popular place. Come early to avoid the crowds and enjoy choosing from a huge seafood menu; reservations are usually necessary. Lunch and dinner. $$

Ramone's Bakery and Cafe. *209 E Street, Eureka 95501; (707) 445–2923.* Where the locals go for cappuccino, killer bagels, breakfast and lunch, homemade soups, salads, sandwiches. $

Where to Stay

Campton House. *305 M Street, Eureka 95501; (800) 772–1622 or (707) 443–1601.* A charming Craftsman-style cottage with three spacious, comfortable bedrooms, two baths, a parlor, dining room, and kitchen—perfect for a big family or a family reunion. Across the street from the Carson Mansion, within walking distance of all the sights and restaurants in town. A simple continental breakfast and afternoon tea are included, and so is use of the pool and sauna at the adjacent motel. $$–$$$

Red Lion Inn. *1929 Fourth Street, Eureka 95501; (800) 547–8010 or (707) 445–0844; www.redlion.com.* A large, family-friendly motel, with a pool, a restaurant, and family suites. $$

Eureka Inn. *518 Seventh Street, Eureka 95501; (707) 442–6441 or (800) 862–4906; www.eurekainn.com.* A fabulous English Tudor–style, half-timbered hotel built in the 1920s, with a huge fireplace in the lobby, a comfy dinner house, a casual cafe, and a poolside dining area, all serving great American food and fresh seafood. Christmastime is festive; a towering, glittering tree is the backdrop for nightly live entertainment. The staff is particularly friendly, and families feel welcome here. Rooms vary in size and amenities. $$$

Thunderbird Inn and Suites. *232 West Fifth Street, Eureka 95501; (800) 521– 6996.* Featuring a heated pool, a recreation and games area, guest laundry facilities, some refrigerators, some two-bedroom units, barbecues, and restaurants. $$

Giant Redwoods RV and Camp. *455 Boy Scout Camp Road, Myers Flat 95554; (707) 943–3198.* Twenty-three acres of riverfront on the Avenue of the Giants, a quiet family camp with full hookups and tent sites. $

For More Information

Eureka/Humboldt County Convention and Visitors Bureau. *1034 Second Street, Eureka 95501; (707) 443– 5097 or (800) 346–3482; www.redwoodvisitor.org. Call for a copy of "Destination Redwood Coast."*

State Park Reservations. *(800) 444–7275.*

Fascinating Facts about Redwood Country

- View sixty percent of the tallest trees in the world along the 31-mile Avenue of the Giants in Humboldt Redwoods State Park.
- The world's tallest living Christmas tree is lit annually in Ferndale.
- Established in 1921, the oldest rodeo in the west is still held in Fortuna in July.
- At 160 feet tall and 57,000 pounds, the tallest totem pole in the country is in McKinleyville.
- The Samoa Cookhouse in Eureka is the last operating lumber camp cookhouse in the west.

Fishing in Redwood Country

Fishing in Redwood Country This is prime ocean- and river-fishing country. For first-timers and beginning fisherpersons, stick to the riverbanks and the piers or go on a guided expedition with a company that provides equipment, transportation, and advice.

- Surf and rock fishing, lingcod, salmon:
  - K Street and the F Street piers in Eureka
  - South jetty, 11 miles south of Eureka
  - North jetty, 6 miles from the west end of Samoa Bridge
- Clamming on beaches near Eureka and Arcata.
- King and silver salmon, as well as steelhead, on the Eel, the Mad, the Van Duzen, the Little River, and Redwood Creek, all near Eureka, and on the Klamath, farther north.
- Twenty lakes in Humboldt County are stocked with trout.
- Fishing conditions: North Coast Fishphone, (707) 444–8041.
- Eel River Headquarters, (707) 946–2311.
- **Celtic Charter Service.** *Woodley Island Marina; (707) 442–7580.* A 50-foot twin-diesel sport-fishing boat takes families on salmon- and rock-cod-fishing and whale-watching expeditions.
- **Rivers West Fishing Expeditions.** *P.O. Box 53, Redcrest; (707) 722–4159.* A veteran jet-boat operator customizes camping, fishing, and sightseeing jaunts on local rivers.
- **Time Flies.** *Eighth and J Streets, Arcata; (707) 822–8331.* Large selection of fresh- and saltwater-fishing gear.
- **Eureka Fly Shop.** *505 H Street, Eureka; (707) 444–2000.* Everything for fly-fishing.

Arcata

Seven miles north of Eureka by way of scenic Highway 255 bordering Humboldt Bay, Arcata is an old loggers' town and the home of Humboldt State University.

Just north, the coastal village of Trinidad on **Trinidad Bay** offers a pier, beaches, fishing access, a few shops, and a handful of terrific restaurants. Trinidad State Park and Patrick's Point State Park are nearby.

Twenty-two miles north of Arcata and stretching more than 40 miles, Redwood National Park is dedicated a World Heritage Site, as "significant to all nations." The national park actually encompasses three state parks: Prairie Creek Redwoods, Del Norte Coast Redwoods, and Jedediah Smith Redwoods.

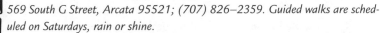

ARCATA MARSH AND WILDLIFE SANCTUARY (all ages)

569 South G Street, Arcata 95521; (707) 826–2359. Guided walks are scheduled on Saturdays, rain or shine.

Spend a couple of hours here on 4.5 miles of quiet footpaths in a stunning bayside setting, with freshwater ponds, a salt marsh, tidal mudflats, and winding water channels alive with birds and ducks. This is also a good place to jog or have a picnic; leashed dogs are allowed. You would never guess this is a waste water reclamation project, and, in fact, a model for the nation. Stop at the interpretive center here for maps and information about birding walks throughout the region, and ask about guided walks at the marsh. In March, the annual spring migration bird festival, called Godwit Days, is a big event, bringing birders from across the country (800–908–WING). For daily bird sightings, call (707) 822–LOON.

HISTORIC LOGGING TRAIL AND COMMUNITY FOREST

Fourteenth and Union Streets, Arcata; (707) 822–3619.

Logging sites and equipment from a century ago, a few old-growth sequoias, and many second-growth trees are here—as are easy, pleasant walking trails, picnic sites, restrooms, and a playground.

HUMBOLDT LAGOONS STATE PARK

Thirty miles north of Eureka on Highway 101, Orick; (707) 488–2171.

It's a 0.75-mile paddle or row to a six-site boat-in campground at Ryan's Cove, located on a mysterious 520-acre lagoon. There is much wildlife to see, including Roosevelt elk. On the edge is a 3-mile, very quiet beach, plus access to the Coastal Trail. For day-use and environmental campsites, enter the park (by car) at Milepost 114.5.

PATRICK'S POINT STATE PARK

Five miles north of Trinidad, on Highway 101; (707) 677–3570.

Forest trails, picnic sites, a sandy beach, and world-class sea views from a vast headland. Developed campsites and showers; RV sites to 31 feet.

REDWOOD NATIONAL PARK (all ages)

Visitor center between the park entrance and the town of Orick; (707) 488–3461.
You will need to get a (**Free**) permit to drive the steep, 170-mile road to Tall Trees Grove, where a 3-mile-round-trip walking trail leads to the world's first, third, and fifth tallest redwoods. There are more than 300 developed campsites in the three state parks within the national park, as well as shoreline trails and beaches, swimming in the Smith River and Redwood Creek, and ranger-guided tours.

PRAIRIE CREEK REDWOODS STATE PARK (all ages)

Six miles north of Orick, take the Elk Prairie Parkway exit off Highway 101. For park information call (707) 464–6101. Some trails are wheelchair accessible.
A World Heritage Site, featuring 12,000 acres of magnificent Coastal Redwoods, 70 miles of mountain-biking and hiking trails, herds of Roosevelt elk, a museum, Gold Bluff Beach, gorgeous campgrounds, and fabulous Fern Canyon, where lush ferns cover 50-foot rock walls. The visitor center is particularly interesting, with a museum, a natural history bookstore and displays. Part of *The Lost World, Jurassic Park* was filmed here. If I were to camp and stay at only one redwood park, this would be the one, because of the almost surreal beauty and the variety of environments and wildlife.

Where to Eat

Plaza Grill. *791 Eighth Street, Arcata 95521; (707) 826–2345.* On the third floor of historic Jacoby's Storehouse, on the town plaza, a casual cafe with a beautiful longbar, a fireplace, and town views. Families love the burgers, sandwiches, fish platters, and the kids menu. $–$$

Wildflower Cafe and Bakery. *1604 G Street, Arcata 95521; (707) 822–0360.* Yummy muffins and pastries to go, and vegetarian cuisine for breakfast, lunch, and dinner. Homemade soup, Mexican and Chinese food, hearty daily specials like quiche and stroganoff. $

Where to Stay

Mad River Quality Inn. *3535 Janes Road, Arcata 95521; (707) 822–0409.* A small resort in a wooded setting, offering pool, tennis, a walking trail, a game room and playground, and basketball; restaurant and grocery here too. $

Mad River Rapid RV Park. *3501 Janes Road, Arcata 95521; (707) 822–7275.* Beautifully landscaped sites with all amenities; game room, pool, tennis; part of the Mad River Quality Inn resort. $

For More Information

Trinidad Chamber of Commerce.
Main Street and Patrick Point Drive, Trindad 95570; (707) 441–9827.

Arcata Chamber of Commerce.
1062 G Street, Arcata 95521; (707) 822–3619; www.urcata.com/chamber.

Ferndale

Five miles off Highway 101 through idyllic dairylands, the village of Ferndale is two long streets of more than 200 glorious Victorian buildings. The entire tiny town is a State Historic Landmark. Pick up a walking tour map at most businesses in town. It will take a couple of hours to stroll Main Street, take pictures of the old buildings, and browse in the shops. Save a roll of film for the **Gingerbread Mansion** on Berding Street, a masterpiece of Victorian architecture.

On the edge of the **Eel River Delta**, a resting point on the Pacific flyway, Ferndale is within minutes of great birdwatching and some nice walks. Running 5 miles west out of town, Centerville Road leads to the beach, where a wide variety of birdlife and animals can be seen on walks north and south— swans, geese, sandpipers, pelicans and cormorants, seals, and whales.

On the east side of town are country lanes leading to the Eel River Estuary, where there are great routes for walking and biking. You can launch canoes and kayaks here in quiet waters or take a guided boat tour of the estuary (Eel River Delta Tours, 707–786–4187). More than 150 feathered species live in or pass through these wetlands, including loons, cormorants, harriers, and egrets. Where the Eel meets the sea, watch for sea lions, seals, and river otters.

GOLDEN GAIT MERCANTILE
421 Main Street, Ferndale 95536; (707) 786–4891.
Time is suspended in the 1850s, with barrels of penny candy, big-wheeled coffee grinders, and glass cases lined with old-fashioned restoratives and hair pomades. Remember Burma Shave?

DAVE'S SADDLERY
491 Main Street, Ferndale 95536; (707) 786–4004.
Cowboy boots, beaded hatbands, hand-tooled saddles, and silver buckles, and Ferndale T-shirts.

FERNDALE ANTIQUE MALL

597 Fernbridge Drive, Ferndale 95536; (707) 725–8820.

On the way into town, watch for a large, light green building with striped awnings and a red door, a veritable bazaar of forty dealers selling everything from estate jewelry to Victorian furniture.

FERNDALE MUSEUM (all ages)

Corner Shaw and Third Street across from Main, Ferndale 95536; (707) 786–4466. Admission for adults $1.00, children 50 cents.

A small but mighty exhibit of Ferndale history and the agriculture of the "Cream City," with period rooms, an operating seismograph, and a blacksmith shop.

KINETIC SCULPTURE MUSEUM

393 Main Street, Ferndale 95536; (707) 786–9259. Free *admission.*

Here, in one of the strangest museums in the world, are some of the wild and weird, handmade, people-powered machines that travel over land, mud, and water in the World Championship Great Arcata to Ferndale Cross-County Kinetic Sculpture Race held annually in May. Called the "triathlon of the art world," this three-day event is great fun to watch, as the fantastical contrivances are driven, dragged, and floated over roads, sand dunes, Humboldt Bay, and the Eel River! Among the machines in past races were "Nightmare of the Iguana" and "Tyrannosaurus Rust," which was powered by cavemen!

Where to Eat

Diane's Cafe and Espresso. *553 Main Street, Ferndale 95536; (707) 786–4950.* Cafe au lait in huge cups, homemade sandwiches, salads, soups. $

Curley's Grill. *460 Main in the Victorian Inn, Ferndale 95536; (707) 786–9696.* California cuisine, homemade soup and foccacia, local fresh fish, grilled sandwiches, and more; served indoors in an old-fashioned dining room or on the patio. Lunch and dinner. $–$$

For More Information

Victorian Village of Ferndale. *248 Francis Street, Ferndale 95536;* *(707) 786–4477; www.victorianferndale. org/chamber.*

General Index

Activities Index

FESTIVALS/CELEBRATIONS

HISTORIC SITES AND LANDMARKS

MUSEUMS

About the Author

A native Northern Californian who lives in Sonoma in the heart of the Wine Country, Karen Misuraca is the author of *Quick Escapes from San Francisco, The California Coast, CitySmart San Francisco,* and *Selling Books in the Bay Area.* Karen specializes in writing about golf travel and international travel, and she is a book publicist. She contributes to magazines and newspapers, including TravelClassics.com, *Alaska Airlines Magazine,* and Copley News Service.

Misuraca and her companion, Michael Capp, explore Northern California's outdoors with her three daughters, five granddaughters, and a grandson.

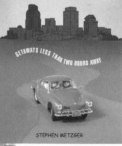